THE COMPLETE
POLYSYLLABIC SPREE

THE COMPLETE
POLYSYLLABIC
SPREE

BY
NICK HORNBY

VIKING
an imprint of
PENGUIN BOOKS

VIKING

Published by the Penguin Group,
Penguin Books Ltd, 80 Strand, London WC2R 0RL, England
Penguin Group (USA) Inc., 375 Hudson Street, New York, New York 10014, USA
Penguin Group (Canada), 90 Eglinton Avenue East, Suite 700, Toronto, Ontario, Canada M4P 2Y3
(a division of Pearson Penguin Canada Inc.)
Penguin Ireland, 25 St Stephen's Green, Dublin 2, Ireland (a division of Penguin Books Ltd)
Penguin Group (Australia), 250 Camberwell Road,
Camberwell, Victoria 3124, Australia (a division of Pearson Australia Group Pty Ltd)
Penguin Books India Pvt Ltd, 11 Community Centre,
Panchsheel Park, New Delhi – 110 017, India
Penguin Group (NZ), cnr Airborne and Rosedale Roads, Albany,
Auckland 1310, New Zealand (a division of Pearson New Zealand Ltd)
Penguin Books (South Africa) (Pty) Ltd, 24 Sturdee Avenue,
Rosebank, Johannesburg 2196, South Africa

Penguin Books Ltd, Registered Offices: 80 Strand, London WC2R 0RL, England

www.penguin.com

First published 2006
1

Copyright © Nick Hornby, 2006

The Acknowledgements on p. 274 constitute an extension of this copyright page

The moral right of the author has been asserted

Set in Bembo
Typeset by Palimpsest Book Production Limited,
Grangemouth, Stirlingshire
Printed in England by Clays Ltd, St Ives plc

A CIP catalogue record for this book is available from the British Library

HARDBACK
ISBN-13: 978–0–670–91666–5
ISBN-10: 0–670–91666–8

TRADE PAPERBACK
ISBN-13: 978–0–670–91672–6
ISBN-10: 0–670–91672–2

For my wife

TABLE OF CONTENTS

TABLE OF CONTENTS

INTRODUCTION

I began writing this column in the summer of 2003. I had just had the reading experience described at the beginning of this book, and it seemed to me that what I had chosen to read in those few weeks contained a narrative, of sorts – that one book led to another, and thus themes and patterns emerged, patterns that might be worth looking at. And, of course, that was pretty much the last time my reading had any kind of logic or shape to it. Ever since then my choice of books has been haphazard, whimsical and entirely shapeless.

It still seemed like a fun thing to do, though, writing about reading, as opposed to writing about individual books. At the beginning of my writing career I reviewed a lot of fiction, but I had to pretend, as reviewers do, that I had read the books outside of space, time and self – in other words, I had to pretend that I hadn't read them when I was tired and grumpy, or drunk, that I wasn't envious of the author, that I had no agenda, no personal aesthetic or personal taste or personal problems, that I hadn't read other reviews of the same book already, that I didn't know who the author's friends and enemies were, that I wasn't trying to place a book with the same publisher, that I hadn't been bought lunch by the book's doe-eyed publicist. Most of all I had to pretend that I hadn't written the review because I was urgently in need of a quick couple of hundred quid. Being paid to read a book and then write about it creates a dynamic which compromises the reviewer in all kinds of ways, very few of them helpful.

So this column was going to be different. Yes, I would be paid for it, but I would be paid to write about what I would have done anyway, which was read the books I wanted to read. And if I felt that mood, morale, concentration levels, weather or family history had affected my relationship with a book, I could and would say so. Inevitably, however, the knowledge that I had to write something for the *Believer* at the end of each month changed my reading habits profoundly. For a start, I probably read more books than I might otherwise have done. I suspect that I used to take a longer break between books, a couple of days, maybe, during which time I'd carry a copy of the *New Yorker* or *Mojo* around with me, but now I push on with the next book, scared I won't have enough to write about (or that I'll look bad, unbookish and unworthy of the space in a publication as smart as the *Believer*). Magazines have been the real casualties of this regime (although the *Economist* has survived, partly to replace the newspapers I'm not reading).

It was the very nature of the *Believer* itself, however, that really shook up my reading, I hope for ever. The magazine, which is five months older than the column, is a broad church, and all sorts of writers (and artists, film-makers and other creative types) are welcome to stand in the pulpit and preach, but it has one commandment: THOU SHALT NOT SLAG ANYONE OFF. As I understand it, the founders of the magazine wanted one place, one tiny corner of the world, in which writers could be sure that they weren't going to get a kicking; predictably and depressingly, this ambition was mocked mercilessly, mostly by those critics whose children would go hungry if their parents weren't able to abuse authors whose books they didn't much like.

I understood and supported the magazine's stance, which seemed admirable and entirely unproblematic to me – until I had to write about the books I'd read which I hadn't much liked. The first couple of times this happened, earnest discussions took place with the magazine's editors, who felt that I'd crossed a line, and I either rewrote the offending passages so that I struck a more conciliatory tone, or the offending books and writers became anonymous. I didn't mind in the least, and in any case it gave me the opportunity to mock the *Believer*'s ambition mercilessly. (For the record: there is no Polysyllabic Spree. I deal with Vendela Vida and Andrew Leland, editor and managing editor of the *Believer* respectively, and they are neither humourless nor evangelical. They even watch television, I think.)

The *Believer*'s ethos did, however, make me think about what and why I read. I didn't want to keep rewriting offending passages in my columns, and I certainly didn't want to keep using the phrases 'Unnameable writer' or 'Anonymous novel'. So what to do? My solution was to try to choose books I knew I would like. I'm not sure this idea is as blindingly obvious as it seems. We often read books that we think we ought to read, or that we think we ought to have read, or that other people think we should read (I'm always coming across people who have a mental, sometimes even an actual, list of the books they think they should have read by the time they turn forty, fifty or dead); I'm sure I'm not the only one who harrumphs his way through a highly praised novel, astonished but actually rather pleased that so many people have got it so wrong. As a consequence, the first thing to be cut from my reading diet was contemporary literary fiction. This seems to me to be the highest-risk category – or the highest risk for me, at any rate, given my tastes.

I am not particularly interested in language. Or rather, I am interested in what language can do for me, and I spend many hours each day trying to ensure that my prose is as simple as it can possibly be. But I do not wish to produce prose that draws attention to itself, rather than the world it describes, and I certainly don't have the patience to read it. (I suspect that I'm not alone here. That kind of writing tends to be admired by critics more than by book-buyers, if the best-seller lists can be admitted as evidence: the literary novels that have reached a mass audience over the last decade or so usually ask readers to look through a relatively clear pane of glass at their characters.) I am not attempting to argue that the books I like are 'better' than more opaquely written novels; I am simply pointing out my own tastes and limitations as a reader. To put it crudely, I get bored, and when I get bored I tend to get tetchy. It has proved surprisingly easy to eliminate boredom from my reading life.

And boredom, let's face it, is a problem that many of us have come to associate with books. It's one of the reasons why we choose to do almost anything else rather than read; very few of us pick up a book after the children are in bed and the dinner has been made and the dirty dishes cleared away. We'd rather turn on the television. Some evenings we'd rather go to all the trouble of getting into a car and driving to a cinema, or waiting for a bus that might take us somewhere near one. This is partly because reading appears to be more effortful than watching TV, and usually it is, although if you choose to watch one of the HBO series, such as

The Sopranos or *The Wire*, then it's a close-run thing, because the plotting in these programmes, the speed and complexity of the dialogue are as demanding as a lot of the very best fiction.

One of the problems, it seems to me, is that we have got it into our heads that books should be hard work, and that unless they're hard work, they're not doing us any good. I recently had conversations with two friends, both of whom were reading a very long political biography that had appeared in many of 2005's 'Books of the Year' lists. They were struggling. Both of these people are parents – they each, coincidentally, have three children – and both have demanding full-time jobs. And each night, in the few minutes they allowed themselves to read before sleep, they ploughed gamely through a few paragraphs about the (very) early years of a major twentieth-century world figure. At the rate of progress they were describing, it would take them many, many months before they finished the book, possibly even decades. (One of them told me that he'd put it down for a couple of weeks, and on picking it up again was extremely excited to see that the bookmark was much deeper into the book than he'd dared hope. He then realized that one of his kids had dropped it, and put the bookmark back in the wrong place. He was crushed.) The truth is, of course, that neither of them will ever finish it – or at least, not in this phase of their lives. In the process, though, they will have reinforced a learned association of books with struggle.

I am not trying to say that the book itself was the cause of this anguish. I can imagine other people racing through it, and I can certainly imagine these two people racing through books that others might find equally daunting. It seems clear to me, though, that the combination of that book with these readers at this stage in their lives is not a happy one. If reading books is to survive as a leisure activity – and there are statistics which show that this is by no means assured – then we have to promote the joys of reading, rather than the (dubious) benefits. I would never attempt to dissuade anyone from reading a book. But please, if you're reading a book that's killing you, put it down and read something else, just as you would reach for the remote if you weren't enjoying a TV programme. Your failure to enjoy a highly rated novel doesn't mean you're dim – you may find that Graham Greene is more to your taste, or Stephen Hawking, or Iris Murdoch or Ian Rankin. Dickens, Stephen King, whoever. It doesn't matter. All I know is that you can get very little from a book that is making you weep with the effort of reading it. You won't remember it, and you'll learn nothing from it, and you'll be less likely to choose a book over *Big Brother* next time you have a choice.

'If reading is a workout for the mind, then Britain must be buzzing with intellectual energy,' said one sarcastic columnist in the *Guardian*. 'Train stations have shops packed with enough words to keep even the most muscular brain engaged for weeks. Indeed, the carriages are full of people exercising their intellects the full length of their journeys. Yet somehow, the fact that millions daily devour thousands of words from *Hello*, the *Sun*, *The Da Vinci Code*, *Nuts* and so on does not inspire the hope that the average cerebrum is in excellent health. It's not just that you read, it's what you read that counts.' This sort of thing – and it's a regrettably common sneer in our broadsheet newspapers – must drive school librarians, publishers and literacy campaigners nuts. In Britain, more than twelve million adults have a reading age of thirteen or under, and yet some clever-dick journalist still insists on telling us that unless we're reading something *proper*, then we might as well not bother at all.

But what's proper? Whose books will make us more intelligent? Not mine, that's for sure. But has Ian McEwan got the right stuff? Julian Barnes? Jane Austen, Zadie Smith, E. M. Forster? Hardy or Dickens? Those Dickens readers who famously waited on the dockside in New York for news of Little Nell – were they hoping to be educated? Dickens is Literary now, of course, because the

books are old. But his work has survived not because he makes
you think, but because he makes you feel, and he makes you laugh,
and you need to know what is going to happen to his characters.
I have on my desk here a James Lee Burke novel, a thriller in the
Dave Robicheaux series, which sports on its covers ringing
endorsements from the *Literary Review*, the *Guardian* and the
Independent on Sunday, so there's a possibility that somebody who
writes for a broadsheet might approve . . . Any chance of this
giving my grey matter a work-out? How much of a stretch is it for
a nuclear physicist to read a book on nuclear physics? How much
cleverer will we be if we read *Of Mice and Men*, Steinbeck's
beautiful, simple novella? Or Tobias Woolf's brilliant *This Boy's
Life*, or *Lucky Jim* or *To Kill a Mockingbird*? Enormous intelligence
has gone into the creation of all of these books, just as it has into
the creation of the iPod, but the intelligence is not transferable. It's
there to serve a purpose.

But there it is. It's set in stone, apparently: books must be hard
work, otherwise they're a waste of time. And so we grind our way
through serious, and sometimes seriously dull, novels, or enormous
biographies of political figures, and every time we do so, books
come to seem a little more like a duty, and *Pop Idol* starts to look
a little more attractive. Please, please, put it down.

And please, please stop patronizing those who are reading a
book – *The Da Vinci Code*, maybe – because they are enjoying it.
For a start, none of us knows what kind of an effort this represents
for the individual reader. It could be his or her first full-length
adult novel; it might be the book that finally reveals the purpose
and joy of reading to someone who has hitherto been mystified by
the attraction books exert on others. And anyway, reading for
enjoyment is what we should all be doing. I don't mean we should
all be reading chick lit or thrillers (although if that's what you want
to read, it's fine by me, because here's something else no one will
ever tell you: if you don't read the classics, or the novel that won

this year's Booker Prize, then *nothing bad will happen to you*; more importantly, *nothing good will happen to you if you do*); I simply mean that turning pages should not be like walking through thick mud. The whole purpose of books is that we read them, and if you find you can't, it might not be *your* inadequacy that's to blame. 'Good' books can be pretty awful sometimes.

The regrettable thing about the culture war we still, after all these years, seem to be fighting is that it divides books into two camps, the trashy and the worthwhile. No one who is paid to talk about books for a living seems to be able to convey the message that this isn't how it works, that 'good' books can provide every bit as much pleasure as 'trashy' ones. Why worry about that if there's no difference anyway? Because it gives you more choice. You may not have to read about conspiracies, or the romantic tribulations of thirtysomething women, in order to be entertained. You may find that you're enthralled by Anthony Beevor's *Stalingrad*, or Donna Tartt's *The Secret History*, or *Great Expectations*. Read anything, as long as you can't wait to pick it up again.

I'm a reader for lots of reasons. On the whole, I tend to hang out with readers, and I'm scared they wouldn't want to hang out with me if I stopped. (They're interesting people, and they know a lot of interesting things, and I'd miss them.) I'm a writer, and I need to read, for inspiration and education and because I want to get better, and only books can teach me how. Sometimes, yes, I read to find things out – as I get older, I feel my ignorance weighing more heavily on me. I want to know what it's like to be him or her, to live there or then. I love the detail about the workings of the human heart and mind that only fiction can provide – film can't get in close enough. But the most important reason of all, I think, is this. When I was nine years old, I spent a few unhappy months in a church choir (my mum's idea, not mine). And two or three times a week, I had to sit through the sermon, delivered by an insufferable old windbag of a vicar. I thought it

would last for ever, and sometimes I thought it would kill me –
that I would, quite literally, die of boredom. The only thing we
were allowed for diversion was the hymn-book, and I even ended
up reading it, sometimes. Books and comics had never seemed so
necessary; even though I'd always enjoyed reading before then, I'd
never understood it to be so desperately important for my sanity.
I've never, ever gone anywhere without a book or a magazine
since. It's taken me all this time to learn that it doesn't have to be
a boring one, whatever the reviews pages and our cultural
commentators tell me; and it took the Polysyllabic Spree, of all
people, to teach me.

Please, please: put it down. You'll never finish it. Start something
else.

SEPTEMBER 2003

BOOKS BOUGHT:

* *Robert Lowell: A Biography* – Ian Hamilton
* *Collected Poems* – Robert Lowell
* *Against Oblivion: Some of the Lives of the 20th-Century Poets* – Ian Hamilton
* *In Search of J. D. Salinger* – Ian Hamilton
* *Nine Stories* – J. D. Salinger
* *Franny and Zooey* – J. D. Salinger
* *Raise High the Roof Beam, Carpenters/Seymour: An Introduction* – J. D. Salinger
* *The Ern Malley Affair* – Michael Heyward
* *Something Happened* – Joseph Heller
* *Penguin Modern Poets 5* – Corso/Ferlinghetti/Ginsberg

BOOKS READ:

* All the Salinger
* *In Search of Salinger* and *Lowell*
* Some of *Against Oblivion*
* *Pompeii* by Robert Harris (not bought)

So this is supposed to be about the how, and when, and why, and what of reading – about the way that, when reading is going well, one book leads to another and to another, a paper trail of theme and meaning; and how, when it's going badly, when books don't stick or take, when your mood and the mood of the book are fighting like cats, you'd rather do anything but attempt the next paragraph, or reread the last one for the tenth time. 'We talked about books,' says a character in Charles Baxter's wonderful *Feast of Love*, 'how boring they were to read, but how you loved them anyway.' Anyone who hasn't felt like that isn't owning up.

But first, some ground rules:

1) I don't want anyone writing in to point out that I spend too much money on books, many of which I will never read. I know that already. I certainly *intend* to read all of them, more or less. My *intentions* are good. Anyway, it's my money. And I'll bet you do it too.

2) Similarly, I don't want anyone pointing out that certain books I write about in this column are by friends – or, in the case of *Pompeii,* by brothers-in-law. A lot of my friends are writers, and so some of my reading time is, inevitably, spent on their books. I won't attempt to disguise the connections, if that makes anyone feel better. Anyway, it's been five years since my brother-in-law, the author of *Fatherland* and *Enigma,* produced a book, so the chances are that I'll have been fired from the *Believer* before he comes up with another one. (I may have been fired even before *this* one is published, in September.)

3) And don't waste your breath trying to tell me that I'm showing off. This month, maybe, I'm showing off a little. (Or am I? Shouldn't I have read some of these books decades ago? *Franny and Zooey?* Jesus. Maybe I'm doing the opposite: maybe I'm humiliating myself. And maybe you have read all these *and loads of others*, in the last fortnight. I don't know you. What's – ahem – a normal amount, for someone with a job and kids, who watches TV?) But next month I may spend my allotted space desperately trying to explain how come I've only managed three pages of a graphic novel and the sports

section of the *Daily Mirror* in four whole weeks – in which case, please don't bother accusing me of philistinism, laziness or pig-ignorance. I read a lot this month (*a*) because it's the summer, and it's been hot, and I haven't been working very hard, and there's no football on TV and (*b*) because my eldest son, for reasons we don't need to go into, has spent even more time than usual stuck in the toilet, and I have to sit outside on a chair. Thus do books get read.

This month, it went something like:

Against Oblivion →
Lowell → *In Search of Salinger* → *Nine Stories* → *Raise High the Roof Beam, Carpenters* → *(Pompeii)* → *Seymour: An Introduction* → *Franny and Zooey*

The Robert Lowell–Ian Hamilton thing began with Anthony Lane's intimidatingly brilliant review of Lowell's collected poems in the *New Yorker*: Lane mentioned in passing that Hamilton's biography was still the best available. Even so, I wouldn't have bothered if it hadn't been for several other factors, the most important of which is that my baby son is called Lowell. We named him thus partly after various musicians – Lowell George and the blues singer Lowell Fulson – and partly because of Robert Lowell, whose work we had never read (in our defence, he is no longer terribly well known here in England, and he isn't taught in school), but whose existence persuaded us, in our untrustworthy hormonal state, that the name had a generic artistic connotation. Our Lowell will almost certainly turn out to be a sales manager for a sportswear firm, whose only contact with literature is when he listens to Tom Clancy audiobooks once a year on holiday – not that there's anything wrong with that.

On top of that, I had recently watched a BBC documentary about Ian Hamilton himself, who was a good poet and a great critic, and a mentor to Barnes, Amis, McEwan, and that whole generation of English writers. (There is, by the way, an exceptionally good new BBC cable channel here, BBC4, which shows documentaries of similar merit and obscurity every night of the week.) And I'd met him a couple of times, and really liked him, not least because he wrote an enthusiastic review of my first book. (Did I mention that he was a great critic?) He died a couple of years ago, and I wish I'd known him better.

I still wouldn't necessarily have tracked down the Lowell biography, however, if I hadn't spent a weekend near Hay-on-Wye. Hay is a weird town on the border of England and Wales that consists almost entirely of secondhand bookshops – there are forty of 'em within a few hundred yards of each other – and one of which is an immaculately stocked poetry store. That's where I found Hamilton's book, as well as the Penguin Modern Poets collection, purchased because Corso's lovely 'Marriage' was read at a friend's wedding recently. I bought the Ern Malley book (for a pound, pure maybe-one-day whimsy, doomed to top-shelf oblivion) and a first edition of *Something Happened* (because it crops up in *Stone Reader*), elsewhere in the town. Buying books is what you do in Hay, in the absence of any other options.

Despite all these various auguries, I hadn't necessarily expected to read every word of the Lowell biography, but Hamilton is such a good writer, and Lowell's life was so tumultuous, that it was gone in a couple of days, like an Elmore Leonard novel. Sometimes, in the hands of the right person, biographies of relatively minor figures (and Lowell's influence seems to be receding fast) are especially compelling: they seem to have their times and cultural environments written through them like a stick of rock, in a way that *sui generis* major figures sometimes don't. Lowell, it turns out, is the guy you can see just behind Zelig's shoulder: he corresponded with Eliot, hung out with Jackie and Bobby K., and travelled around with Eugene McCarthy in '68. He also beat up his own father, had endless strange, possibly sexless extramarital affairs with innumerable young women, and endured terrible periods of psychosis, frequently accompanied by alarming rants about Hitler. In other words, it's one of those books you thrust on your partner with an incredulous cry of 'This is *me!*'

And as a bonus, I felt I learned more about the act of creating poetry from this one book than I did in my entire educational career. (A line from a letter Lowell wrote to Randall Jarrell that I shall endeavour to remember: 'In prose you have to be interested in *what* is being said . . . it's very exciting for me, like going fishing.') In the end, the psychotic periods make for a wearying rhythm to the book, and perhaps Hamilton's criticism of the poems tends to be a little too astringent – the *Collected Poems* runs to twelve hundred pages, but Hamilton seems to argue that we could live without a good eleven hundred and fifty of them. And this is a poet he clearly loves . . .

But it's a great biography, and now I was off on this Hamilton kick. I bought *Against Oblivion,* his book of little essays about every major twentieth-century poet bar four – Eliot, Auden, Hardy and Yeats – absent because their work is, in the critic's view, certain to survive; it's in the bathroom, and I've got through half of it. (Shock news: grown-up critics think e. e. Cummings sucks. I honestly didn't know. I read him at school, put him in the 'good' box, and left him there.) I vaguely remembered the story of Hamilton's attempt to write a biography of Salinger: it ended up in court, and Salinger actually broke cover to give a deposition to Hamilton's lawyer. Hamilton admits that Salinger's victory left gaping holes in the book he wanted to write. He was denied permission to quote from letters that are freely available for inspection in various libraries. I'm still glad I read it, though. I learned things – that you could earn $2,000 for a short story in the 1930s, for example. The stories about Salinger hustling for work, and dining gaily with the Oliviers in London, make one feel almost giddy, so unlikely do they sound now; and when the Hamilton mind goes to work on the stories, it's something to see.

The realization that you could polish off a major author's entire oeuvre in less than a week was definitely part of the appeal – you won't catch Dickens being pushed around like that – but it was still tougher work than I thought it would be. Just about every one of *Nine Stories* is perfect, and *Raise High the Roof Beam, Carpenters* is fresh and funny, but *Seymour: An Introduction* . . . Man, I really didn't want to know about Seymour's ears. Or his eyes. Or whether he could play sports. The very first time I met him he blew his brains out (in 'A Perfect Day for Bananafish'), so to be brutal, I never really developed as much curiosity about him as Salinger seems to want of me. But whereas I was expecting something light and sweet, I ended up with this queasy sense of the psychodramatic: I knew that I wouldn't be able to separate the stories from the Story, but I hadn't expected the author to collude in the confusion. Hamilton is especially good on how Buddy Glass, apparently Salinger's mouthpiece, creates and perpetuates myths about his alter ego.

I read *Pompeii* in between *Nine Stories* and *Raise High the Roof Beam* . . . It has to be a rule, I think, that when a family member gives you his new book, you stop what you're doing and read it. Having a brother-in-law for a writer could have turned out really, really badly. He could have been more or less successful than me. Or he could have written books that I hated, or found impossible to get through. (Imagine if your brother-in-law wrote *Finnegans Wake,* and you were really busy at work. Or you weren't really a big reader.) Luckily, his books are great, and a pleasure to read, and despite my trepidation – I couldn't see how he was going to pull off a thriller that ends with the biggest *deus ex machina* the world has ever known – this is, I reckon, his best one. Oh, and he read just about every book there is on volcanology and Roman water systems, as well as every word Pliny wrote, so my admiration for my sister has increased even further. Has she been sitting there listening to stuff about Roman water systems for the last three years? I now understand why her favourite film of recent years is *Legally Blonde*. How could it not be?

I read 55 per cent of the books I bought this month – five and a half out of ten. Two of the unread books, however, are volumes of poetry, and, to my way of thinking, poetry books work more like books of reference: they go up on the shelves straightaway (as opposed to on to the bedside table), to be taken down and dipped into every now and again. (And, before any outraged poets explode, I'd like to point out that I'm one of the seventy-three people in the world who buys poetry.) And anyway, anyone who is even contemplating ploughing straight through over a thousand pages of Lowell's poetry clearly needs a cable TV subscription, or maybe even some friends, a relationship and a job. So if it's OK with you, I'm taking the poetry out, and calling it five and a half out of eight – and the Heller I've read before, years ago, so that's six and a half out of eight. I make that 81¼ per cent! I am both erudite and financially prudent! I admit it: I haven't read a book about an Australian literary hoax (which, I repeat, I bought for a quid), and a handful of essays about people like James Wright, Robinson Jeffers and Norman Cameron. Maybe there are slumbering pockets of ignorance best left undisturbed; no one likes a know-it-all. ✶

OCTOBER 2003

If you write books – or a certain kind of book, anyway – you can't resist a scan round the hotel swimming pool when you go on holiday. You just can't help yourself, despite the odds: you need to know, straight off, whether anyone is reading one of yours. You imagine spending your days under a parasol watching, transfixed and humbled, as a beautiful and intelligent young man or woman, almost certainly a future best friend, maybe even spouse, weeps and guffaws through three hundred pages of your brilliant prose, too absorbed even to go for a swim, or take a sip of Evian. I was cured of this particular fantasy a couple of years ago, when I spent a week watching a woman on the other side of the pool reading my first novel, *High Fidelity*. Unfortunately, however, I was on holiday with my sister and brother-in-law, and my brother-in-law provided a gleeful and frankly unfraternal running commentary. 'Look! Her lips are moving.' 'Ha! She's fallen asleep! Again!' 'I talked to her in the bar last night. Not a *bright* woman, I'm afraid.' At one point, alarmingly, she dropped the book and ran off. 'She's gone to put out her eyes!' my brother-in-law yelled triumphantly. I was glad when she'd finished it and moved on to *Harry Potter* or Dr Seuss or whatever else it was she'd packed.

I like to think that, once he'd recovered from the original aesthetic shock, Jonathan Lethem wouldn't have winced too often if he'd watched me reading *The Fortress of Solitude* by the pool this month. I was pinned to my lounger, and my lips hardly moved at all. In fact, I was so determined to read his novel on holiday that the first half of the reading month started with a mess. It went something like, *Being* **The** *John McEnroe* Stop-Time **Fortress of Solitude**. I'd just started Tim Adams's short book on McEnroe when an advance copy of *Fortress* came in the post, and I started reading that – but because it seemed so good, so much my kind of book, I wanted to save it, and I went back to the McEnroe. Except then the McEnroe turned out to be *too* short, and I'd finished it before the holiday started, so I needed something to fill in, which is why I reread *Stop-Time*. (And *Stop-Time* turned out to be too long, and I didn't get on to *Fortress* until the third day of the seven-day holiday.)

Last month I read a lot of Salinger, and he pops up in all three of these books. Tim Adams remembers reading *Raise High the Roof Beam, Carpenters* while queuing to watch McEnroe at Wimbledon in 1981; the seventeen-year-old Adams had a theory that McEnroe 'was, in fact, a latter-day Holden Caulfield, unable and unwilling to grow up . . . constantly railing against the phonies – dozing linesmen, tournament organizers with walkie-talkies – in authority'. Later, he points out that McEnroe went to

Buckley Country Day School – 'one model for Holden Caulfield's Pencey Prep'. Frank Conroy, meanwhile, attended P.S. 6, 'of J. D. Salinger fame'. (Adams's book is great, by the way. It's witty and smart, and has ideas about sport that don't strain for significance. It's also oddly English, because it's about the collision of McEnroe and Wimbledon – in other words, McEnroe and one version of England – and about how McEnroe was a weirdly timely illustration of Thatcherism. My favourite McEnroe tirade, one I hadn't heard before: 'I'm so disgusting you shouldn't watch. Everybody leave!')

And then, at the beginning of *The Fortress of Solitude*, I came across the following, describing a street ball game: 'A shot . . . which cleared the gates on the opposite side of the street was a home run. Henry seemed to be able to do this at will, and the fact that he didn't each time was mysterious.' Compare that to this, from *Seymour: An Introduction*: 'A home run was scored only when the ball sailed just high and hard enough to strike the wall of the building on the opposite street . . . Seymour scored a home run nearly every time he was up. When other boys on the block scored one, it was generally regarded as a fluke . . . but Seymour's failures to get home runs looked like flukes.' Weird, huh? (And that's all it is, by the way – there's nothing sinister going on here. Lethem's book is probably over a hundred thousand words long, and bears no resemblance to anything Salinger wrote, aside from this one tiny echo.) All three books are in part about being young and mixed-up and American, and even though this would appear to be a theme so broad that no one can claim it as their own, somehow Salinger has managed to copyright it (and you wouldn't put it past him); there is clearly some law compelling you to acknowledge somewhere in your book, however obliquely, that he got there first.

A confession, for the record: I know Jonathan Lethem. Or rather, I've met him, and we have exchanged emails on occasions. But I don't know him so well that I had to read his book, if you see what I mean. I could easily have gotten away with not reading it. I could have left the proof copy his publisher sent me sitting around unopened, and no social embarrassment would have ensued. But I wanted to read it; I loved *Motherless Brooklyn*, and I knew a little bit about this book before I started it – I knew, for example, that a lot of funk records and Marvel comics were mentioned by name. In other words, it wasn't just up my street; it was actually knocking on my front door and peering through the letterbox to see if I was in. I was, however, briefly worried about the title, which sounds portentously and alarmingly Literary, until I was reminded that it refers to Superman.

The Fortress of Solitude is one of those rare novels that felt as though it had to be written; in fact, it's one of those novels that deals with something so crucial – namely, the relationship between a middle-class white boy and black culture – that you can't believe it hasn't been written before. Anyone who has grown up listening to black music, or even white music derived from black music, will have some point of connection to this book; but Dylan Ebdus, Lethem's central character, is a kind of walking, talking embodiment of a cultural obsession. He's the only white kid in his street (in Brooklyn, pre-gentrification), and one of a handful of white kids in his school; Mick Jagger would have killed for his experience, and Mick Jagger would have suffered in exactly the same ways.

This is a painful, beautiful, brave, poetic and definitive book (anyone who attempts to enter this territory again will be found out, not least because Lethem clearly knows whereof he speaks), and though it has its flaws, the right reader will not only forgive them but love them – just as the right listener loves the flaws in, say, *The Wild, the Innocent & the E Street Shuffle*. They are the flaws that come of ambition, not of ineptitude. I think this is a book that people might argue about, but it will also be a book that a sizable number of people cherish and defend and reread, despite its density and length, and as an author you can't really ask for much more than that.

Three of the books on the 'read' list — by Patrick Neate, Ian MacDonald and Peter Guralnick — I reviewed for *The Times Literary Supplement,* and I'm not going to write about them again at any length here. But *Where You're At* is in part about a middle-class white boy's obsession with hip-hop, and *Feel Like Going Home* is fuelled by a middle-class white boy's love for R&B and blues; reading them only served to underline why *The Fortress of Solitude* is so necessary.

I do seem, however, to have spent a disproportionate amount of time reading about Stuyvesant High School this month. That's where Dylan Ebdus escapes to, and it's also where Frank Conroy went when he could be bothered. I'm guessing that Stuyvesant is decent enough, but I'm sure its students would be perplexed to hear that an Englishman spent an entire holiday in France reading about alumni both fictional and real. I even ended up checking out the Stuyvesant website, just to see what the place looked like. (It looked like a high school.)

I reread *Stop-Time* because Frank Conroy is so eloquent and moving about books and their power at the end of *Stone Reader.* I don't reread books very often; I'm too conscious of both my ignorance and my mortality. (I recently discovered that a friend who was rereading *Bleak House* had done no other Dickens apart from *Barnaby Rudge.* That's just weird. I shamed and nagged him into picking up *Great Expectations* instead.) But when I tried to recall anything about it other than its excellence, I failed. Maybe there was something about a peculiar stepfather? Or was that *This Boy's Life*? And I realized that, as this is true of just about every book I consumed between the ages of, say, fifteen and forty, I haven't even read the books I think I've read. I can't tell you how depressing this is. What's the fucking point?

Apart from Stuyvesant and Salinger, the recurring theme

of the month was Paula Fox. Fox has given blurbs for both *The Fortress of Solitude* and Zoë Heller's novel; Lethem has given a blurb to *Desperate Characters*. I know I'm wrong about this book, because everyone else in the world, including writers I love, thinks it's fantastic, but it Wasn't For Me. It's brilliantly written, I can see that much, and it made me think, too. But mostly I thought about why I don't know anyone like the people Fox writes about. Why are all my friends so dim and unreflective? Where did I go wrong?

Towards the end of the book, Otto and Sophie, the central couple, go to stay in their holiday home. Sophie opens the door to the house, and is immediately reminded of a friend, an artist who used to visit them there; she thinks about him for a page or so. The reason she's thinking about him is that she's staring at something he loved, a vinegar bottle shaped like a bunch of grapes. The reason she's staring at the bottle is because it's in pieces. And the reason it's in pieces is because someone has broken in and trashed the place, a fact we only discover when Sophie has snapped out of her reverie. At this point, I realized with some regret that not only could I never write a literary novel, but I couldn't even be a character in a literary novel. I can only imagine myself, or any character I created, saying, 'Shit! Some bastard has trashed the house!' No rumination about artist friends – just a lot of cursing, and maybe some empty threats of violence.

Zoë Heller's *Notes on a Scandal*, about a fortysomething pottery teacher who has an affair with a fifteen-year-old pupil, was moving along nicely until a character starts talking about football. He tells a teaching colleague that he's been to see Arsenal, and that 'Arsenal won Liverpool 3-0.' Readers of this column will have realized by now that I know almost nothing about anything, but if I were forced to declare one area of expertise, it would be what people say to each other after football matches. It's not much, I know, but it's mine. And I am positive that no one has ever said 'Arsenal won Liverpool 3-0' in the entire history of either Arsenal Football Club or the

English language. 'Beat', 'thrashed', 'did' or 'done', 'trounced', 'thumped', 'shat all over', 'walloped', etc., yes; 'won', emphatically, no. And I think that my dismay and disbelief then led me to question other things, and the fabric of the novel started to unravel a little. Can you really find full-time pottery teachers in modern English state schools? Would a contemporary teenager really complain about being treated as 'the Kunta Kinte round here' when asked to do some housework? I like Zoë Heller's writing, and this book has a terrific narrative voice that recalls Alan Bennett's work; I just wish I wasn't so picky. This is how picky I am. You know the Arsenal bit? It wasn't just the unconvincing demotic I objected to; it was the score. Arsenal haven't beaten Liverpool 3-0 at Highbury since 1991. What chance did the poor woman have?

I haven't finished the Richard Yates biography yet. I will, however, say this much: it is 613 pages long. Despite the influence Yates had on a generation of writers, it's hard enough finding people who've read the great *Revolutionary Road,* let alone people who will want to read about its author's grandparents. I propose that those intending to write a biography should first go to the National Biography Office to get a permit that tells you the number of pages you get. (There will be no right of appeal.) It's quite a simple calculation. Nobody wants to read a book longer than – what? – nine hundred pages? OK, a thousand, maybe. And you can't really get the job done in less than 250. So you're given maximum length if you're doing Dickens, say – someone who had an enormous cultural impact, wrote enormous books and had a life outside them. And everyone else is calculated using Dickens as a yardstick. By this reckoning, Yates is a three-hundred-page man – maybe 315 tops. I'm on page 194 as we speak, and I'm going to stick with it – the book is compelling and warm and gossipy. But on page 48, I found myself reading a paragraph about the choice of gents' outfitters facing the pupils at Yates's school; I felt, personally speaking, that it could have gone.

I reread two other books this month: *How to Stop Smoking and Stay Stopped for Good* and *Quitting Smoking – The Lazy Person's Guide!* I reread them for obvious reasons; I'll be rereading them again, too. They're good books, I think, sensible and helpful. But they're clearly not perfect. If I do stop smoking, it may be because I don't want to read Gillian Riley any more. ✷

NOVEMBER 2003

Unfinished, abandoned, abandoned, unfinished. Well, you can't say I didn't warn you. In the first of these columns, I voiced the suspicion that my then-current reading jag was unsustainable: I was worried, I seem to recall, about the end of the summer, and the forthcoming football season, and it's true that both of these factors have had an adverse effect on book consumption. (Words added to ongoing novel since autumnal return to work: not many, but more than the month before. Football matches watched in the last month: seven whole ones, four of them live in the stadium, and bits and pieces of probably half a dozen others.) Of the two books I started and finished this month, one I read in a day, mostly on a plane, during a day trip to Amsterdam. And it was a book about football.

It is not only sport and work that have slowed me up, however; I would have to say that the ethos of the *Believer* has inhibited me a little too. As you are probably aware by now, the *Believer* has taken the honourable and commendable view that, if it is attacks on contemporary writers and writing you wish to read, then you can choose from an endless range of magazines and newspapers elsewhere – just about all of them, in fact – and that therefore the *Believer* will contain only acid-free literary criticism.

This position is, however, likely to cause difficulties if your brief is simply to write honestly about the books you have been reading: boredom and, very occasionally, despair are part of the reading life, after all. Last month, mindful of the *Believer's raison d'être*, I expressed mild disappointment with a couple of the books I had read. I don't remember the exact words; but I said something to the effect that, if I were physically compelled to express a view as to whether the Disappointing Novel was better or worse than *Crime and Punishment*, then I would keep my opinion to myself, no matter how excruciating the pain, such was my respect for the editorial credo. If, however, the torturers threatened my children, then I would – with the utmost reluctance – voice a very slight preference for *Crime and Punishment*.

Uproar ensued. Voicing a slight preference for *Crime and Punishment* over the Disappointing Novel under threat of torture to my children constituted a Snark, it appeared, and I was summoned to appear before the *Believer* committee – twelve rather eerie young men and women (six of each, naturally), all dressed in white robes and smiling maniacally, like a sort of literary equivalent of the Polyphonic Spree. I was given a severe dressing-down, and only avoided a three-issue suspension by promising never to repeat the offence. Anyway, We (i.e., the Polysyllabic Spree) have decided that if it looks as though I might not enjoy a book, I will abandon it immediately, and not mention it by name. This is what happened with the Literary Novel and the Work of Non-fiction – particularly regrettable in the latter case, as I was supposed to be reviewing it for a London newspaper. The loss of income there, and the expense of flying from London to San Francisco to face the committee (needless to say, those bastards wouldn't stump up), means that this has been an expensive month.

I did, however, finish the biography of Richard Yates that I started last month. I haven't changed my view that it could easily have afforded to shed a few of its six-hundred-plus pages – Yates doesn't sell his first story until page 133 – but I'm glad I stuck with it. Who'd have thought that the author of *Revolutionary Road* wrote speeches for Robert Kennedy, or provided the model for Alton Benes, the insane writer-father of *Seinfeld*'s Elaine? (Yates's daughter Monica, an ex-girlfriend of Larry David, was apparently an inspiration for Elaine herself.) And who'd have thought that the author of an acknowledged American classic, as well as several other respected novels and an outstanding collection of short stories, could have ended up living and then dying in such abject penury? *A Tragic Honesty*, like the Ian Hamilton biography of Lowell that I read recently, is a sad and occasionally terrifying account of how creativity can be simultaneously fragile and self-destructive; it also made me grateful that I am writing now, when the antidepressants are better, and we all drink less. Stories about contemporary writers being taken away in straitjackets are thin on the ground – or no one tells them to me, anyway – but it seemed to happen to Lowell and Yates all the time; there are ten separate page references under 'breakdowns' in the index of *A Tragic Honesty*.

Just as frightening to anyone who writes (or who is connected intimately to a writer) is Yates's willingness to cannibalize his life –

friends, lovers, family, work – for his fiction: just about everyone he ever met was able to find a thinly disguised, and frequently horrific, version of themselves in a novel or a story somewhere. Those who have read *The Easter Parade* will recall the savagely drawn portrait of Pookie, the pathetic, vain, drunken mother of the Grimes sisters; when I tell you that Yates's mother was known to everyone as 'Dookie', you will understand just how far Yates was prepared to go.

It was something of a relief to turn to Jasper Rees's biography of Arsène Wenger – not just because it's short, but because Wenger's career as a football manager is currently both highly successful and unfinished. I don't often pick up books about football any more – I wrote one once, and though the experience didn't stop me from wanting to watch the sport, as I feared it might, it did stop me from wanting to read about it – but I love Arsène, who, weirdly and neatly, coaches my team, Arsenal, and who would probably feature at about number eight in a list of People Who Have Changed My Life for the Better. He transformed a mediocre, plodding side into a thing of beauty, and on a good day, Arsenal plays the best football that anyone in England has ever seen. He was the first foreign manager to win an English championship, and his influence is such that everyone now wants to employ cool, cerebral Europeans. (The previous fashion was for ranting, red-faced Scotsmen.) Even the English national team has one now, much to the disgust of tabloid sportswriters and the more rabidly patriotic football fans.

I gave an interview to Rees for his book, but despite my contribution it's a pretty useful overview of his career to date. I couldn't, hand on heart, argue that it transcends the genre, and you probably only really need to read it if you have an Arsenal season ticket. And if there is one single *Believer* reader who is also an Arsenal season-ticket holder, I'll buy you a drink next home game. What the hell – I'll buy you a car.

I received *How to Breathe Underwater* and the Wilkie Collins novel in the same Jiffy envelope, sent to me by a friend at Penguin, who publishes all three of us in the UK; this friend is evangelical about both books, and so I began one, loved it, finished it, and then started the other. Usually, of course, I treat personal book recommendations with the suspicion they deserve. I've got enough to read as it is, so my first reaction when someone tells me to read something is to find a way to doubt their credentials, or to try to dredge up a conflicting view from the memory. (Just as stone always blunts scissors, a lukewarm 'Oh, it was OK', always beats a 'You have to read this.' It's less work that way.) But every now and again, the zealous gleam in someone's eye catches the attention, and anyway Joanna, jaded as she is by her work, doesn't make loose or unnecessary recommendations. She keeps her powder dry.

She was right, luckily for her: *How to Breathe Underwater* is an outstanding collection of stories. Orringer writes about the things that everyone writes about – youth, friendship, death, grief, etc. – but her narrative settings are fresh and wonderfully knotty. So, while her themes are as solid and as recognizable as oak trees, the stuff growing on the bark you've never seen before. If you wanted to be reductive, 'The Smoothest Way Is Full of Stones' would collapse neatly into a coming-of-age story with a conventional two-girls-and-a-guy triangle at its core. But one of the girls comes from a ferociously orthodox Jewish family, and the other one has a mother who's in the hospital after the loss of a baby, and the boy has this pornographic book stashed away, and the whole thing is so beautifully and complicatedly imagined that you don't want to boil it down to its essence. 'Pilgrims', the first story in the book, makes you feel panicky and breathless, and is destined, I suspect, to be taught in creative writing classes everywhere. The moment I'd finished I bought myself a first edition, and then another, for a friend's birthday. It's that sort of book. I'll tell you how much I liked it: one paragraph in the story 'When She Is Old and I Am

Famous' contained the words 'gowns', 'pumps', 'diva hairdos', 'pink chiffon', 'silk roses', 'couture' and '*Vogue*', and, after the briefest shudder, I read on anyway.

I'm a couple of hundred pages into *No Name*, and so far it's everything I'd hoped it would be. It was sold to me – or given to me free, anyway – as a lost Victorian classic (and I'd never even heard of it), and it really hits the spot: an engrossing, tortuous plot, quirky characters, pathos, the works. If you pick up the Penguin Classics edition, however, don't read the blurb on the back. It more or less blows the first (fantastic) plot twist on the grounds that it's 'revealed early on' – but 'early on' turns out to be page ninety-six, not, say, page eight. Note to publishers: some people read nineteenth-century novels for fun, and a lot of them were written to be read that way too.

I should, perhaps, attempt to explain away the ludicrous number of books bought this month. Most of them were second-hand paperbacks; I bought the Pete Dexter, the Murakami and *The Poet and the Murderer* on a Saturday afternoon spent wandering up and down Stoke Newington Church Street with the baby, and I bought *Leadville* and *Master Georgie* from a bookstall at a local community festival. *Leadville* is a biography of the A40, one of London's dreariest arterial roads, and the desperately unpromising nature of the material somehow persuades me that the book has to be great. And I'd like to point out that *The Poet and the Murderer* is the second cheap paperback about a literary hoax that I've bought since I started writing this column. I cannot really explain why I keep buying books about literary hoaxes that I never seriously intend to read. It's a quirk of character that had remained hitherto unrevealed to me.

I picked up the Styron in a remainder shop while I was reading the Yates biography – Yates spent years adapting it for a film that was never made. *Genome* and *Six Days of War* I bought on a visit to the *London Review of Books*' slightly scary new shop near the

British Museum. I'm not entirely sure why I chose those two in particular, beyond the usual attempts at reinvention that periodically seize one in a bookstore. (When I'm arguing with St Peter at the Pearly Gates, I'm going to tell him to ignore the Books Read column, and focus on the Books Bought instead. 'This is *really* who I am,' I'll tell him. 'I'm actually much more of a *Genome* guy than an Arsène Wenger guy. And if you let me in, I'm going to prove it, honest.') I got the CDs at the *LRB* shop, too. They're actually pretty amazing: the recordings are taken from the British Library Sound Archive, and all the writers featured were born in the nineteenth century – Conan Doyle, Virginia Woolf, Joyce, Yeats, Kipling, Wodehouse, Tolkien and, astonishingly, Browning and Tennyson, although to be honest you can't really hear Browning, who was recorded at a dinner party in 1889, trying and failing to remember the words of 'How They Brought the Good News from Ghent to Aix'. Weirdly, everyone sounds the same: very posh and slightly mad.

I read about a third of *Bush at War*, and I may well return to it at some stage, but the mood that compelled me to begin it passed quickly, and in any case it wasn't quite what I wanted: Woodward's tone is way too matey and sympathetic for me. I did, however, learn that George W. Bush was woken up by the Secret Service at 11:08 p.m. on 9/11. Woken up! He didn't work late that night? And he wasn't too buzzy to get off to sleep? See, if that had been me, I would have been up until about six, drinking and smoking and watching TV, and I would have been useless the next day. It can't be right, can it, that world leaders emerge not through their ability to solve global problems, but to nod off at the drop of a hat? Most decent people can't sleep easily at night, and that, apparently, is precisely why the world is in such a mess. ✶

DECEMBER 2003/
JANUARY 2004

First, an apology. Last month, I may have inadvertently given the impression that *No Name* by Wilkie Collins was a lost Victorian classic (the misunderstanding may have arisen because of my loose use of the phrase 'lost Victorian classic'), and that everyone should rush out and buy it. I had read over two hundred pages when I gave you my considered verdict; in fact, the last four hundred and eighteen pages nearly killed me, and I wish I were speaking figuratively. We fought, Wilkie Collins and I. We fought bitterly and with all our might, to a standstill, over a period of about three weeks, on trains and aeroplanes and by hotel swimming pools. Sometimes – usually late at night, in bed – he could put me out cold with a single paragraph; every time I got through twenty or thirty pages, it felt to me as though I'd socked him good, but it took a lot out of me, and I had to retire to my corner to wipe the blood and sweat off my reading glasses. And still he kept coming back for more. Only in the last fifty-odd pages, after I'd landed several of these blows, did old Wilkie show any signs of buckling under the assault. He was pretty tough for a man of nearly one hundred and eighty. Hats off to him. Anyway, I'm sorry for the bum steer, and readers of this column insane enough to have run down to their nearest bookstore as a result of my advice should write to the *Believer*, enclosing a receipt, and we will refund your $14. It has to say *No Name* on the receipt, though, because we weren't born yesterday, and we're not stumping up for your Patricia Cornwell novels. You can pay for them yourselves.

In his introduction to my Penguin edition, Mark Ford points out that Collins wrote the closing sections of the novel 'in both great pain and desperate anxiety over publishers' deadlines'. (In fact, Dickens, who edited the magazine in which *No Name* was originally published, *All the Year Round*, offered to nip down to London and finish the book off for him: 'I could take it up any time and do it . . . so like you as that no-one should find out the difference.' That's literature for you.) It is not fair to wonder why Collins bothered: *No Name* has lots going for it, including a driven, complicated and morally ambiguous central female character, and a tremendous first two hundred pages. But it's certainly reasonable to wonder why a sick man should have wanted to overextend a relatively slight melodrama to the extent that people want to fight him. *No Name* is the story of a woman's attempt to reclaim her rightful inheritance from cruel and heartless relatives, and one of the reasons the book didn't work for me is that one has to quiver with outrage throughout at the prospect of this poor girl having to work for a living, as a governess or something equally demeaning. It could be, of course, that the book seems bloated because Collins simply wasn't as good at handling magazine serialization as Dickens, and that huge chunks of the novel, which originally came in forty-four parts, were written only to keep the end well away from the beginning. I'm only guessing, but I'd imagine that many subscribers to *All the Year Round* between May 1862 and early January 1863 felt exactly the same way. I'm guessing, in fact, that there were a few cancelled subscriptions, and that *No Name* is the chief reason you can no longer find *All the Year Round* alongside the *Believer* at your nearest newsstand.

There are two sides to every fight, though, and Wilkie would point out that I unwisely attempted to read the second half of *No Name* during a trip to LA. Has anyone ever attempted a Victorian novel in Los Angeles, and if so, why? In England, we read Victorian novels precisely because they're long, and we have nothing else to do. LA is too warm, too bright, there's too much sport on TV, and the sandwiches are too big (and come with chips/'fries'). English people shouldn't attempt to do anything in LA; it's all too much. We should just lie in a darkened room with a cold flannel until it's time to come home again.

With the exception of *The Sirens of Titan*, bought secondhand from a Covent Garden market stall, all this month's books were purchased at Book Soup in LA. (Book Soup and the Tower Records directly opposite have become, in my head, what Los Angeles *is*.) Going to a good US bookshop is still ludicrously exciting – unless I'm on book tour, when the excitement tends to wear off a little. As I don't see American books-pages, I have no idea whether one of my favourite authors – Charles Baxter, for example, on this trip – has a new book out, and there's every chance that it won't be published in the UK for months, if at all. There is enough money in the music and movie industries to ensure that we get to hear about most things that might interest us; books have to remain a secret, to be discovered only when you spend time browsing. This is bad for authors, but good for the assiduous shopper.

Mark Salzman's book about juvenile offenders I read about in the *Believer*. I met Mark after a reading in LA some years ago, and one of the many memorable things he told me was that he'd written a large chunk of his last novel almost naked, covered in aluminium foil, with a towel round his head, sitting in a car. His reasons for doing so, which I won't go into here, were sound, and none of them were connected with mental illness, although perhaps inevitably he had caused his wife some embarrassment – especially when she brought friends back to the house. Jincy Willett, whose work I had never heard of, I bought because of her blurbs, which, I'm afraid to say, only goes to show that blurbs do work.

I was in the US for the two epic playoff series, between the Cubs and the Marlins, and the Red Sox and the Yankees, and I became temporarily fixated with baseball. And I'd read something about *Moneyball* somewhere, and it was a staff pick at Book Soup, and when, finally, *No Name* lay vanquished and lifeless at my feet, it was Lewis's book I turned to: it seemed a better fit. *Moneyball* is a rotten title, I think. You expect a subtitle something along the lines of *How Greed Killed America's National Pastime*, but actually the book isn't like that at all – it's the story of how Billy Beane, the GM of the Oakland As, worked out how to buck the system and win lots of games despite being hampered by one of the smallest payrolls in baseball. He did this by recognizing (*a*) that the stats traditionally used to judge players are almost entirely worthless, and (*b*) that many good players are being discarded by the major leagues simply because they don't *look* like good players.

The latter discovery in particular struck a chord with me, because my football career has been blighted by exactly this sort of prejudice. English scouts visiting my Friday morning five-a-side game have (presumably) discounted me on peripheral grounds of age, weight, speed, amount of time spent lying on the ground weeping with exhaustion, etc.; what they're not looking at is *performance*, which is of course the only thing that counts. They'd have made a film called *Head It Like Hornby* by now if Billy Beane were working over here. (And if I were any good at heading, another overrated and peripheral skill.) Anyway, I understood about one word in every four of *Moneyball*, and it's still the best and most engrossing sports book I've read in years. If you know anything about baseball, you will enjoy it four times as much as I did, which means that you might explode.

I have an autistic son, but I don't often read any books about autism. Most of the time, publishers seem to want to hear from or about autists with special talents, as in *Rain Man* (my son, like the vast majority of autistic kids and contrary to public perception, has no special talent, unless you count his remarkable ability to hear the opening of a crisp packet from several streets away), or from parents who believe that they have 'rescued' or 'cured' their autistic child (and there is no cure for autism, although there are a few weird stories, none of which seem applicable to my son's condition). So most books on the subject tend to make me feel alienated, resentful, cynical or simply baffled. Granted, pretty much any book on any subject seems to make me feel this way, but I reckon that in this case, my personal experience of the subject means I'm entitled to feel anything I want.

I read Charlotte Moore's book because I agreed to write an introduction for it, and I agreed to write an introduction because, in a series of brilliant columns in the *Guardian*, she has managed not only to tell it like it is, but to do so with enormous good humour and wit – *George and Sam* (Moore has three sons, two of whom are autistic) is, believe it or not, the funniest book I've read this year. I'm not sure I would have found it as funny six or seven years ago, when Danny was first diagnosed and autism wasn't a topic that made me laugh much; but now that I'm used to glancing out of the window on cold wet November nights and suddenly seeing a ten-year-old boy bouncing naked and gleeful on a trampoline, I have come to relish the stories all parents of autistic kids have.

The old cliché 'You couldn't make it up' is always dispiriting to anyone who writes fiction – if you couldn't make it up, then it's probably not worth talking or writing about anyway. But autism is worth writing about – not just because it affects an increasingly large number of people, but because of the light the condition shines down on the rest of us. And though you can predict that autistic kids are likely to behave in peculiar obsessive-compulsive ways, the details of these compulsions and obsessions are always completely unimaginable and frequently charming in their strangeness. Sam, the younger of Moore's two autistic boys, has an obsession with oasthouses – he once escaped from home in order to explore a particularly fine example a mile and a half away. 'Its owner, taking an afternoon nap, was startled to be joined in bed by a small boy still wearing his Wellington boots.'

George, meanwhile, is compelled to convince everyone that he doesn't eat, even though he does. After his mum has made his breakfast she has to reassure him that it's for Sam, and then turn her back until he's eaten it. (Food has to be smuggled into school, hidden inside his swimming things.) Sam loves white goods, especially washing machines, so during a two-week stay in London he was taken to a different launderette each day, and nearly combusted with excitement; he also likes to look at bottles of lavatory cleaner through frosted glass. George parrots lines he's learned from videotapes: 'The Government has let me down,' he told his trampoline teacher recently. (For some reason, trampolines are a big part of our lives.) 'This would make Ken Russell spit with envy,' he remarked enigmatically on another occasion. Oasthouses, washing machines, pretending not to eat when really you do . . . see? You really couldn't make it up.

I don't want to give the impression that living with an autistic child is *all* fun. If you have a child of the common or garden-variety, I wouldn't recommend, on balance, that you swap him (most autistic kids are boys) for a child with a hilarious obsession. Hopefully I need hardly add that there's some stuff that . . . well, that, to understate the case, isn't quite as hilarious. I am merely pointing out, as Moore is doing, that if you are remotely interested in the strangeness and variety and beauty of humankind, then there is a lot in the condition to marvel at. This is the first book about autism I've read that I'd recommend to people who want to know what it is like; it's sensible about education, diet, possible causes, just about everything that affects the quotidian lives of those dealing with the condition. It also made this parent feel better about the compromises one has to make: 'This morning George breakfasted on six After Eights [After Eights are 'sophisticated' chocolate mints] and some lemon barley-water. I was pleased − *pleased* − because lately he hasn't been eating at all . . .' In our house it's salt-and-vinegar crisps.

I can imagine *George and Sam* doing a roaring trade with grandparents, aunts and uncles tough enough to want to know the truth. I read it while listening to Damien Rice's beautiful *O* for the first time, and I had an unexpectedly transcendent moment: the book coloured the music, and the music coloured the book, and I ended up feeling unambivalently happy that my son is who he is; those moments are precious. I hope *George and Sam* finds a US publisher.

A couple of months ago, I became depressed by the realization that I'd forgotten pretty much everything I've ever read. I have, however, bounced back: I am now cheered by the realization that if I've forgotten everything I've ever read then I can read some of my favourite books again *as if for the first time*. I remembered the punch line of *The Sirens of Titan*, but everything else was as fresh as a daisy, and Vonnegut's wise, lovely, world-weary novel was a perfect way to cap Charlotte Moore's book: she'd prepared the way beautifully for a cosmic and absurdly reductive view of our planet. I'm beginning to see that our appetite for books is the same as our appetite for food, that our brain tells us when we need the literary equivalent of salads, or chocolate, or meat and potatoes. When I read *Moneyball*, it was because I wanted something quick and light after the 32-oz steak of *No Name*; *The Sirens of Titan* wasn't a reaction against *George and Sam*, but a way of enhancing it. So what's that? Mustard? MSG? A brandy? It went down a treat, anyway.

Smoking is rubbish, most of the time. But if I'd never smoked, I'd never have met Kurt Vonnegut. We were both at a huge party in New York, and I sneaked out on to the balcony for a cigarette, and there he was, smoking. So we talked – about C. S. Forester, I seem to remember. (That's just a crappy and phoney figure of speech. Of course I remember.) So tell your kids not to smoke, but it's only fair to warn them of the downside, too: that they will therefore never get the chance to offer the greatest living writer in America a light. ✶

A *selection from*

GEORGE AND SAM:
AUTISM IN THE FAMILY

by CHARLOTTE MOORE

✶ ✶ ✶

Monday morning. We're in a hurry – of course we are. Every working mother with three school-age sons is in a hurry on a Monday morning.

George is nearly thirteen. The physical process of puberty is beginning, but he seems unaware of this, just as he's always been unaware of the effect his exceptional good looks have on people. He wanders into the kitchen, naked. He climbs on to the Aga, and sits there twiddling a piece of cardboard. I send him to get dressed; his skin is red and mottled from the heat. He returns with all his clothes on the wrong way round.

I fill a lunchbox for eleven-year-old Sam. Plain crisps, gluten-free biscuits, marzipan, an apple that I know he won't eat, but I suppose I live on in hope. George doesn't have a lunchbox, because George maintains the fiction that he doesn't eat anything at all, and a lunchbox is too blatant a reminder that this cannot be the case. I smuggle his food supplies – mainly Twiglets and choco-late – into his school taxi, underneath his swimming things.

I make George's breakfast – but I have to pretend it's not his breakfast. 'I'm making this for Sam,' I announce, pointedly. I toast two slices of rice bread; Sam's diet excludes wheat, oats, barley, rye and all dairy products. I place them on two plates which George has selected by sniffing. I spread Marmite in an even layer right up to the edge of the crusts, cut them into quarters, then busy myself elsewhere. George slips down from the Aga; as long as my back's turned, he'll risk the toast. 'These are for Sam,' he states as he starts to eat. 'Yes, they're for Sam,' I confirm, without looking round.

Sam's always the last up. He's awake, but he's under his duvet, murmuring; his vocalization is somewhere between a hum and a chant, and is almost completely incomprehensible. He fingers the toy owl he's had since babyhood. The owl has no name, no character; Sam has never played with him, but then, he's rarely played with any toy. The owl is a tactile comforter, not a friend.

Sam won't get up and dress until the taxi driver rings the doorbell. I did try ringing it myself, to get him moving, but Sam's not daft. He only fell for that once. And the dressing process can be infuriatingly slow. Pants on – pants off again. Shirt inside out – outside in – inside out once more. Six pairs of identical tracksuit trousers rejected – the seventh finally, mysteriously, acceptable. Socks stuffed down into the toes of his trainers, pulled out, stuffed in again. One step forward, two steps back – and endless little rituals about touching things and moving things in his bedroom. If I try to intervene, the whole process starts all over again.

At last he's dressed – no time for niceties like washing or brushing teeth. Now Sam has to get down the stairs all in one go. If anything blocks his way, or if he has a crisis of confidence halfway down, he'll freeze. He takes the stairs at a gallop, gets as far as the front door. I open the door for him. Mistake! Sam has to do everything for himself. He opens and shuts the door six times before he can bring himself to leave the house.

George's taxi arrives. I note with pleasure that the toast has been eaten – but where is George? In the lavatory of course, where he spends about a quarter of his waking hours. He emerges, and makes for the front door – but wait, there's something odd about his gait. He's pulled up his trousers, but forgotten about his pants. I ignore his protests, hoick up his pants, waft a brush over his uncut hair, and propel him towards the taxi. 'Don't wave! Don't say goodbye!' he commands, and hands me a fragment of sweet paper to add to the collection that already covers the kitchen table. Two empty Fanta bottles, eight yellow lollipop sticks, silver foil, Softmint wrappers . . . hoarding litter is George's latest obsession.

A call from the playroom reminds me of the existence of my youngest child. *Blue Peter* has finished; Jake, four, wants his Ready Brek. He chats as he eats; he'd like to meet Gareth Gates, he'd like to be Young Sportsman of the Year. Have I found his reading book? Can he have three kinds of sugar on his cereal?

I take Jake to the local primary school, where he is in Reception. He greets his friends on the way in, dismisses me with a hug and a kiss. Neither George nor Sam ever embrace me in greeting or salute.

As I leave, I peep through the window. Jake is cross-legged in the middle of the group; he is listening to what the teacher has to say. His hand shoots up. He's right in there, a proper schoolboy, a social animal. He couldn't be more different from his older brothers – but then, Jake's not autistic. ✶

FEBRUARY 2004

My first book was published just over eleven years ago and remains in print, and though I observed the anniversary with only a modest celebration (a black-tie dinner for forty of my closest friends, many of whom were kind enough to read out the speeches I had prepared for them), I can now see that I should have made more of a fuss: in *Enemies of Promise*, which was written in 1938, the critic Cyril Connolly attempts to isolate the qualities that make a book last for ten years.

Over the decades since its publication, *Enemies of Promise* has been reduced pretty much to one line: 'There is no more sombre enemy of good art than the pram in the hall,' which is possibly why I was never previously very interested in reading it. What are you supposed to do if the pram in the hall is already there? You could move it out into the garden, I suppose, if you have a garden, or get rid of it and carry the little bastards everywhere, but maybe I'm being too literal-minded.

Enemies of Promise is about a lot more than the damaging effects of domesticity, however; it's also about prose style, and the perils of success, and journalism, and politics. Anyone who writes, or wants to write, will find something on just about every single page that either endorses a long-held prejudice or outrages, and that makes it a pretty compelling read. Ironically, the copy I found on the shelf belongs to one of the mothers of my children. I wonder if she knew, when she bought it twenty years ago, that she would one day partially destroy a literary career? Connolly would probably argue that she did. He generally takes a pretty dim view of women, who 'make crippling demands on [a writer's] time and money, especially if they set their hearts on his popular success'. Bless 'em, eh? I'm presuming, as Connolly does, that you're a man. What would a woman be doing reading a literary magazine anyway?

Connolly spends the first part of the book dividing writers into two camps, the Mandarin and the Vernacular. (He is crankily thorough in this division, by the way. He even goes through the big books of the twenties year by year, and marks them with a V or an M: '1929 – H. Green, *Living* (V); W. Faulkner, *The Sound and the Fury* (M); Hemingway, *A Farewell to Arms* (V); Lawrence, *Pansies* (V); Joyce, *Fragments of a Work in Progress* (M)', and so on. One hesitates to point it out – it's too late now – but shouldn't Connolly have been getting on with his writing, rather than fiddling around with lists? That's one of your enemies, right there.) And then, having thus divided, he spends a lot of time despairing of both camps. 'The Mandarin style . . . is beloved of literary pundits, by those who would make the written word as unlike as possible to the spoken one. It is the title of those writers whose tendency is to make their language convey more than they mean or more than they feel.' (Yay, Cyril! Way to go!) Meanwhile, 'According to Gide, a good writer should navigate against the current; the practitioners in the new vernacular are swimming with it; the familiarities of the advertisements in the morning paper, the matey leaders in the *Daily Express*, the blather of the film critics, the wisecracks of the newsreel commentators, the know-all autobiographies of political reporters, the thrillers and 'teccies . . . are all swimming with it too.' (Cyril, you utter *ass*. You think Hemingway wrote like that lot? Have another look, mate.) Incidentally, the 'know-all auto-biographies of political reporters' – that was a whole *genre* in the nineteen-thirties? Boy.

The invention of paperbacks, around the time Connolly was writing *Enemies of Promise*, changed everything. Connolly's ten-year question could fill a book in 1938 because the answer was genuinely complicated then; books really could sit out the vicissitudes of fashion on library shelves, and then dust themselves off and climb back down into readers' laps. Paperbacks and chain bookstores mean that a contemporary version of *Enemies of Promise* would consist of one simple and uninteresting question: 'Well, did it sell in its first year?' My first book did OK; meanwhile, books that I reviewed and loved in 1991 and 1992, books every bit as good or better than mine, are out of print, simply because they never found a readership then. They might have passed all the Connolly tests, but they're dead in the water anyway.

You end up muttering back at just about every ornately constructed *pensée* that Connolly utters, but that's one of the joys of this book. At one point, he strings together a few sentences by Hemingway, Isherwood and Orwell in an attempt to prove that their prose styles are indistinguishable. But the point, surely, is that though you can make Connolly's sentence-by-sentence case easily enough, you'd never confuse a book by Orwell with a book by Hemingway – and that's what they were doing, writing books. Look, here's a plain, flat, vernacular sentence:

> So I bought a little city (it was Galveston, Texas) and told everybody that nobody had to move, we were going to do it just gradually, very relaxed, no big changes overnight.

This is the tremendous first line of Donald Barthelme's story 'I Bought a Little City' (V); one fears that Connolly might have spent a lot of time looking at the finger, and ignored what it was pointing at. ('See, he bought a whole *city*, Cyril! Galveston, Texas! Oh, forget it.') The vernacular turned out to be far more adaptable than Connolly could have predicted.

Reading the book now means that one can, if one wants, play Fantasy Literature – match writers off against each other and see who won over the long haul. (M) or (V)? Faulkner or Henry Green? I reckon the surprise champ was P. G. Wodehouse, as elegant and resourceful a prose stylist as anyone held up for our inspection here; Connolly is sniffy about him several times over the course of *Enemies of Promise*, and presumes that his stuff won't last five minutes, but he has turned out to be as enduring as anyone apart from Orwell. Jokes, you see. People do like jokes.

The Polysyllabic Spree, the twelve terrifyingly beatific young men and woman who run the *Believer*, have been quiet of late – they haven't been giving me much trouble, anyway. A friend who works in the same building has heard the ominous rustle of white robes upstairs, however, and he reckons they're planning something pretty big, maybe something like another Jonestown. (That makes sense, if you think about it. The robes, the eerie smiles, 'the *Believer*' . . . if you find a free sachet of powdered drink, or – more likely – an edible poem in this month's issue, don't touch it.) Anyway, while they're thus distracted, I shall attempt to sneak a snark under the wire: Tobias Wolff's *Old School* is too short. Oh, come on, guys! That's different from saying it's too long! Too long means you didn't like it! Too short means you did!

The truth is, I've been reading more short books recently because I need to bump up the numbers in the Books Read column – six of this month's seven were really pretty scrawny. But *Old School* I would have read this month, the month of its publication, no matter how long it was: Wolff's two volumes of memoir, *This Boy's Life* and *In Pharaoh's Army*, are perennial sources of writerly inspiration, and you presumably know how good his stories are. *Old School* is brilliant – painful, funny, exquisitely written, acute about writers and literary ambition. (*Old School* is set right at the beginning of the sixties, in a boys' private school, and you get to meet Robert Frost and Ayn Rand.) But the problem with short novels is that you can take liberties with them: you know you're going to get through them no matter what, so you never set aside the time or the commitment that a bigger book requires. I fucked *Old School* up; I should have read it in a sitting, but I didn't, and I never gave it a chance to leave its mark. We are never allowed to forget that some books are badly written; we should remember that sometimes they're badly read, too.

Eats, Shoots and Leaves (the title refers to a somewhat laboured joke about a misplaced comma and a panda) is Britain's number-one best seller at the moment, and it's about punctuation, and no, I don't get it, either. It's a sweet, good-humoured book, and it's grammatically sound and all, but, you know . . . it really is all about how to use a semicolon and all that. What's going on? One writer I know suspects that the book's enormous success is due to the disturbing rise of the Provincial Pedant, but I have a more benign theory: that when you hear about it (and you hear about it a lot, at the moment), you think of someone immediately, someone you know and love, whose punctuation exasperates you and fills them full of self-loathing. I thought of Len, and my partner thought of

Emily, neither of whom could place an apostrophe correctly if their lives depended on it. (Names have been changed, by the way, to protect the semiliterate.) And I'm sure Len and Emily will receive a thousand copies each for Christmas and birthdays, and other people will buy a thousand copies for their Lens and Emilys, and in the end the book will sell a quarter of a million copies, *but only two hundred different people will own them.* I enjoyed the fearful bashing that Lynn Truss gives to the entertainment industry – the Hugh Grant movie *Two Weeks Notice* (*sic*), *Who Framed Roger Rabbit* (*sic*), the fabricated English pop band Hear'Say (*sic*) – and the advice she quotes from a newspaper style manual: 'Punctuation is a courtesy designed to help readers understand a story without stumbling', which helps to explain a lot of literary fiction. I had never before heard of the Oxford comma (used before the 'and' that brings a list to a close), and I didn't know that Jesus never gets a possessive 's', just because of who He is. I never really saw the possessive 's' as profane, or even very secular, but there you go.

The most irritating book of the month (can't you feel the collective heart of the Spree beating a little faster?) was Joe Pernice's *Meat Is Murder*. One can accept, reluctantly, Pernice's apparently inexhaustible ability to knock out brilliant three-minute pop songs – just about any Pernice Brothers record contains half a dozen tunes comparable to Elvis Costello's best work. But now it turns out that he can write fiction too, and so envy and bitterness become unavoidable. *Meat Is Murder* and Warren Zanes's *Dusty in Memphis* are both part of a new and neat little '33 ⅓' series published by Continuum; Pernice is the only writer who has chosen to write a novella about a favourite album, rather than an essay; his story is set in 1985, and is about high school and suicide and teen depression and, tangentially, the Smiths. Warren Zanes's effort, almost the polar opposite of Pernice's, is a long, scholarly and convincing piece of non-fiction analysing the myth of the American South. Endearingly, neither book mentions the relevant records as much as you'd expect: the music is a ghostly rather than physical presence. I liked Art Linson's *What Just Happened?*, one of those scabrous, isn't-Hollywood-awful books written by someone – a producer, in this case (and indeed in most other cases, e.g. Julia Phillips, Lynda Obst) – who knows what he's talking about. I can't really explain why I picked it up, however; perhaps I wanted to be made grateful that I work in publishing, rather than film, and that's what happened.

Clockers was my big book of the month, the centrepiece around which I can now arrange the short books so that they look functional – pretty, even, if I position them right. I cheated a little, I know – *Clockers* is essentially a thriller, so it didn't feel as though I'd had to work for my 650 pages – but it was still a major reading job. Why isn't Richard Price incredibly famous, like Tom Wolfe? His work is properly plotted, indisputably authentic and serious-minded, and it has soul and moral authority.

Clockers asks – almost in passing, and there's a lot more to it than this – a pretty interesting question: if you choose to work for the minimum wage when everyone around you is pocketing thousands from drug deals, then what does that do to you, to your head and to your heart? Price's central characters, brothers Strike (complicatedly bad, a crack dealer) and Victor (complicatedly good, the minimum-wage guy), act out something that feels as inevitable and as durable as a Bible story, except with a lot more swearing and drugs. *Clockers* is – eek – really about the contradictions of capitalism.

I've been trying to write a short story that entails my knowing something about contemporary theories of time – hence *Introducing Time* – but every time I pick up any kind of book about science I start to cry. This actually inhibits my reading pretty badly, due to not being able to see. I'm OK with time theorists up until, say, St Augustine, and then I start to panic, and the panic then gives way to actual weeping. By my estimation, I should be able to understand Newton by the time I'm 850 years old – by which time I'll probably discover that some smartass has invented a new theory, and he's out of date anyway. The short story should be done some time shortly after that. Anyway, I hope you enjoy it, because it's killing me. ✷

MARCH 2004

BOOKS BOUGHT:

* *The Amateur Marriage* – Anne Tyler
* *The Eclipse* – Antonella Gambotto
* *The Complete Richard Hannay* – John Buchan
* *Selected Letters* – Gustave Flaubert
* *Vietnam-Perkasie* – W. D. Ehrhart

BOOKS READ:

* Some of Flaubert's letters
* *Not Even Wrong* – Paul Collins
* *How Mumbo-Jumbo Conquered the World* – Francis Wheen
* *Liar's Poker* – Michael Lewis
* Some of *Greenmantle* – John Buchan
* *How to Stop Smoking and Stay Stopped for Good* – Gillian Riley

S o this last month was, as I believe you people say, a bust. I had high hopes for it, too; it was Christmastime in England, and I was intending to do a little holiday comfort reading – *David Copperfield* and a couple of John Buchan novels, say, while sipping an eggnog and heroically ploughing my way through some enormous animal carcass or other. I've been a father for ten years now, and not once have I been able to sit down and read several hundred pages of Dickens during the Christmas holidays. Why I thought it might be possible this year, now that I have twice as many children, is probably a question best discussed with an analyst – somewhere along the line, I have failed to take something on board. (Hey, great idea: if you have kids, give your partner reading vouchers next Christmas. Each voucher entitles the bearer to two hours' reading-time *while kids are awake*. It might look like a cheapskate present, but parents will appreciate that it costs more in real terms than a Lamborghini.)

If I'm honest, however, it wasn't just snot-nosed children who crawled between and all over me and Richard Hannay. One of the reasons I wanted to write this column, I think, is because I assumed that the cultural highlight of my month would arrive in book form, and that's true, for probably eleven months of the year. Books are, let's face it, better than everything else. If we played Cultural Fantasy Boxing League, and made books go fifteen rounds in the ring against the best that any other art form had to offer, then books would win pretty much every time. Go on, try it. *The Magic Flute* v. *Middlemarch*? *Middlemarch* in six. *The Last Supper* v. *Crime and Punishment*? Fyodor on points. See? I mean, I don't know how scientific this is, but it feels like the novels are walking it. You might get the occasional exception – *Blonde on Blonde* might mash up *The Old Curiosity Shop*, say, and I wouldn't give much for *Pale Fire*'s chances against *Citizen Kane*. And every now and again you'd get a shock, because that happens in sport, so *Back to the Future III* might land a lucky punch on *Rabbit, Run*; but I'm still backing literature twenty-nine times out of thirty. Even if you love movies and music as much as you do books, it's still, in any given four-week period, way, *way* more likely you'll find a great book you haven't read than a great movie you haven't seen, or a great album you haven't heard: the assiduous consumer will eventually exhaust movies and music. Sure, there will always be gaps and blind spots, but I've been watching and listening for a long time, and I'll never again have the feeling everyone has with literature: that we can't get through the good novels published in the last six months, let alone those published since publishing began. This month, however, the cultural highlight was a rock-and-roll show – two shows, actually, one of which took place in a pub called the Fiddler's Elbow in Kentish Town, North London. The Fiddler's Elbow is not somewhere you would normally expect to find your most memorable drink of the month, let alone your most memorable spiritual moment, but there you go: God really is everywhere. Anyway, against all the odds, and even though they were fighting above their weight, these shows punched the books to the floor. And they were good books, too.

Five or six years ago, a friend in Philly introduced me to a local band called Marah. Their first album had just come out, on an indie label, and it sounded great to me, like the Pogues reimagined by the E Street Band, full of fire and tunes and soul and banjos. There was a buzz about it, and they got picked up by Steve Earle's label, E-Squared; their next album got noticed by Greil Marcus and Stephen King (who proudly wore a Marah T-shirt in a photo-shoot) and Springsteen himself, and it looked like they were off and away. Writing this down, I can suddenly see the reason why it didn't happen for them, or at least, why it hasn't happened yet. Steve Earle, Stephen King, Greil Marcus, Bruce, me . . . none of us is under a hundred years old. The band is young, but their refer-ents, the music they love, is getting on a bit, and in an attempt to address this problem, they attempted to alienate their ancient fans with a noisy modern rock album. They succeeded in the alien-ation, but not in finding a new audience, so they have been forced to retreat and retrench and rethink. At the end of the Fiddler's Elbow show they passed a hat around, which gives you some indi-cation of the level of retrenchment going on. They'll be OK. Their next album will be a big hit, and they'll sell out Madison Square Garden, and you'll all be boasting that you read a column by a guy who saw them in the Fiddler's Elbow.

Anyway, the two shows I saw that week were spectacular, as

good as anything I've seen with the possible exception of the Clash in '79, Prince in '85, and Springsteen on the *River* tour. Dave and Serge, the two brothers who are to Marah what the Gallaghers are to Oasis, played the Fiddler's Elbow as if it were Giants Stadium, and even though it was acoustic, they just about blew the place up. They were standing on chairs and lying on the floor, they were funny, they charmed everyone in the pub apart from an old drunk sitting next to the drum kit (a drummer turned up halfway through the evening with his own set, having played a gig elsewhere first), who put his fingers firmly in his ears during Serge's extended harmonica solo. (His mate, meanwhile, rose unsteadily to his feet and started clapping along.) It was utterly bizarre and very moving: most musicians wouldn't have bothered turning up, let alone almost killing themselves. And I was re-minded – and this happened the last time I saw them play, too – how rarely one feels included in a live show. Usually you watch, and listen, and drift off, and the band plays well or doesn't and it doesn't matter much either way. It can actually be a very lonely experience. But I felt a part of the music, and a part of the people I'd gone with, and, to cut this short before the encores, I didn't want to read for about a fortnight afterward. I wanted to write, but I couldn't because of the holidays, and I wanted to listen to Marah, but I didn't want to read no book. I was too itchy, too energized, and if young people feel like that every night of the week, then, yes, literature's dead as a dodo. (In an attempt to get myself back on course, I bought Bill Ehrhardt's book *Vietnam-Perkasie*, because he comes Marah-endorsed, and provided the inspiration for 'Round Eye Blues', one of their very best songs. I didn't read the thing, though. And their next album is tentatively entitled *20,000 Streets Under the Sky*, after a Patrick Hamilton novel – I'm going to order that and not read it, too.)

It wasn't as if I didn't try; it was just that very little I picked up fit very well with my mood. I bought Flaubert's letters after reading the piece about Donald Barthelme's required reading list in the *Believer* [October 2003], but they weren't right – or at least, they're not if one chooses to read them in chronological order. The young Flaubert wasn't very rock and roll. He was, on this evidence, kind of a prissy, nerdy kid. 'friend, I shall send you some of my political speeches, liberal constitutionalist variety,' he wrote to Ernest Chevalier in January 1831; he'd just turned nine years old. Nine! Get a life, kid! (Really? You wrote those? They're pretty good books. Well . . . Get another one, then.) I am probably taking more pleasure than is seemly in his failure to begin the sentence with a capital letter. You know, as in, Jesus, he didn't know the first thing about basic punctuation! How did this loser ever get to be a writer?

Francis Wheen's *How Mumbo-Jumbo Conquered the World* was a better fit, because, well, it rocks: it's fast and smart and very funny, despite being about how we have betrayed the Enlightenment by retreating back to the Dark Ages. Wheen wrote a warm, witty biography of Marx a few years back and has a unique, sharp, enviable and trustworthy mind. Here he dishes it out two-fisted to Tony Blair and George W. Bush, Deepak Chopra and Francis Fukuyama, Princess Diana and Margaret Thatcher, Hillary Clinton and Jacques Derrida, and by the end of the book you do have the rather dizzying sensation that you, the author, and maybe Richard Dawkins are the only remotely sane people in the entire world. It's difficult to endorse this book without committing a few cardinal *Believer* sins: as you may have noticed, some of the people that Wheen accuses of talking bullshit are, regrettably, writers, and in a chapter entitled 'The Demolition Merchants of Reality', Wheen lumps deconstructionism in with creationism. In other words, he claims there isn't much to choose from between Pat Buchanan and Jacques Lacan when it comes to mumbo-jumbo, and I'm sorry to say that I laughed a lot. The next chapter, 'The Catastrophists', gives homoeopathy, astrology and UFOlogy a good kicking, and you'll find yourself conveniently forgetting the month you gave up coffee and mint because you were taking arnica three times a day. (Did you know that Jacques Benveniste, one of the world's leading homoeopathic 'scientists', now claims that you can *email* homoeopathic remedies? Yeah, see, what you do is you can take the 'memory' of the diluted substance out of the water electromagnetically, put it on your computer, email it, and play it back on a sound card into new water. I mean, that could work, right?)

Richard Dawkins, Wheen recalls, once pointed out that if an alternative remedy proves to be efficacious – that is to say, if it is shown to have curative properties in rigorous medical trials – then 'it ceases to be an alternative; it simply becomes medicine'. In other words, it's only 'alternative' so long as it's been shown not to be any bloody good. I found it impossible not to apply this helpful observation to other areas of life. Maybe a literary novel is just a novel that doesn't really work, and an art film merely a film that people don't want to see . . . *How Mumbo-Jumbo Conquered the World* is a clever-clogs companion to Michael Moore's *Stupid White Men*; and as it's about people of both sexes and every conceivable hue, it's arguably even more ambitious.

I read *Liar's Poker*, Michael Lewis's book about bond-traders in the eighties, for two reasons, one of which was Wheen-inspired: he made me want to try to be more clever, especially about grown-up things like economics. Plus I'd read Lewis's great *Moneyball* a couple of months previously [see p. 38], so I already knew that he was capable of leading me through the minefields of my own ignorance. It turns out, though, that the international money markets are more complicated than baseball. These guys buy and sell mortgages! They buy and sell risk! But I haven't got a clue what any of that actually means! This isn't Michael Lewis's fault – he really did try his best, and in any case you kind of romp through the book anyway: the people are pretty compelling, if completely unlike anyone you might meet in real life. At one point, Lewis describes an older trader throwing a ten-dollar bill at a young colleague about to take a business flight. 'Hey, take out some crash insurance for yourself in my name,' the older guy says. 'I feel lucky.' As a metaphor for what happens on the trading floor, that's pretty hard to beat.

Francis Wheen's book and Paul Collins's *Not Even Wrong* were advance reading copies that arrived through the post. I'm never going to complain about receiving free early copies of books, because quite clearly there's nothing to complain about, but it does introduce a rogue element into one's otherwise carefully plotted reading schedule. I had no idea I wanted to read Wheen's book until it arrived, and it was because of Wheen that I read Lewis, and then *Not Even Wrong* turned up and I wanted to read that too, and Buchan's *Greenmantle* got put to one side, I suspect for ever. Being a reader is sort of like being president, except reading involves fewer state dinners, usually. You have this agenda you want to get through, but you get distracted by life events, e.g., books arriving in the mail/ World War III, and you are temporarily deflected from your chosen path.

Having said that I hardly ever read books about autism, I have now read two in the last few weeks. Paul Collins, occasionally of this parish, is another parent of an autistic kid, and *Not Even Wrong*, like Charlotte Moore's *George and Sam*, is a memoir of sorts. The two books are complementary, though; while writing unsentimentally but movingly about his son Morgan's diagnosis and the family's response, Collins trawls around, as is his wont, for historical and contemporary illustration and resonance, and finds plenty. There's Peter the Wild Boy, who became part of the royal household in the early eighteenth century, and who met Pope, Addison, Steele, Swift and Defoe – he almost certainly played for our team. (Autistic United? Maybe Autistic Wanderers is better.) And Collins finds a lot of familiar traits among railway-timetable collectors, and

Microsoft boffins, and outsider artists . . . I'm happy that we're living through these times of exceptionally written and imaginative memoirs, despite the incessant whine you hear from the books-pages; Collins's engaging, discursive book isn't as raw as some, but in place of rawness there is thoughtfulness, and thoughtfulness is never a bad thing. I even learned stuff, and you can't often say that of a memoir.

New Year, New Me, another quick read of Gillian Riley's *How to Stop Smoking and Stay Stopped for Good.* I have now come to think of Riley as our leading cessation theorist; she's brilliant, but now I need someone who deals with the practicalities. ✶

APRIL 2004

L ast month I was banging on about how books were better than anything – how just about any decent book you picked would beat up anything else, any film or painting or piece of music you cared to match it up with. Anyway, like most theories advanced in this column, it turned out to be utter rubbish. I read four really good books this month, but even so, my cultural highlights of the last four weeks were not literary. I went to a couple of terrific exhibitions at the Royal Academy (and that's a hole in my argument right there – one book might beat up one painting, but what chance has one book, or even four books, got against the collected works of Guston and Vuillard?); I saw Jose Antonio Reyes score his first goal for Arsenal against Chelsea, a thirty-yard screamer, right in the top corner; and someone sent me a super-lative Springsteen bootleg, a '75 show at the Main Point in Bryn Mawr with strings, and a cover of 'I Want You', and I don't know what else. Like I said, I loved the books that I read this month, but when that Reyes shot hit the back of the net, I was four feet in the air. (The Polysyllabic Spree hates sport, especially soccer, because it requires people to expose their arms and legs, and the Spree believes that all body parts must be covered at all times. So even though I'm not allowed to talk about Reyes at any length, he does look to be some player.) Anyway, Patrick Hamilton didn't even get me to move my feet. I just sat there – lay there, most of the time – throughout the whole thing. So there we are, then. Books: pretty good, but not as good as other stuff, like goals, or bootlegs.

I spent a long time resisting *The Curious Incident of the Dog in the Night-Time* because I got sent about fifteen copies, by pub-lishers and agents and magazines and newspapers, and it made me recalcitrant and reluctant, truculent, maybe even perverse. I got sent fifteen copies because the narrator of *The Curious Incident* has Asperger's syndrome, which places him on the autistic spectrum, although way over the other side from my son. I can see why publishers do this, but the books that arrive in the post tend to be a distorted and somewhat unappetizing version of one's life and work. And what one wants to read, most of the time, is something that bears no reference to one's life and work.

(Twice this week I have been sent manuscripts of books that remind their editors, according to their covering letters, of my writing. Like a lot of writers, I can't really stand my own writing, in the same way that I don't really like my own cooking. And, just as when I go out to eat, I tend not to order my signature dish – an overcooked and overspiced meat-stewy thing containing something inappropriate, like tinned peaches, and a side order of undercooked and flavourless vegetables – I really don't want to read anything that I could have come up with at my own computer. What I produce on my computer invariably turns out to be an equivalent of the undercooked overcooked stewy thing, no matter how hard I try to follow the recipe, and you really don't want to eat too much of that. I'd love to be sent a book with an accompanying letter that said, 'This is nothing like your work. But as a man of taste and discernment, we think you'll love it anyway.' That never happens.)

Anyway, I finally succumbed to Mark Haddon's book, simply because it had been recommended to me so many times as a piece of fiction, rather than as a recognizable portrait of my home life. It's the third book about autism I've read in three months, and each book – this one, Charlotte Moore's *George and Sam* and Paul Collins's *Not Even Wrong* – contains a description of the classic test devised to demonstrate the lack of a theory of mind in autistic children. I'll quote Paul Collins's succinct summary:

> Sally and Anne have a box and a basket in front of them. Sally puts a marble in the basket. Then she leaves the room. While Sally is gone, Anne takes the marble out of the basket and puts it in the box. When Sally comes back in, where will she look for her marble?

If you ask ordinary kids, even ordinary three-year-olds, to observe Sally and Anne and then answer the question, they'll tell you that Sally will look in the basket. An autistic kid, however, will always tell you that Sally should look in the box, because an autistic kid is unable to imagine that someone else knows (or feels, or thinks) anything different from himself. In *The Curious Incident*, Christopher attempts to solve a murder-mystery, and one would imagine that of all the career-paths closed off to autists, the path leading to a desk at the FBI is probably the least accessible. If you are profoundly unable to put yourself in someone else's shoes, then a job involving intuition and empathy, second-guessing and psychology is probably not the job for you. Haddon has Christopher, his narrator, refer to the theory-of-mind experiment, and it's the one moment in the book where the author nearly brings his otherwise smartly imagined world crashing about his and our ears. Christopher talks about his own failure in the test, and then says, 'That was because when I was little I didn't understand about other people having minds. And Julie said to Mother and Father that I would always find this very difficult. Because I decided it was a kind of puzzle, and if something is a puzzle there is always a way of solving it.'

'*I decided it was a kind of puzzle . . .*' Hold on a moment: that means – what? – that every Asperger's kid could do this, if they so chose? That the most debilitating part of the condition – effectively, the condition itself – could be removed by an application of will? This is dangerous territory, and I'm not sure Haddon crosses it with absolute conviction. *The Curious Incident* is an absorbing, entertaining, moving book, but when truth gets bent out of shape in this way in order to serve the purposes of a narrative, then maybe it's a book that can't properly be described as a work of art? I don't know. I'm just asking the question. Happily, the detective element of the novel has been pretty much forgotten by the second half, and one description – of Christopher trying and failing to get on a crowded tube train, and then another, and then another, until hours and hours pass – is unforgettable, and very, very real.

In an online interview, Haddon quotes one of his Amazon reviewers, someone who hated his novel, saying, 'the most worrying thing about the book is that Christopher says he dislikes fiction, and yet the whole book is fiction'. And that, says the author, 'puts at least part of the problem in a nutshell'. It doesn't, I don't think, because the Amazon reviewer is too dim to put anything in a nutshell. I suspect, in fact, that the Amazon reviewer couldn't put anything in the boot of his car, let alone a nutshell. (Presumably you couldn't write a book about someone who couldn't read, either, or someone who didn't like paper, because the whole book is paper. Oh, man, I hate Amazon reviewers. Even the nice ones, who say nice things. They're bastards too.) But Haddon is right if what he's saying is that picking through a book of this kind for inconsistencies is a mug's game, and I'm sorry if that's what I've done. The part that made me wince a little seemed more fundamental than an inconsistency, though.

This comes up again in Patrick Hamilton's brilliant *Hangover Square*, where the central character suffers from some kind of schizophrenia. At periodic intervals he kind of blacks out, even though he remains conscious throughout the attacks. ('It was as though a shutter had fallen'; 'as though one had blown one's nose too hard and the outer world had become suddenly dim'; 'as though he had been watching a talking film, and all at once the sound-track had failed' – because George Bone cannot properly recall the last attack, he searches for fresh ways to describe each new one.) And of course it doesn't quite make sense, because he doesn't know what he's doing when the attacks occur, except he does, really; and he doesn't know who anyone is any more, except he manages to retain just enough information to make Hamilton's plot work. And it really doesn't matter, because this book isn't about schizophrenia. It's about an exhausted city on the brink of war – it's set in London at the beginning of 1939 – and about shiftless drunken fuckups, and it feels astonishingly contemporary and fresh. You may remember that I wanted to read Hamilton because my current favourite rock-and-roll band is naming an album after one of his books, and if that seems like a piss-poor (and laughably unliterary) reason to dig out a neglected minor classic, well, I'm sorry. But I got there in the end, and I'm glad I did. Thank you, Marah. Oh, and George Bone in schizophrenic mode has a hilarious and unfathomable obsession with a town called Maidenhead, which is where I grew up, and which has been for the most part overlooked, and wisely so, throughout the entire history of the English novel. Bone thinks that when he gets to Maidenhead, everything's going to be all right. Good luck with that, George!

I bought Mark Salzman's *True Notebooks* a couple of months ago, after an interview with the author in the *Believer*. I am beginning belatedly to realize that discovering books through reading about them in the *Believer*, and then writing about them in the *Believer* – as I have done once or twice before – is a circular process that doesn't do you any favours. You'd probably like to read about a book you didn't read about a while back. Anyway, as the interview implied, this is a pretty great book, but, *boy* is it sad.

True Notebooks is about Mark Salzman's gig teaching writing at Central Juvenile Hall in LA, where just about every kid is awaiting trial on a gang-related murder charge. Salzman's just the right person to attempt a book of this kind. He's empathetic and compassionate and all that jazz, but he's no bleeding-heart liberal. At the beginning of the book, he lists all the reasons why he shouldn't get involved in this kind of thing. They include 'Students all gangbangers', 'Still angry about getting mugged in 1978', and, even less ambiguously, 'Wish we could tilt LA County and shake it until everybody with a shaved head and tattoos falls into the ocean.' Towards the end of the book, he attends the trial of the student he loves the most, listens to all the extenuating circumstances, and finds himself going to bed that night with a broken heart, just as he feared he would. However, his sadness is engendered 'not because of what the legal system was doing to young people . . . I had to wrap my mind around the fact that someone I had grown so fond of, and who seemed so gentle, had been foolish enough to go to a movie theater carrying a loaded gun, violent enough to shoot three people with it – two of them in the back – and then callous enough to want to go to a movie afterwards.'

I don't want to give the impression that *True Notebooks* is unreadable in its grey-grimness, or unpalatably preachy. It's consistently entertaining, and occasionally bleakly funny. '"How about describing a time you helped someone?"' Salzman suggests to a student who is struggling for a topic to write about.

'Mm . . . I never did anything that nice for anybody.'

'It can be a small thing.'

'Mm . . . it's gonna have to be real small, Mark.'

This is one of those books where the characters learn and grow and change, and we've all read countless novels and seen countless films like that, and we know what to expect: redemption, right? But *True Notebooks* is real, so the characters learn and grow and change, and then get sentenced to thirty-plus years in prison, where God knows what fate awaits them. In the acknowledgements at the end of the book, Salzman thanks the students for making him decide to have children of his own. It might not be much when set against the suffering and pain both caused and experienced by the kids he teaches, but it's all we've got to work with, and I'm disproportionately glad he mentioned it: when I'd finished *True Notebooks*, Salzman's kids were all I had to keep me going. I'm enjoying *The Long Firm*, Jake Arnott's clever and vivid novel about London's gangland in the 1960s, but I think perhaps *True Notebooks* spoiled it for me a little. Gangland, gangs, guns, murder . . . none of it is as much fun as you might think.

Next month I'm going to read *David Copperfield*, the only major Dickens I haven't done yet. I'll probably still be reading it the month after, too, so if you want to take a break from this column, now would probably be the time to do it. I've been putting it off for a while, mostly because of the need to read loads of stuff that I can use to fill up these pages, but I'm really feeling the need for a bit of Dickensian nutrition. I don't know what I'll find to say about it, though, and I'm really hoping that Jose Antonio Reyes can help me out of a hole. Are thirty-yard thunderbolts better than Dickens at his best? I'll bet you can't wait to find out. ✶

MAY 2004

Anyone and everyone taking a writing class knows that the secret of good writing is to cut it back, pare it down, winnow, chop, hack, prune and trim, remove every superfluous word, compress, compress, compress. What's that chinking noise? It's the sound of the assiduous creative-writing student hitting bone. You can't read a review of, say, a Coetzee book without coming across the word 'spare', used invariably with approval; I just Googled 'J. M. Coetzee + spare' and got 907 hits, almost all of them different. 'Coetzee's spare but multi-layered language', 'detached in tone and spare in style', 'layer upon layer of spare, exquisite sentences', 'Coetzee's great gift – and it is a gift he extends to us – is in his spare and yet beautiful language', 'spare and powerful language', 'a chilling, spare book', 'paradoxically both spare and richly textured', 'spare, steely beauty'. Get it? Spare is good.

Coetzee, of course, is a great novelist, so I don't think it's snarky to point out that he's not the funniest writer in the world. Actually, when you think about it, not many novels in the Spare tradition are terribly cheerful. Jokes you can usually pluck out whole, by the roots, so if you're doing some heavy-duty prose-weeding, they're the first things to go. And there's some stuff about the whole winnowing process that I just don't get. Why does it always stop when the work in question has been reduced to sixty or seventy thousand words – entirely coincidentally, I'm sure, the minimum length for a publishable novel? I'm sure you could get it down to twenty or thirty, if you tried hard enough. In fact, why stop at twenty or thirty? Why write at all? Why not just jot the plot and a couple of themes down on the back of an envelope and leave it at that? The truth is, there's nothing very utilitarian about fiction or its creation, and I suspect that people are desperate to make it sound like manly, back-breaking labour because it's such a wussy thing to do in the first place. The obsession with austerity is an attempt to compensate, to make writing resemble a real job, like farming, or logging. (It's also why people who work in advertising put in twenty-hour days.) Go on, young writers – treat yourself to a joke, or an adverb! Spoil yourself! Readers won't mind! Have you ever looked at the size of books in an airport bookstall? The truth is that people like superfluity. (And, conversely, the writers' writers, the pruners and the winnowers, tend to have to live off critical approval rather than royalty cheques.)

Last month, I ended by saying that I was in need of some Dickensian nutrition, and maybe it's because I've been sucking on the bones of pared-down writing for too long. Where would

David Copperfield be if Dickens had gone to writing classes? Probably about seventy minor characters short, is where. (Did you know that Dickens is estimated to have invented thirteen thousand characters? Thirteen thousand! The population of a small town! If you want to talk about books in terms of back-breaking labour, then maybe we should think about how hard it is to write a lot – long books, teeming with exuberance and energy and life and comedy. I'm sorry if that seems obvious, but it can't always be true that writing a couple of hundred pages is harder than writing a thousand.) At one point near the beginning of the book, David runs away, and ends up having to sell the clothes he's wearing for food and drink. It would be enough, maybe, to describe the physical hardship that ensued; but Dickens being Dickens, he finds a bit part for a real rogue of a secondhand clothes merchant, a really scary guy who smells of rum and who shouts things like 'Oh, my lungs and liver' and 'Goroo!' a lot.

As King Lear said – possibly when invited into Iowa as a visiting speaker – 'Reason not the need.' There is no *need*: Dickens is having fun, and he extends the scene way beyond its function. Rereading it now, it seems almost to have been conceived as a retort to spareness, because the scary guy insists on paying David for his jacket in halfpenny instalments over the course of an afternoon, and thus ends up sticking around for two whole pages. Could he have been cut? Absolutely he could have been cut. But there comes a point in the writing process when a novelist – any novelist, even a great one – has to accept that what he is doing is keeping one end of a book away from the other, filling up pages, in the hope that these pages will move, provoke and entertain a reader.

Some random observations:

1) *David Copperfield* is Dickens's *Hamlet*. *Hamlet* is a play full of famous quotes; *Copperfield* is a novel full of famous

characters. I hadn't read it before, partly because I was under the curious misapprehension that I could remember a BBC serialization that I was forced to watch when I was a child, and therefore would be robbed of the pleasures of the narrative. (It turns out that all I could remember was the phrase 'Barkis is willing', and Barkis's willingness isn't really the book's point.) So I really had no idea that I was going to run into both Uriah Heep and Mr Micawber, as well as Peggotty, Steerforth, Betsey Trotwood, Little Em'ly, Tommy Traddles and the rest. I'd presumed Dickens would keep at least a couple of those back for some of the other novels I haven't read – *The Pickwick Papers*, say, or *Barnaby Rudge*. But he's blown it now. That might be an error on his part. We shall see, eventually.

2) Why do people keep trying to make movie or TV adaptations of Dickens novels? In the first issue of the *Believer*, Jonathan Lethem asked us to reimagine the characters in *Dombey and Son* as animals, in order to grasp the essence of these characters, and it's true that only the central characters in a Dickens novel are human. Here's Quilp, in *The Old Curiosity Shop*, terrifying Kit's mother with 'many extraordinary annoyances; such as hanging over from the side of the coach at the risk of his life, and staring in with his great goggle eyes . . . dodging her in this way from one window to another; getting nimbly down whenever they changed horses and thrusting his head in at the window with a dismal squint . . .' And here's Uriah Heep: 'hardly any eyebrows, and no eyelashes, and eyes of a red-brown, so unsheltered and unshaded, that I remember wondering how he went to sleep . . . high-shouldered and bony . . . a long, lank skeleton hand . . . his nostrils, which were thin and pointed, with sharp dints in them, had a singular and most uncomfortable way of

expanding and contracting themselves; that they seemed to twinkle instead of his eyes, which hardly ever twinkled at all.' So who would *you* cast as these two? If the right actors ever existed, I'm betting that they wouldn't be much fun to hang out with on set, what with having no social lives, or girl-friends, or prospects of working in anything else ever, apart from *Copperfield 2: Heep's Revenge*. And once these cartoon gremlins take corporeal form, they lose their point anyway. Memo to studios: a mix of CGI and live action is the only way forward. True, it would be expensive, and true, no one would ever want to pay to watch. But if you wish to do the great man justice – and I'm sure that's all you Hollywood execs think about, just as I'm sure you're all subscribers to the *Believer* – then it's got to be worth a shot.

3) In *The Old Curiosity Shop* I discovered that in the character of Dick Swiveller, Dickens provided P. G. Wodehouse with pretty much the whole of his oeuvre. In *David Copperfield*, David's bosses Spenlow and Jorkins are what must be the earliest fictional representations of good cop/bad cop.

4) I have complained in this column before about how everyone wants to spoil plots of classics for you. OK, I should have read *David Copperfield* before, and therefore deserve to be punished. But even the snootiest critic/publisher/what-ever must presumably accept that we must all, at some point, read a book for the first time. I know that the only thing brainy people do with their lives is reread great works of fiction, but surely even James Wood and Harold Bloom read before they reread? (Maybe not. Maybe they've only ever reread, and that's what separates them from us. Hats off to them.) Anyway, the great David Gates gives away two or three major narrative developments in the *very first paragraph*

of his introduction to my Modern Library edition (and I think I'm entitled to read the first paragraph, just to get a little context or biographical detail); I tried to check out the film versions on Amazon, and an Amazon reviewer point-lessly gave away another in a three-line review. That wouldn't have happened if I'd been looking for a Grisham adaptation.

5.) At the end of last year, I was given a first edition *David Copperfield* as a prize, and I had this fantasy that I was going to sit in an armchair and read a few pages of it, and feel the power of the great man enter me at my fingertips. Well, I tried it, and nothing happened. Also, the print was really small, and I was scared of dropping it in the bath, absentmindedly putting a cigarette out on it, etc. I actually ended up reading four different copies of the book. An old college Penguin edition fell apart in my hands, so I bought a Modern Library edition to replace it. Then I lost the Modern Library copy, temporarily, and bought another cheap Penguin to replace it. It cost £1.50! That's only about ninety dollars! (That was my attempt at edgy *au courant* humour. I won't bother again.)

There was a moment, about a third of the way through, when I thought that *David Copperfield* might become my new favourite Dickens novel – which, seeing as I believe that Dickens is the greatest novelist who ever lived, would mean that I might be in the middle of the best book I'd ever read. That superlative way of thinking ceases to become very compelling as you get older, so the realization wasn't as electrifying as you might think. I could see the logic, in the same way that you can see the logic of those ontolog-ical arguments that the old philosophers used to trot out to prove that God exists: Dickens = best writer, *DC* = his best book, there-fore *DC* = best book ever written – without feeling it. But, in the end, there was too much wrong. The young women, as usual, are weedy. Bodies start to pile up in uncomfortable proximity – there are four deaths, if you count drippy Dora's bloody dog, which I don't but Dickens does – between pages 714 and 740. And just when you want the book to wrap up, Dickens inserts a pointless and dull chapter about prison reform, twenty pages from the end. (He's against solitary confinement. Too good for 'em.)

What puts *David Copperfield* right up there with *Bleak House* and *Great Expectations*, however, is its sweet nature, and its surprising modernity. There's some metafictional stuff going on, for example: David grows up to be a novelist, and the full title of the book, according to Edgar Johnson's biography (not that I can find any evidence of this anywhere), is *The Personal History, Experience and Observations of David Copperfield the Younger of Blunderstone Rookery, which he never meant to be published on any account*. And there's a point to the metafictional stuff, too. The last refuge of the scoundrel-critic is any version of the sentence, 'Ultimately, this book is about fiction itself/this film is about film itself.' I have used the sentence myself, back in the days when I reviewed a lot of books, and it's bullshit: invariably all it means is that the film or novel has drawn attention to its own fictional state, which doesn't get us very far, and which is why the critic never tells us exactly what the novel has to say about fiction itself. (Next time you see the sentence, which will probably be some time in the next seven days if you read a lot of reviews, write to the critic and ask for elucidation.)

Anyway, David Copperfield's profession allows him these piercing little moments of regret and nostalgia; there's a lot about memory in this book, and in an autobiographical novel, memory and fiction get all tangled up. Dickens uses the tangle to his advantage, and I can't remember being so moved by one of his novels. The other thing that seems to me different about *David Copperfield* is the sophistication of a couple of the characters and relationships. Dickens isn't the most sophisticated of writers, and when he does attain complexity, it's because subplot is layered upon subplot, and character over character, until he can't help but get something going. But there's a startlingly contemporary admission of marital dissatisfaction in *Copperfield*, for example, an acknowledgement of lack and of an unspecified yearning that you'd associate more with Rabbit Angstrom than with someone who spends half the novel quaffing punch with Mr Micawber. Dickens eventually takes the Victorian way out of the twentieth-century malaise, but even so . . . Making notes for this column, I find that I wrote 'He's from another planet'; 'Was he a Martian?' David Gates asks in the introduction. And to think that some people don't rate him! To think that some people have described him as 'the worst writer to plague the English language'! Yeah, well. You can believe them or you can side with Tolstoy, Peter Ackroyd and David Gates. And me. Your choice.

For the first time since I've been writing this column, the completion of a book has left me feeling bereft: I miss them all. Let's face it: usually you're just happy as hell to have chalked another one up on the board, but this last month I've been living in this hyperreal world, full of memorable, brilliantly eccentric people, and laughs (I hope you know how funny Dickens is), and proper bendy stories you want to follow. I suspect that it'll be difficult to read a pared-down, stripped-back, skin-and-bones novel for a while. ✱

A *selection from*

DAVID COPPERFIELD

by CHARLES DICKENS

★ ★ ★

Into this shop, which was low and small, and which was darkened rather than lighted by a little window, overhung with
clothes, and was descended into by some steps, I went with a palpi-
tating heart; which was not relieved when an ugly old man, with
the lower part of his face all covered with a stubbly grey beard,
rushed out of a dirty den behind it, and seized me by the hair of
my head. He was a dreadful old man to look at, in a filthy flannel
waistcoat, and smelling terribly of rum. His bedstead, covered with
a tumbled and ragged piece of patchwork, was in the den he had
come from, where another little window showed a prospect of
more stinging nettles, and a lame donkey.

'Oh, what do you want?' grinned this old man, in a fierce,
monotonous whine. 'Oh, my eyes and limbs, what do you want?
Oh, my lungs and liver, what do you want? Oh, goroo, goroo!'

I was so much dismayed by these words, and particularly by the
repetition of the last unknown one, which was a kind of rattle in
his throat, that I could make no answer; hereupon the old man, still
holding me by the hair, repeated —

'Oh, what do you want? Oh, my eyes and limbs, what do you
want? Oh, my lungs and liver, what do you want? Oh, goroo!' —
which he screwed out of himself, with an energy that made his
eyes start in his head.

'I want to know,' I said, trembling, 'if you would buy a jacket.'

'Oh, let's see the jacket!' cried the old man. 'Oh, my heart on
fire, show the jacket to us! Oh, my eyes and limbs, bring the jacket
out!'

With that he took his trembling hands, which were like the claws of a great bird, out of my hair; and put on a pair of spectacles, not at all ornamental to his inflamed eyes.

'Oh, how much for the jacket?' cried the old man, 'no! Oh, my eyes, no! Oh, my limbs, no! Eighteenpence. Goroo!'

Every time he uttered this ejaculation, his eyes seemed in danger of starting out; and every sentence he spoke, he delivered in a sort of tune, always exactly the same, and more like a gust of wind, which begins low, mounts up high, and falls again, than any other comparison I can find for it.

'Well,' I said, glad to have closed the bargain, 'I'll take eighteenpence.'

'Oh, my liver!' cried the old man, throwing the jacket on a shelf. 'Get out of the shop! Oh, my eyes and limbs – goroo! – don't ask for money; make it an exchange.'

I was never so frightened in my life, before or since; but I told him humbly that I wanted money, and that nothing else was of any use to me, but that I would wait for it, as he desired, outside, and had no wish to hurry him. So I went outside, and sat down in the shade in a corner. And I sat there so many hours, that the shade became sunlight, and the sunlight became shade again, and still I sat there waiting for the money.

There was never such another drunken madman in that line of business, I hope. That he was well known in the neighbourhood, and enjoyed the reputation of having sold himself to the devil, I soon understood from the visits he received from the boys, who continually came skirmishing about the shop, shouting that legend, and calling to him to bring out his gold. 'You ain't poor, you know, Charley. Rip it open and let's have some!' This, and many offers to lend him a knife for the purpose, exasperated him to such a degree, that the whole day was a succession of rushes on his part, and flights on the part of the boys. Sometimes in his rage he would take me for one of them, and come at me, mouthing as if he were going to tear me in pieces; then, remembering me, just in time, would dive into the shop, and lie upon his bed, as I thought from the sound of his voice, yelling in a frantic way, to his own windy tune, the Death of Nelson; with an Oh! before every line, and innumerable Goroos interspersed. As if this were not bad enough for me, the boys, connecting me with the establishment, on account of the patience and perseverance with which I sat outside, half-dressed, pelted me, and used me very ill all day.

He made many attempts to induce me to consent to an exchange; at one time coming out with a fishing-rod, at another with a fiddle, at another with a cocked hat, at another with a flute. But I resisted him all these overtures, and sat there in desperation; each time asking him, with tears in my eyes, for my money or my jacket. At last he began to pay me in halfpence at a time; and was full two hours getting by easy stages to a shilling.

'Oh, my eyes and limbs!' he cried, peeping hideously out of the shop, after a long pause, 'will you go for twopence more?'

'I can't,' I said, 'I shall be starved.'

'Oh, my lungs and liver, will you go for threepence?'

'I would go for nothing, if I could,' I said, 'but I want the money badly.'

'Oh, go-roo!' (it is really impossible to express how he twisted this ejaculation out of himself, as he peeped round the door-post at me, showing nothing but his crafty old head;) 'will you go for fourpence?'

I was so faint and weary that I closed with this offer; and taking the money out of his claw, not without trembling, went away more hungry and thirsty than I had ever been, a little before sunset. But at an expense of threepence I soon refreshed myself completely; and, in being in better spirits then, limped seven miles upon my road. *

JUNE 2004

The Polysyllabic Spree – the ninety-nine young and menacingly serene people who run the *Believer* – recently took their regular columnists out for what they promised would be a riotous and orgiastic night on the town. Now, I have to confess that I've never actually seen a copy of this magazine, due to an ongoing dispute with the Spree (I think that as a contributor I should be entitled to a free copy, but they are insisting that I take out a ten-year subscription – does that sound right to you?), so I was completely unaware that there is only one other regular columnist, the Croatian sex lady, and she didn't show. I suspect that she'd been given a tip-off, probably because she's a woman (the Spree hold men responsible for the death of Virginia Woolf) and stayed at home. It shouldn't have made much difference, though, because you can have fun with a hundred people, right?

Wrong. The Spree's idea of a good time was to book tickets for a literary event – a reading given by all the nominees for the National Book Critics' Circle Awards – and sit there for two and a half hours. Actually, that's not quite true: they didn't sit there. Such is their unquenchable passion for the written word that they were too excited to sit. They stood, and they wept, and they hugged each other, and occasionally they even danced – to the poetry recitals, and some of the more up-tempo biography nominees. In England we don't often dance at dances, let alone readings, so I didn't know where to look. Needless to say, drink, drugs, food and sex played no part in the festivities. But who needs any of that when you've got literature?

I did, however, discover a couple of books as a result of the evening: Tony Hoagland's *What Narcissism Means to Me*, which didn't win the poetry award, and Adrian Nicole LeBlanc's *Random Family*, which didn't win the non-fiction award. I haven't read the books that did win, and therefore cannot comment on the judges' inexplicable decisions, but they must be pretty good, because Hoagland's poems and LeBlanc's study of life in the Bronx were exceptional.

Middle-class people – especially young middle-class people – spend an awful lot of time and energy attempting to familiarize themselves with what's going down on the street. *Random Family* is a one-stop shop: it tells you everything you need to know, and may even stop you from hankering after a gun or a crack habit as a quick way out of the graduate-school ghetto. And yes, I know that all reality is mediated, and so on and so forth, but this book does a pretty good job of convincing you that it knows whereof it speaks.

Random Family is about two women, Coco and Jessica; LeBlanc's story, which took her ten years to write and research, begins when they're in their mid-teens, and follows them through the next couple of decades. Despite the simplicity of the setup, it's not always an easy narrative to follow. If LeBlanc were a novelist, you'd have to observe that she's screwed up by overpopulating her book, but Coco and Jessica and the Bronx don't give her an awful lot of choice, because *Random Family* is partly about overpopulation. Coco and Jessica have so many babies, by so many fathers, and their children have so many half-siblings, that at times it's impossible to keep the names straight. By the time the two women are in their early thirties, they have given birth to Mercedes, Nikki, Nautica, Pearl, LaMonte, Serena, Brittany, Stephany, Michael and Matthew, by Cesar, Torres, Puma (or maybe Victor), Willy (or maybe Puma), Kodak, Wishman and Frankie. This is a book awash with sperm (Jessica even manages to conceive twins while in prison, after an affair with a guard), and at one stage I was wondering whether it was medically possible for a man to become pregnant through reading it. I think I'm probably too old.

The combination of LeBlanc's scrupulous attention to quotidian detail and her absolute refusal to judge is weirdly reminiscent of Peter Guralnick's approach to Elvis in his monumental two-volume biography. Those of you who read the Elvis books will know that though Presley's baffling, infuriating last decade gave Guralnick plenty of opportunity to leap in and tell you what he thinks, he never once does so. LeBlanc's stern neutrality is generous and important: she hectors nobody, and the space she leaves us allows us to think properly, to recognize for ourselves all the millions of complications that shape these lives.

There are many, many things, a *zillion* things, that make my experiences different from those of Coco and Jessica. But it was remembering my first pregnancy scare that helped me to fully understand the stupidity and purposelessness of the usual conservative rants about responsibility and fecklessness and blah blah blah. It was the summer before I went to college, and my girlfriend's period was late, and I spent two utterly miserable weeks convinced that my life was over. I'd have to get, like, an office job, and I'd miss out on three years pissing around at university, and my brilliant career as a . . . as a something or other would be over before it had even begun. We'd used birth control, of course, because failing to do so would cost us everything, including a very great deal of money, but we were still terrified: I would just as soon have gone to prison as started a family. What *Random Family* explains, movingly and convincingly and at necessary length, is that the future as Coco and Jessica and the fathers of their children see it really isn't worth the price of a condom, and they're right. I eventually became a father for the first time around the same age that Jessica became a grandmother.

As I hadn't noticed the publication of *Random Family*, I caught up with the reviews online. They were for the most part terrific, although one or two people wondered aloud whether LeBlanc's presence might not have affected behaviour and outcome. (Yeah, right. I can see how that might work for an afternoon, but a whole decade? Stick a writer in a corner of the room and watch the combined forces of international economics, the criminal justice system, and the drug trade wither before her pitiless gaze.) 'I believe I had far less effect than anybody would imagine,' LeBlanc said in an interview, with what I like to imagine as wry understatement. I did come across this, however, the extraordinary conclusion to a review in the *Guardian*:

> It is only by accident, in the acknowledgements, that the book finally confronts the reader with the 'American experience of class injustice' that is ostensibly its subject. So many institutions, so many funds and fellowships, retreat centres and universities, publishers, mentors, editors, friends, formed a net to support this one writer.

Nothing comparable exists to hold up the countless Cocos and Jessicas . . .

But the tougher question is why the stories of poor people – and not just any poor people but those acquainted with chaos and crime, those the overclass likes to call the underclass – are such valuable raw material, creating a frisson among the literary set and the buyers of books? Why are their lives and private griefs currency for just about anyone but themselves?

First of all: 'by accident'? 'BY ACCIDENT'? Those two words, so coolly patronizing and yet, paradoxically, so dim, must have made LeBlanc want to buy a gun. And I think a decent lawyer could have gotten her off, in the unfortunate event of a shooting. She spends ten years writing a book, and a reviewer in a national newspaper doesn't even notice what it's about. (It's about the American experience of class injustice, among other things.) Second: presumably the extension of the argument about grants and fellowships and editors is that they are only appropriate for biographies of bloody, I don't know, Vanessa Bell; I doubt whether 'the support net' has ever been put to better social use.

And last: if you get to the end of *Random Family* and conclude that it was written to create 'a frisson', then, I'm sorry, but you should be compelled to have your literacy surgically removed, without anaesthetic. The lives of Coco and Jessica are 'valuable raw material' because people who read books – quite often people who are very quick to judge, quite often people who make or influence social policy – don't know anyone like them, and certainly have no idea how or sometimes even why they live; until we all begin to comprehend, then nothing can even begin to change. Oh, and there's no evidence to suggest that Coco and Jessica resented being used in this way; there is plenty of evidence to suggest that they got it. But what would they know, right?

It's not humourless, either, although of necessity the humour tends to be a little bleak. When Coco is asked, as part of her application, for an essay entitled 'Why I Want to Live in Public Housing', she writes simply, 'Because I'm homeless.' And a description of the office Christmas party thrown by Jessica's major-duty drug-dealing boyfriend Boy George is hilarious, if you're able to laugh at the magnitude of your misapprehensions concerning the wages of sin. (The party took place on a yacht. There were 121 guests, who ate steak tartare and drank twelve grand's worth of Moët, and who won Hawaiian trips and Mitsubishis in the raffle. The Jungle Brothers, Loose Touch and Big Daddy Kane performed. Are you listening, Spree?)

George is banged up in the end, of course, so mostly Jessica and Coco are eating rice and beans, when they're eating at all, and moving from one rat-infested dump to the next. Luckily we don't have poverty in England, because Tony Blair eradicated it shortly after he came to power in 1997. (Note to *Guardian* reviewer – that was a joke.) But American people should really read this book. That's 'should' as in, It's really good, and 'should' as in, You're a bad person if you don't.

I warned you that this was going to be a non-fiction month. I started three novels, all of them warmly recommended by friends or newspapers, and I came to the rather brilliant conclusion that not one of them was *David Copperfield*, the last novel I read, and the completion of which has left a devastating hole in my life. So it seemed like a good time to find out about Coco and Jessica and Bobby Fischer, real people I knew nothing about. *Bobby Fischer Goes to War* isn't the most elegantly written book I've ever read, but the story it tells is so compelling – so hilarious, so nutty, so resonant – that you forgive it its prose trespasses.

When Fischer played Spassky in Reykjavik in 1972 I was fifteen, and not yet worrying about whether anyone was pregnant. You heard about chess all the time that summer, on the TV and on the radio, and I presumed that you always heard about chess in the year of a World Chess Championship, that I'd simply been too young to notice the previous tournament. That happened all the time when you were in your early teens: things that only rolled around every few years, like elections and Olympics, suddenly assumed a magnitude you'd never known they possessed, simply because you were more media-aware. The truth in this case was, of course, that no one had ever talked about chess before, and no one ever would again, really. Everyone was talking about Fischer: Fischer and his refusal to play, Fischer and his demands for more money (he just about bankrupted an entire country by demanding a bigger and bigger chunk of the purse, and then refusing to allow the Icelanders to recoup it through TV and film coverage), Fischer and his forfeit of the second game, Fischer and his absence from the opening ceremony . . . You could make an absolutely gripping film of Reykjavik '72 that would end with the very first move of the very first match, and that would be about pretty much everything.

Tony Hoagland is the sort of poet you dream of finding but almost never do. His work is relaxed, deceptively easy on the eye and ear, and it has jokes and unexpected little bursts of melancholic resonance. Plus, I pretty much understand all of it, and yet it's clever — as you almost certainly know, contemporary poetry is a kind of Reykjavik, a place where accessibility and intelligence have been fighting a Cold War by proxy for the last half-century. If something doesn't give you even a shot at comprehension in the first couple of readings, then my motto is 'Fuck it', but I never swore once. They can use that as a blurb, if they want. They should. Who wouldn't buy a poetry book that said 'I never swore once' on the cover? Everyone would know what it meant. And isn't *What Narcissism Means to Me* a great title?

I cheated a little with *What Narcissism Means to Me* — I read it last month, immediately after my night on the town with the Spree. But I wanted this clean *Copperfield* line in my last column, and anyway I was worried that I'd be short of stuff this month, not

least because it's been a big football month. Arsenal lost the
Champions League quarterfinal to Chelsea, lost the FA Cup semi
to Man Utd, and then, just this last weekend, won the Championship. (The two losses were in knock-out competitions. The
Championship is what counts, really. That's what we're all telling
ourselves here in Highbury.) So on Sunday night, when I should
have been reading stuff, I was in a pub called the Bailey, as has
become traditional on Championship nights, standing on a chair
and singing a comical song about Victoria Beckham. To be honest,
I thought if I threw in some poetry, you might like me more. I
thought I might even like myself more. Anyway, the standing on
the chair and singing wasn't as much fun as the consumption of
contemporary literature, obviously, but, you know. It was still
pretty good. ✷

IMPOSSIBLE DREAM

by TONY HOAGLAND

✷ ✷ ✷

In Delaware a congressman
          accused of sexual misconduct
says clearly at the press conference
          speaking
                   right into the microphone
that he would like very much
               to do it again.

It was on the radio
          and Carla laughed
as she painted, *Die, You Pig*
              in red nail polish
on the back of a turtle
she plans to turn loose tomorrow
             in Jerry's backyard

We lived near the high school that year
and in the afternoons, in autumn,
you could hear the marching-band rehearsals
from the stadium:
          off-key trumpets smeared and carried by the wind,
drums and weirdly-bent trombones:

a ragged 'Louie Louie'
          or sometimes, 'The Impossible Dream'.
I was reading a book about pleasure,
how you have to glide through it
          without clinging,

like an arrow,
passing through a target,
                coming out the other side and going on.

Sitting at the picnic table
carved with the initials of the previous tenants;
                thin October sunlight
blessing the pale grass –
you would have said we had it all –

But the turtle in Carla's hand
churned its odd, stiff legs like oars,
as if it wasn't made for holding still,

and the high-school band played
                worse than ever for a moment
as if getting the song right
                was the impossible dream.

JULY 2004

I f you wanted to draw a family tree of everything I read and bought this month – and you never know, it could be fun, if you're a writer, say, or a student, and there are several large holes in your day – you'd have to put *McSweeney's* 13 and Pete Dexter's novel *Train* right at the top.[2] They're the Adam and Eve here, or

---

[1] I bought so many books this month it's obscene, and I'm not owning up to them all: this is a selection. And to be honest, I've been economical with the truth for months now. I keep finding books that I bought, didn't read and didn't list.

[2] [We do indeed pay Nick Hornby to write his monthly column, but we didn't pay him to mention *McSweeney's* 13. – *Ed.*]

they would be if Adam and Eve had been hermaphrodites, each able to give birth independently of the other. *McSweeney's* 13 and *Train* never actually mated to produce a beautiful synthesis of the two; and nor did any of the other books actually get together, either. So it would be a pretty linear family tree, to be honest: one straight line coming out of *McSweeney's* 13, because *McSweeney's* begat a bunch of graphic novels (*McSweeney's* 13, edited by Chris Ware, is a comics issue, if you're not from 'round these parts), and another straight line coming out of *Train*, which leads to a bunch of non-fiction books, for reasons I will come to later. *Train* didn't directly beget anything, although it did plant some seeds. (I know what you're thinking. You're thinking, Well, if *Train* and *McSweeney's* 13 never actually mated, and if *Train* never directly begat anything, then how good is this whole family-tree thing? And my answer is, Oh, it's good. Trust me. I have a writer's instinct.) Anyway, if you do decide to draw the family tree, the good news is that it's easy; the bad news is that it's boring, pointless and arguably makes no sense. Up to you.

Pete Dexter's *Train* was carefully chosen to reintroduce me to the world of fiction, a world I have been frightened of visiting ever since I finished *David Copperfield* a couple of months back. I've read Dexter before – *The Paperboy* is a terrific novel – and the first couple of chapters of *Train* are engrossing, complicated, fresh and real, and I really thought I was back on the fictional horse. But then, in the third chapter, there is an episode of horrific violence, graphically rendered, and suddenly I was no longer under the skin of the book, the way I had been; I was on the outside looking in. What happens is that in the process of being raped, the central female character gets her nipple sliced off, and it really upset me. I mean, I know I was supposed to get upset. But I was bothered way beyond function. I was bothered to the extent that I struck up a conversation with the author at periodic intervals thereafter. 'Did the nipple really have to go, Pete? Explain to me why. Couldn't it have just . . . nearly gone? Or maybe you could have left it alone altogether? I mean, come on, man. Her husband has just been brutally murdered. She's been raped. We get the picture. Leave the nipple alone.'

I am, I think, a relatively passive reader, when it comes to fiction. If a novelist tells me that something happened, then I tend to believe him, as a rule. In his memoir *Experience*, Martin Amis recalls his father, Kingsley, saying that he found Virginia Woolf's fictional world 'wholly contrived: when reading her he found that he kept interpolating hostile negatives, murmuring "Oh no she didn't" or "Oh no he hadn't" or "Oh no it wasn't" after each and every authorial proposition'; I only do that when I'm reading something laughably bad (although after reading that passage in *Experience*, I remember it took me a while to shake off Kingsley's approach to the novel). But in the nipple-slicing incident in *Train*, I thought I could detect Dexter's thumb on the scale, to use a brilliant Martin Amis phrase from elsewhere in *Experience*. It seemed to me as though poor Norah lost her nipple through a worldview rather than through a narrative inevitability; and despite all the great storytelling and the muscular, grave prose, and the richness and resonance of the setup (Train is a golf caddy in 1950s LA, and the novel is mostly about race) I just sort of lost my grip on the book. Also, someone gets shot dead at the end, and I wasn't altogether sure why. That's a sure sign that you haven't been paying the right kind of attention. It should always be clear why someone gets shot. If I ever shoot you, I promise you there will be a really good explanation, one you will grasp immediately, should you live.

While I was in the middle of *Train*, I went browsing in a remainder bookshop, and came across a copy of Frank Kermode's memoir *Not Entitled*. I knew of Kermode's work as a critic, but I didn't know he'd written a memoir, some of which is about his childhood on the Isle of Man, and when I saw it, I was seized by a need to own it. This need was entirely created by poor Norah in *Train*. There would be no nipple-slicing in *Not Entitled*, I was sure of it. I even started to read the thing in a cab on the way home, and although I gave up pretty quickly (it probably went too far the other way – it's a delicate balance I'm trying to strike here), it was very restorative.

I bought Claire Tomalin's gripping, informative *The Invisible Woman* at the Dickens Museum in Doughty Street, London, which is full of all sorts of cool stuff: marked-up reading copies that say things like 'SIGH here', letters, the original partwork editions of the novels, and so on. The thing is, I really want to read a Dickens biography, but they're all too long. Ackroyd's is a frankly hilarious 1,140 pages, excluding notes and postscript. (It has a great blurb on the front, the Ackroyd: 'An essential book for anyone who has ever loved *or read* Dickens,' says P. D. James [my italics]. Can you imagine? You flog your way through *Great Expectations* at school, hate it, and then find you've got to read a thousand pages of biography! What a pisser!) So both the museum visit and the Tomalin book – about his affair with the actress Nelly Ternan – were my ways of fulfilling a need to find out more about the great man without killing myself.

Here's something I found out in *The Invisible Woman*: the son of Charles Dickens's mistress died during my lifetime. He wasn't Dickens's son, but even so: I could have met a guy who said, 'Hey, my mum slept with Dickens.' I wouldn't have understood what he meant, because I was only two, and as Tomalin makes clear, he wouldn't have wanted to own up anyway, because he was traumatized by what he found out about his mother's past. It's still weird, though, I think, to see how decades – centuries – can be eaten up like that.

Ackroyd, by the way, disputes that Ternan and Dickens ever had an affair. He concedes that Chas set her up in a couple of houses, one in France, and disappeared for long stretches of time in order to visit her, but he won't accept that Dickens was an adulterer: that sort of explanation might work for an ordinary man, he says, but Dickens 'was not "ordinary" in any sense'. *The Invisible Woman* is such a formidable work of scholarship, however, that it leaves very little room for doubt. Indeed, Claire Tomalin is so consumed by her research, so much the biographer, that she actually takes Dickens to task for destroying evidence of his relationship with Nelly Ternan. 'Dickens himself would not have welcomed our curiosity,' she says. 'He would have been happier to have every letter he ever wrote dealt with as Nelly . . . dealt with the bundles of twelve years' intimate correspondence. [She destroyed it all.] He was wrong by any standards.'

Don't you love that last sentence? The message is clear: if you're a writer whose work will interest future generations, and you're screwing around, don't delete those emails because Claire Tomalin and her colleagues are going to need them. Zadie Smith and Michael Chabon and the rest of you, watch out. (I'm not implying, of course, that either of you is screwing around, and I'm sorry if you made that inference. It was supposed to be a compliment. It just came out wrong. Forget it, OK? And sue the Spree, not me. It was their sloppy editing.)

This Is Serbia Calling, Matthew Collin's book about the Belgrade radio station B92 and the role it played in resisting Milosevic, has been lying around my house for a while. But when my post-*McSweeney's* 13 research into comic books led me to conclude that I should buy, among other things, Joe Sacco's *Safe Area Gorazde*, I wanted to do a little extra reading on the Yugoslavian wars, and Collin's book is perfect: it gives you a top-notch potted history, as well as an enthralling and humbling story about very brave young people refusing to be cowed by a brutal regime. It's pretty funny, too, in places. If you have a taste for that hopelessly bleak Eastern European humour, then the Serbian dissenter of the 1990s is your sort of guy. You've got warring nationalist groups, and an inflation rate in January '94 of 313,563,558 percent (that's on the steep side, for those of you with no head for economics) that resulted in a loaf of bread costing 4,000,000,000 dinars. You've got power cuts, rigged elections, a government too busy committing genocide to worry about the niceties of free speech and, eventually, NATO bombs. There are good jokes to be made, by those with the stomach for them. 'The one good thing about no electricity,' one cynic remarked during the power failures, 'is that there's no television telling us we've got electricity.' *This Is Serbia Calling* is essential reading if you've ever doubted the power or the value of culture, of music, books, films, theatre; it also makes a fantastic case for Sonic Youth and anyone else who makes loud, weird noises. When your world is falling round about your ears, Tina Turner isn't going to do it for you.

Y: The Last Man is a comic-book series about a world run by women, after every man but one has been wiped out by a mysterious plague. It's a great premise, and full of smart ideas: the Democrats are running the country, because the only Republican women are Republican wives; Israel is cleaning up in the Middle East, because they have the highest proportion of trained female combat soldiers. It's strange, reading a comic – a proper comic, not a graphic novel – in which a woman says, 'You can fuck my tits if you want' (and I can only apologize, not only for repeating the expression, but for the number of references to breasts in this month's column. I'm pretty sure it's a coincidence, although we should, I suppose, recognize the possibility that it marks the beginning of a pathetic middle-aged obsession). Is that what happens in comics now? Is this the sort of stuff your ten-year-old boy is reading? Crikey. When I was ten, the only word I'd have understood in the whole sentence would have been 'you', although not necessarily in this context. Daniel Clowes's *David Boring* – yeah, yeah, late again – is partly about large bottoms, but as one of the reviews quoted on the back called the book 'perverse and fetishistic', I'd have wanted my money back if it hadn't been. It's also clever, and the product of a genuinely odd imagination.

There's no rule that says one's reading has to be tonally consistent. I can't help but feel, however, that my reading has been all over the place this month. *The Invisible Woman* and *Y: The Last Man* were opposites in just about every way you can imagine; they even had opposite titles. A woman you can't see versus a guy whose mere existence attracts the world's attention. Does this matter? I suspect it might. I was once asked to DJ at a *New Yorker* party, and the guy who was looking after me (in other words, the guy who was actually playing the records) wouldn't let me choose the music I wanted because he said I wasn't paying enough attention to the beats per minute: according to him, you can't have a differential of more than, I don't know, twenty bpm between records. At the time, I thought this was a stupid idea, but there is a possibility that it might apply to reading. *The Invisible Woman* is pacy and engrossing, but it's no graphic novel, and reading Tomalin's book after *The Last Man* was like playing John Lee Hooker after the Chemical Brothers – in my opinion, John Lee Hooker is the greater artist, but he's in no hurry, is he? Next month, I might try starting with the literary equivalent of a smoocher, and move on to something a bit quicker. And I promise that if there are any breasts, I won't mention them. In fact, I won't even look at them. ✶

AUGUST 2004

BOOKS BOUGHT:
* *Prayers for Rain* – Dennis Lehane
* *Mystic River* – Dennis Lehane
* *Jesse James: Last Rebel of the Civil War* – T. J. Stiles
* *The Line of Beauty* – Alan Hollinghurst
* *Like a Fiery Elephant* – Jonathan Coe

BOOKS READ:
* *Prayers for Rain* – Dennis Lehane
* *Mystic River* – Dennis Lehane
* *Like a Fiery Elephant* – Jonathan Coe

Shortly after I submitted my copy for last month's column, my third son was born. I mention his arrival not because I'm after your good wishes or your sympathy, but because reading is a domestic activity, and is therefore susceptible to any changes in the domestic environment. And though it's true that the baby is responsible for everything I read this month, just about, he's been subtle about it: he hasn't made me any more moronic than I was before, and he certainly hasn't prevented me from reading. He could argue, in fact, that he has actually encouraged reading in our household, through his insistence on the increased consciousness of his parents. (Hey — if you lot are all so brainy and so serious about books, how come you're still using contraception?)

Shortly after the birth of a son, I panic that I will never be able to visit a bookshop again, and that therefore any opportunity I have to buy printed matter should be exploited immediately. Jesse (and yes, the T. J. Stiles bio was bought as a tribute) was born shortly before 7 a.m.; three or four hours later I was in a news-agent's, and I saw a small selection of best-selling paperbacks. There wasn't an awful lot there that I wanted, to be honest; but because of the consumer fear, something had to be bought, right there and then, just in case, and I vaguely remembered reading something good about Dennis Lehane's *Mystic River*. Well, the shop didn't have a copy of *Mystic River*, but they did have another Dennis Lehane book, *Prayers for Rain*: that would have to do. Never mind that, as regular readers of this column know, I have over the last few months bought several hundred books I haven't yet read. And never mind that, as it turned out, I found myself passing a book-shop the very next day, and the day after that (because what else is there to do with a new baby, other than mooch around bookshops with him?), and was thus able to buy *Mystic River*. I didn't know for sure I'd ever go to a bookshop again; and if I never went to a bookshop again, how long were those several hundred books going to last me? Nine or ten years at the most. No, I needed that copy of *Prayers for Rain*, just to be on the safe side.

And then, when the baby was a couple of weeks old, I became convinced that I was turning into a vegetable, and so took urgent corrective action: I bought and read, in its entirety, Jonathan Coe's five-hundred page biography of B. S. Johnson, an obscure experi-mental novelist — again, just to be on the safe side, just to prove I still could, even though I never did. I'm hoping that the essential anti-vegetative nutrients and minerals I ingested will last me for a while, that they won't be expelled from the brain via snot or saliva,

THE COMPLETE POLYSYLLABIC SPREE

because I'm not sure when I will next get the chance to read a few hundred pages about a difficult writer I've never read. It almost certainly won't be for a couple of months.

They actually make a very nice theoretical contrast, Johnson and Dennis Lehane. Johnson thought that our need for narrative, our desire to find out what happens next, was 'primitive' and 'vulgar', and if you took that vulgarity out of *Prayers for Rain*, there wouldn't be an awful lot left. *Prayers for Rain* is 'a Kenzie and Gennaro novel', and if I'd spotted those words on the cover, I probably wouldn't have read it. I appreciate that I'm in a minority here, but I just don't get the appeal of the reappearing hero. I don't get Kay Scarpetta, or James Bond, or Hercule Poirot; I don't even get Sherlock Holmes. My problem is that, when I'm reading a novel, I have a need – a childish need, B. S. Johnson would argue – to believe that the events described therein are definitive, that they really matter to the characters. In other words, if 1987 turned out to be a real bitch of a year for Winston Smith, then I don't want to be wasting my time reading about what happened to him back in '84. The least one can ask, really, is that fictional characters should be able to remember the stuff that's happened to them, but I get the impression that Kenzie and Gennaro would struggle to distinguish the psycho killer they're tracking down in *Prayers for Rain* from the psycho killers they've tracked down in other books.

There is a rather dispiriting moment in *Prayers for Rain* that seems to confirm this suspicion. Angie Gennaro, who is involved both professionally and romantically with Patrick Kenzie, asks whether she can shave off his stubble – stubble that he has grown to cover scars. 'I considered it,' Kenzie tells us. 'Three years with protective facial hair. Three years hiding the damage delivered on the worst night of my life . . .' Hang on a moment. The worst night of your life was *three years ago*? So what am I reading about now? The fourth-worst night of your life? Sometimes, when you walk into a pub in the centre of town mid-evening, you get the feeling that you've missed the moment: all the after-work drinkers have gone home, and the late-night drinkers haven't arrived, and there are empty glasses lying around (and the ashtrays are full, if you're drinking in a civilized country), and you didn't make any of the mess . . . Well, that's kind of how I felt reading *Prayers for Rain*.

I liked Lehane's writing, though. It's humane, and humorous at the right moments, and he has a penchant for quirky cultural references: I hadn't expected a discussion about David Denby's film criticism, for example. (On the other hand: would someone who reads Denby accuse someone who uses the word 'finite' of showing off?) I was more than happy to plough straight on into the next one. And the next one was absolutely fantastic.

Why hasn't anyone ever told me that *Mystic River* is right up there with *Presumed Innocent* and *Red Dragon*? Because I don't know the right kind of people, that's why. In the last three weeks, about five different people have told me that Alan Hollinghurst's *The Line of Beauty* is a work of genius, and I'm sure it is; I intend to read it soonest. (Luckily, I happened to be passing a bookshop with the baby, and I was able to pick up a copy.) I'm equally sure, however, that I won't walk into a lamp-post while reading it, like I did with *Presumed Innocent* all those years ago; you don't walk into lamp-posts when you're reading literary novels, do you? How are we supposed to find out about landmark thrillers like *Mystic River*? Anyway, if you haven't seen the movie (and the same goes for *Presumed Innocent* and *Red Dragon*) then take *Mystic River* with you next time you get on a plane, or a holiday, or a toilet, or into a bath, or a bed. On to or into anything.

Years and years ago, I read a great interview with Jam and Lewis, the R&B producers, in which they described what it was like to be members of Prince's band. They'd sit down, and Prince would tell them what he wanted them to play, and they'd explain that they couldn't – they weren't quick enough, or good enough. And Prince would push them and push them until they mastered it, and then, just when they were feeling pleased with themselves for accomplishing something they didn't know they had the capacity for, he'd tell them the dance steps he needed to accompany the music.

This story has stuck with me, I think, because it seems like an encapsulation of the very best and most exciting kind of creative process, and from the outside, the craft involved in the creation of *Mystic River* looks as though it must have involved the same stretch. Lehane has done everything that a literary novelist is supposed to be able to do (this is a novel about grief, a community, the childhood ties that bind); the intensely satisfying whodunit element is the equivalent of the dance step on top. Indeed, Lehane has ended up making it look so effortless that no one I've ever met seems to have noticed he's done anything much at all. But then, the lesson of literature over the last eighty-odd years is the old maths teacher's admonishment: 'SHOW YOUR WORKINGS!' Otherwise, how is anyone to know that there are any?

In *Prayers for Rain*, Lehane piles complication upon complication in order to keep his detectives guessing, and there is a certain readerly pleasure to be had from that, of course; but it just seems like a more routine pleasure, compared to what he does in *Mystic River*. There, Lehane peers into the deep, dark hole that the murder of a young girl leaves in various lives, and tries to make sense of everything revealed therein; everything seems organic, nothing – or almost nothing, anyway – feels contrived. I'm happy to have friends who recommend Alan Hollinghurst, really I am. They're all nice, bright people. I just wish I had friends who could recommend books like *Mystic River*, too. Are you that person? Do you have any vacancies for a pal? If you can't be bothered with a full-on friendship, with all the tearful, drunken late-night phone calls and bitter accusations and occasional acts of violence thus entailed (the violence is always immediately followed by an apology, I hasten to add), then maybe you could just tell me the titles of the books.

At the time of writing, *Like a Fiery Elephant*, Jonathan Coe's brilliant biography of B. S. Johnson, doesn't have a US publisher, which seems absurd. Your guys seem to have been frightened off by Johnson's obscurity, but we've never heard of him, either; the book works partly because its author anticipates our ignorance. It also works because Jonathan Coe, probably the best English novelist of his generation (my generation, as bad luck would have it), has been imaginative and interrogative about the form and shape of the book, and because it's a book about writing, perhaps more than anything else. Johnson may have been a 1960s experimentalist who hung out with Beckett and cut holes in his books, but he was as egocentric and arrogant and bitter and money-obsessed as the rest of us. Johnson was a depressive who eventually killed himself; his suicide note read:

This is my last

word.

But he was a great comic character, too, almost Dickensian in his appetites and his propensity for pomposity. Whenever he wrote to complain to publishers, or agents, or even printers – and he complained a lot, not least because he got through a large number of publishers, agents and printers – he was never backwards in coming forwards, as we say here, and he included the same self-promoting line again and again. 'In reviewing my novel *Albert Angelo*, the *Sunday Times* described me as "one of the best writers we've got," and the *Irish Times* called the book "a masterpiece" and put me in the same class as Joyce and Beckett,' he wrote to Allen Lane, the founder of Penguin, demanding to know why he wasn't interested in paperback rights. 'The *Sunday Times* called me "one of the best writers we've got," and the *Irish Times* called the book a masterpiece and put me in the same class as James Joyce and

Samuel Beckett,' he wrote to his foreign-rights agent, demanding to know why there had been no Italian publication of his first novel. 'You ignorant unliterary Americans make me puke,' he wrote to Thomas Wallace of Holt, Rinehart and Winston, Inc. after Wallace had turned him down. (Maybe Coe should write a version of the same letter, if you ignorant unliterary Americans still refuse to publish his book.) 'For your information, *Albert Angelo* was reviewed by the *Sunday Times* here as by "one of the best writers we've got," and the *Irish Times* called the book a masterpiece and put me in the same class as Joyce and Beckett.' And then, finally and gloriously:

> . . . The *Sunday Times* called me 'one of the best writers we've got,' and the *Irish Times* called the book a masterpiece, and compared me with Joyce and Beckett.
>
> However, it seems that I am to be denied the opportunity of a most profound and enormous experience: of being present with my wife Virginia when our first child is born at your hospital on or about July 24th . . .

This last letter was to the Chief Obstetrician of St Bartholomew's Hospital in London, after Johnson had discovered that it was not the hospital's policy to allow fathers to attend a birth. It's the 'However' kicking off the second paragraph that's such a brilliant touch, drawing attention as it does to the absurdity of the contradiction. 'I can understand you keeping out the riff-raff, your Flemings and your Amises and the rest of the what-happened-next brigade,' it implies. 'But surely you'll make an exception for a genius?' In the end, it's just another variation on 'Don't you know who I am?' – which in Johnson's case was an even more unfortunate question than it normally is. Nobody knew then, and nobody knows now.

Johnson had nothing but contempt for the enduring influence

of Dickens and the Victorian novel; strange, then, that in the end he should remind one of nobody so much as the utilitarian school inspector in the opening scene of *Hard Times*. Here's the school inspector: 'I'll explain to you . . . why you wouldn't paper a room with representations of horses. Do you ever see horses walking up and down the sides of rooms in reality – in fact? . . . Why, then, you are not to see anywhere what you don't see in fact; you are not to have anywhere what you don't have in fact. What is called Taste is only another name for Fact.' And here's Johnson: 'Life does not tell stories. Life is chaotic, fluid, random; it leaves myriads of ends untied, untidily. Writers can extract a story from life only by strict, close selection, and this must mean falsification. Telling stories really is telling lies.' Like communists and fascists, Johnson and the dismal inspector wander off in opposite directions, only to discover that the world is round. I'm glad that they both lost the cultural Cold War: there's room for them all in our world, but there's no room for *Mystic River* in theirs. And what kind of world would that be? ★

SEPTEMBER 2004

BOOKS BOUGHT:
* *Twenty Thousand Streets Under the Sky* – Patrick Hamilton
* Unnamed Literary Novel – Anonymous
* *The Letters of Charles Dickens, Vol. 1*
* *Through a Glass Darkly: The Life of Patrick Hamilton* – Nigel Jones

BOOKS READ:
* *The Midnight Bell* – Patrick Hamilton
* *Blockbuster* – Tom Shone
* *We're in Trouble* – Chris Coake
* Literary novel (unfinished)
* Biography (unfinished)

Twelve months! A whole year! I don't think I've ever held down a job for this long. And I have to say that when I first met the Polysyllabic Spree, the eighty-four chillingly ecstatic young men and women who run the *Believer*, I really couldn't imagine contributing one column, let alone a dozen. The Spree all live together in Believer Towers, high up in the hills somewhere; they spend their days reading Montaigne's essays aloud to each other (and laughing ostentatiously at the funny bits), shooting at people who own TV sets, and mourning the deaths of every single

writer since the Gawain-Poet, in chronological order. When I first
met them, they'd got up to Gerard Manley Hopkins. (They
seemed particularly cut up about him. It may have been the Jesuit
thing, kindred spirits and all that.) I was impressed by their seriousness and their progressive sexual relationships, but they really
didn't seem like my kind of people.

And yet here we are, still. I'm beginning to see through the
white robes to the people beneath, as it were, and they're really not
so bad, once you get past the incense, the vegan food and the
communal showers. They've definitely taught me things: they've
taught me, for example, that there is very little point in persisting
with a book that isn't working for me, and even less point in
writing about it. In snarky old England, we're used to working the
other way around – we only finish books that aren't working for
us, and those are definitely the only ones we write about. Anyway,
as a consequence, my reading has become more focused and less
chancy, and I no longer choose novels that I know in advance will
make me groan, snort and guffaw.

I still make mistakes, though, despite the four-hundred-page
manual they make you read before you can contribute to the
Believer, and I made two in the last four weeks. The biography I
abandoned was of a major cultural figure of the twentieth century
– he died less than forty years ago – so when you see, in the
opening chapter, the parentheses '(1782–1860)' after a name, it's
really only natural that you become a little disheartened: you're a
long, long way from the action. I made it through to the subject's
birth, but then got irritated by a long-winded story about a prank
he played on a little girl when he was seven. I had always
suspected, even before I knew anything about him, that this major
cultural figure was once a small boy, so the confirmation was
superfluous. And the prank was so banal that he could just as
easily have grown up to be Hemingway, or Phil Silvers, or any
other midcentury colossus. It wasn't, like, a revealingly or quint-

essentially ____esque prank. At that point I threw the book down in disgust, and it went straight through the bedroom floor, only just missing a small child. Please, biographers. Please, please, please. Have mercy. Select for us. We have jobs, kids, DVD players, season tickets. But that doesn't mean we don't want to know about stuff.

My other mistake was a literary first novel, and I've probably broken every rule in the Spree manual just by saying that much. I took every precaution, I promise: I was reading a paperback that came garlanded with superlative reviews, and there were a couple of recommendations involved, although I can see now that they came from untrustworthy sources. I ignored the most boring opening sentence I have ever read in my life and ploughed on, prepared to forgive and forget; I got halfway through before its quietness and its lack of truth started to get me down. I don't mind nothing happening in a book, but nothing happening in a phoney way – characters saying things people never say, doing jobs that don't fit, the whole works – is simply asking too much of a reader. Something happening in a phoney way must beat nothing happening in a phoney way every time, right? I mean, you could prove that, mathematically, in an equation, and you can't often apply science to literature.

Here's Tom Shone writing about Spielberg's *Jaws* in his book *Blockbuster*:

> What stays with you, even today, are less the movie's big action moments than the crowning gags, light as air, with which Spielberg gilds his action – Dreyfuss crushing his Styrofoam cup, in response to Quint's crushing of his beercan, or Brody's son copying his finger-steepling at the dinner table . . .
>
> To get anything resembling such fillets of improvised character-isation, you normally had to watch something far more boring – some chamber piece about marital disintegration by John Cassavetes, say – and yet here were such things, popping up in a

movie starring a scary rubber shark. It was nothing short of revolutionary: you could have finger-steepling and scary rubber sharks *in the same movie*. This seemed like important information. Why had no one told us this before?

If this column has anything like an aesthetic, it's there: you can get finger-steepling and sharks in the same book. And you really need the shark part, because a whole novel about finger-steepling – and that's a fair synopsis of both the Abandoned Literary Novel and several thousand others like it – can be on the sleepy side. You don't have to have a shark, of course; the shark could be replaced by a plot, or, say, thirty decent jokes.

Tom Shone is a friend, and I've known him for ages – he's younger than me, but I'm pretty sure he was the first person ever to phone me up and ask me to write something for him, when he was the literary editor of a now-defunct newspaper in London. That doesn't mean I owe him anything, and it certainly doesn't mean I have to be nice about his book. He gave me something like one hundred and fifty quid for a thousand-word piece, so he probably still owes me. In England, writers are never nice about their friends' books: I read out a terrific sentence from *Blockbuster* with the express purpose of making a mutual friend groan with horrified envy, and it worked a treat.

With a heavy heart, then, I must tell you that *Blockbuster* is compelling, witty, authoritative and very, very smart. Subtitled *How Hollywood Learned to Stop Worrying and Love the Summer*, it's an alternative view of the film universe to that expounded in *Easy Riders, Raging Bulls*; where Peter Biskind believes that Spielberg and Lucas murdered movies, Shone takes the view that they breathed a whole new life into them. 'It seems worth pointing out: the art of popular cinema was about to get, at a rough estimate, a bazillion times better.' He's not philistine about it – he doesn't think that blockbusters have gotten better and better with each successive summer, for example, and he despairs in all the right places.

Indeed, he manages to put his finger on something that had always troubled my populist soul: he explains why breaking all box-office records has become a meaningless feat, almost certainly indicative of lack of quality rather than the opposite, over the last few years. *Raiders of the Lost Ark* took $8 million in its opening weekend, but then went on to make $209 million. By contrast, the big movies of 2001 – *AI, Jurassic Park III, Pearl Harbor, The Mummy Returns, Planet of the Apes* – all opened big, and then disappeared fast. 'By the time we've all seen that it sucked, it's a hit. The dollar value of our bum on seat has never been greater, but what it signifies has never meant less.'

There is, in the end, something untrustworthy about the film critics who have sat in an audience spellbound by *Close Encounters of the Third Kind* and then gone on to slag it off at some stage in their careers. There's certainly something untrustworthy about them as critics, and I would argue that there is something untrust-worthy about them as people: what was it that prevented them from responding in the way we all responded, those of us who were old enough to go to a cinema in 1977? What bit of them is missing? *Star Wars, Raiders, ET, Close Encounters* and the rest clearly worked for discriminating cinema audiences; Tom Shone demon-strates that all his bits are where they should be by writing with acuity and enthusiasm about how and why they worked. This may be a strange thing to say about a book that embraces the evil Hollywood empire so warmly, but *Blockbuster* is weirdly humane: it prizes entertainment over boredom, and audiences over critics, and yet it's a work of great critical intelligence. It wouldn't kill me, I suppose, to say I'm proud of the boy.

I know Chris Coake, too. I taught him for a week a couple of years ago – by which I mean that I read a couple of his stories, scratched my head while trying to think of some way they could be improved, gave up the unequal struggle, and told him they were terrific. I would like to claim that I discovered him, but you can't really discover writers like this: the quality of the work is so blindingly obvious that he was never going to labour in obscurity for any length of time, and the manuscript he sent me has already been bought by Harcourt Brace in the United States, Penguin in the UK, Guanda in Italy, and so on. You won't be able to read his book until next year, but when you see the reviews, you'll be reminded that you heard about it here first – which is, after all, how you usually hear about most things, apart from sports results.

We're in Trouble is, for the most part, a book about death – quite often, about how death affects the young. 'In the Event' takes place over the course of a few hours: it begins in the early morning, just after a car crash that has killed the parents of a three-year-old boy, and ends shortly before the boy wakes up to face his terrible new world. In between times, the child's youthful and untogether godfather, who will raise the child, has a very long and very dark night of the soul. In the collection's title story, death casts a shadow over three relationships, at various stages of maturity, and with increasing directness. Sometimes, when you're reading the stories, you forget to breathe, which probably means that you read them with more speed than the writer intended. Are they literary? They're beautifully written, and they have bottom, but they're never dull, and they all contain striking and dramatic narrative ideas. And Coake never draws attention to his own art and language; he wants you to look at his people, not listen to his voice. So they're literary in the sense that they're serious, and will probably be nominated for prizes, but they're unliterary in the sense that they could end up mattering to people.

Patrick Hamilton, who died in 1962, is my new best friend. I read his most famous book, *Hangover Square*, a couple of months back; now a trilogy of novels, collectively entitled *Twenty Thousand Streets Under the Sky*, has just been republished here in the UK, and the first of them, *The Midnight Bell*, seemed to me to be every bit as good as *Hangover Square*. Usually, books have gone out of print for a reason, and that reason is they're no good, or, at least, of very marginal interest. (Yeah, yeah, your favourite book of all time is currently out of print, and it's a scandal. But I'll bet you any money you like it's not as good as *The Catcher in the Rye*, or *The Power and the Glory*, or anything else still available that was written in the same year.) Hamilton's books aren't arcane, or difficult, although they're dated in the sense that the culture that produced them has changed beyond recognition. Tonally, though, they're surprisingly modern: they're gritty, real, tough and sardonic, and they deal with dissipation. And we love a bit of dissipation, don't we? We're always reading books about that. Or at least, someone's always writing one. Hamilton's version, admittedly, isn't very glamorous – people sit in pubs and get pissed. But if you were looking to fly from Dickens to Martin Amis with just one overnight stop, then Hamilton is your man. Or your airport, or whatever.

Doris Lessing called him 'a marvellous novelist who's grossly neglected', and she felt that he suffered through not belonging to the 1930s Isherwood clique. She also thought, in 1968, that 'his novels are true now. You can go into any pub and see it going on.' This, however, is certainly no longer the case – our pub culture here in London is dying. Pubs aren't pubs any more – not, at least, in the metropolitan centre. They're discos, or sports bars, or gastro-pubs, and the working- and lower-middle-class men that Hamilton writes about with such appalled and amused fascination don't go anywhere near them. That needn't bother you, however. You're all smart enough to see that the author's central theme – men are vile and stupid, women are vile and manipulative – is as meaningful today as it ever was. I have only just started to read Nigel Jones's biography, but I suspect that Hamilton wasn't the happiest of chaps.

Thank you, dear reader, for your time over these last twelve months, if you have given any. And if you haven't, then thank you for not complaining in large enough numbers to get me slung out. I reckon I've read at least a dozen wonderful books since I began this column. I've read *Hangover Square*, *How to Breathe Underwater*, *David Copperfield*, *The Fortress of Solitude*, *George and Sam*, *True Notebooks*, *Random Family*, Ian Hamilton's Lowell biography, *The Sirens of Titan*, *Mystic River*, *Clockers*, *Moneyball* . . . And there'll be the same number this coming year, too. More, if I read faster. What have you done twelve times over the last year that was so great, apart from reading books? Fibber. ✶

OCTOBER 2004

Sex with cousins: are you for or against? I only ask because the first two books I read this month, Maile Meloy's *Liars and Saints* and Meg Rosoff's *How I Live Now*, answer the question with a resounding affirmative. (It's a long story, but in *Liars and Saints*, the couple in question is under the impression that they're actually uncle and niece, rather than cousins – and even that doesn't stop 'em! Crikey!) People are always plighting their troth to and/or screwing their cousins in Hardy and Austen, but I'd always presumed that this was because of no watercoolers, or speed-dating, or college dances; what is so dispiriting about *Liars and Saints* and *How I Live Now* is that they are set in the present, or even in the

near-future, in the case of the latter book. No offence to my cousins
– or, indeed, to *Believer* readers who prefer to keep things in the
family – but is that really all we have to look forward to?

I know that when it comes to subconscious sexual deviation
there's no such thing as coincidence, but I swear I haven't been
scouring the bookshops for novels about the acceptable face of
incest. I picked up *Liars and Saints* because it's been blurbed by
both Helen Fielding and Philip Roth, and though I enjoyed the
book, that conjunction set up an expectation that couldn't ever be
fulfilled: sometimes blurbs can be too successful. I was hoping for
something bubbly and yet achingly world-weary, something
diverting and yet full of lacerating and unforgettable insights about
the human condition, something that was fun while being at the
same time no fun at all, in a bracing sort of a way, something that
cheered me up while making me want to hang myself. In short, I
wanted Roth and Fielding to have cowritten the book, and poor
Maile Meloy couldn't deliver. *Liars and Saints* is a fresh, sweet-
natured first novel, but it's no Nathan Zuckerman's *Diary*.
(Cigarettes – 23, attacks of *Weltschmerz* – 141, etc.)

How I Live Now has had amazing reviews here in England –
someone moderately sensible called it 'a classic' – and although
that might sometimes be enough to persuade me to shell out (cf.
Seven Types of Ambiguity, which has received similar press), normally that wouldn't be enough to persuade me to read the thing.
Rosoff's book, however, is delightfully short, and aimed at
teenagers, and the publishers sent me a copy, so you can see the
thinking here: knock off a classic in a day or so, at no personal
expense, and bulk this column out a little. And that's pretty much
how things worked out.

I'm not sure that *How I Live Now* is a classic, though, even if a
book can achieve that kind of status in the month of its publication. It's set in a war-torn England a few years from now, and
though the love affair between the cousins has a dreamy intensity,

and Rosoff's teenage voice is strong and true, her war is a little shoddy, if you ask me. London has been occupied, but by whom no one, not even the adults, seems quite sure: it could be the French, it could be the Chinese. What sort of war is that? Rosoff is aiming for a fog of half-truth and rumour, the sort of fog that most teenagers live in most of the time, and yet one is given the impression that not even Seymour Hersh would be able to shed much light on the matter of who invaded Britain and why.

I've been meaning to read Edmund Gosse's *Father and Son* for about ten years; the only thing that was stopping me from reading it was the suspicion that it might be unreadable – miserable and dreary and impossibly remote. First published (anonymously) in 1907, *Father and Son* describes Edmund's relationship with his father, Philip, a marine biologist of some distinction who was also a member of the Plymouth Brethren, and whose fierce, joyless evangelism crippled his son's childhood. In fact, *Father and Son* is a sort of Victorian *This Boy's Life*: it's inevitably, unavoidably painful, but it's also tender and wry. OK, sometimes it reads like that Monty Python sketch about the Yorkshiremen, constantly trying to trump each other's stories of deprivation ('You lived in a hole in the road? You were lucky.'): when Gosse's mother was dying of cancer, and too sick to travel from one London borough to another for the hopeless last-chance quack treatment she was trying, she and her young son stayed in a grim boarding house in Pimlico, where Edmund was allowed to entertain her by reading from religious tracts. His pathetic treat, at the end of the day, was to read her a hymn – in the Gosse family, that was what passed for fun.

My first book, *Fever Pitch*, was a memoir, and I own a copy of *Father and Son* because some clever-dick reviewer somewhere compared the two. (I seem to remember that the comparison did me no favours, before you accuse me of showing off. Someone must have been dissed, and I can't imagine it was Gosse.) My young life was blighted by my devotion to Arsenal Football Club, a team so dour and joyless during the late sixties and seventies that they would have been rather intimidated by the comparative exuberance and joie de vivre of the Plymouth Brethren. It's always weird, though, for a writer to spot the same impulses and ambitions in another, especially when the two are separated by history, culture, environment, belief and just about anything else you can think of, and I identified absolutely with more or less every page in Gosse's book. I had hoped, when I wrote mine, that even if I were to allow myself the indulgence of writing in detail about 1960s League Cup finals, people might be prepared to put up with it if they thought there was something else going on as well; Gosse's football-sized hole was created by religion, and filled by marine biology, so he was, in effect, both damaged and repaired by his father's twin obsessions. (His father, meanwhile, was almost split in two by them − Darwin's theories were more devastating for the evangelical naturalist than for just about anyone else in the country.) *Father and Son* is an acknowledged classic, so I had expected it to be good, but I hadn't expected it to be lovable, or modern, nor had I expected it to speak to me. *How I Live Now*, by contrast, felt as if it was talking to everyone else but me − I was watching from the wings as its author addressed the multitudes. Maybe that's why you have to give books time to live before you decide that they're never going to die. You have to wait and see whether anyone in that multitude is really listening.

Every time I read a biography of a novelist, I discover that the novels in question are autobiographical to an almost horrifying degree. In Blake Bailey's book about Richard Yates, for example, we learn that Yates fictionalized his mother by changing her name from Dookie to Pookie (or perhaps from Pookie to Dookie, I can't remember now). In Nigel Jones's *Through a Glass Darkly* we learn that, like Bob in *The Midnight Bell*, Patrick Hamilton had a disastrous crush on a prostitute, and that, like Bone in *Hangover Square*, his obsession with a young actress (Geraldine Fitzgerald, who appeared in *Wuthering Heights* alongside Laurence Olivier and Merle Oberon) was deranged, although he stopped short of murdering her. And, of course, like all of his characters, Hamilton was a drunk. I'm sure that a biography of Tolkien would reveal that *The Lord of the Rings* was autobiographical, too – that Tolkien actually fell down a hole and found a place called Central Earth, where there were a whole bunch of Hobbits. Some people – critics, mostly – would argue that this diminishes the achievement somehow, but it's the writing that's hard, not the invention.

See, some of us just don't come from the right kind of background to be the subject of a literary biography. Hamilton's father was left a hundred thousand pounds in 1884, and pissed it all away during a lifetime of utter indolence and dissolution; his first wife was a prostitute whom Hamilton Sr imagined he could save from the streets, but the marriage didn't work out. 'Snot fair! Why didn't my dad ever have a thing with prostitutes? (Note to *Believer* fact-checker: I'll give you his number, but I'm not making the call. He's pretty grouchy at the best of times.)

Jenny, the prostitute in *The Midnight Bell*, takes centre stage in *The Siege of Pleasure*, the second novel in the *Twenty Thousand Streets Under the Sky* trilogy. Hamilton was a Marxist for much of his life, and though he ended up voting Conservative, as so many English Marxists did, in his case it was because the Tories hated the Labour Party as much as he did, which at least shows a warped kind of ideological consistency. *The Siege of Pleasure* is in part a careful, convincing analysis of the economic and social pressures that forced Jenny on to the streets and out of her life below stairs. It's more fun than this sounds, because Hamilton, who wrote the play *Rope*, which Hitchcock later filmed, loves his ominous narratives. He's a sort of urban Hardy: everyone is doomed, right from the first page. Hamilton isolates Jenny's plight to an evening spent boozing with a tarty friend; she gets plastered, wakes up late in the house of a man she doesn't know, and fails to turn up at her new job, skivvying for a comically incapable trio of old people. It's sad, but Hamilton's laconic narrative voice is always a joy to read, and as a social historian, Hamilton is unbeatable. Who knew that you could get waiter service in pubs in the 1920s? And plates of biscuits? Biscuits! What sort of biscuits? Hamilton doesn't say.

In *So Many Books*, Gabriel Zaid attempts to grapple with the question that seems constantly to arise in this column, namely, Why bloody bother? Why bother reading the bastards, and why bother writing them? I'm not sure he gets a lot further than I've ever managed, but there are some great stats here: Zaid estimates, for example, that it would take us fifteen years simply to read a list of all the books ever published. ('Author and title' – he's very precise. You can, presumably, add on another seven or eight years if you want to know the names of the publishers.) I think he intends to make us despair, but I was actually rather heartened: not only can I now see that it's possible – I'd be finished some time in my early sixties – but I'm seriously tempted. A good chunk of coming across as educated, after all, is just a matter of knowing who wrote what: someone mentions Patrick Hamilton, and you nod sagely and say, *Hangover Square*, and that's usually enough. If I read the list, something might stick in the memory, because God knows that the books themselves don't.

Zaid's finest moment, however, comes in his second paragraph, when he says that 'the truly cultured are capable of owning thousands of unread books without losing their composure or their desire for more'.

That's me! And you, probably! That's us! 'Thousands of unread books'! 'Truly cultured'! Look at this month's list: Chekhov's letters, Amis's letters, Dylan Thomas's letters . . . What are the chances of getting through that lot? I've started on the Chekhov, but the Amis and the Dylan Thomas have been put straight into their permanent home on the shelves, rather than on to any sort of temporary pending pile. The Dylan Thomas I saw remaindered for fifteen quid (down from fifty) just after I'd read a terrific review of a new Thomas biography in the *New Yorker*; the Amis letters were a fiver. But as I was finding a home for them in the Arts and Lit non-fiction section (I personally find that for domestic purposes, the Trivial Pursuit system works better than Dewey), I suddenly had a little epiphany: all the books we own, both read and unread, are the fullest expression of self we have at our disposal. My music is me, too, of course – but as I only really like rock and roll and its mutations, huge chunks of me – my rarely examined operatic streak, for example – are unrepresented in my CD collection. And I don't have the wall space or the money for all the art I would want, and my house is a shabby mess, ruined by children . . . But with each passing year, and with each whimsical purchase, our libraries become more and more able to articulate who we are, whether we read the books or not. Maybe that's not worth the thirty-odd quid I blew on those collections of letters, admittedly, but it's got to be worth something, right? ✷

TWENTY THOUSAND
STREETS UNDER THE SKY

by PATRICK HAMILTON

✶ ✶ ✶

T he first to enter the Saloon Bar that night was Mr Wall. This was a very sprightly little man, and another habitué. He had a red face, fair hair, twinkling blue eyes, a comic little moustache, and a bowler hat. He was obscurely connected with motors in Great Portland Street, and incorrigible. His incorrigibility was his charm. Indeed, he kept his company perpetually diverted. But this was not because his jokes and innuendoes were good, but because they were so terribly, terribly bad. You couldn't believe that anyone could behave so badly and awfully, and you loved to hear him exceed himself. Against all your sense of propriety you were obscurely tickled – simply because he was at it again. There was no doing anything with him.

His jokes, like all bad jokes, were mostly tomfooleries with the language. To call, for instance, 'The Four Horsemen of the Apocalypse' 'The Four Horsemen of the Eucalyptus' was, to him, quite tremendous in its sly and impudent irony. But he was not always as subtle as this. Having a wonderful comic susceptibility to words, and particularly those with as many as, or more than, four syllables in them, he could hardly let any hopeful ones go by without raillery. Thus, if in the course of conversation you happened innocently to employ the word 'Vo*cab*ulary' he would instantly cry out 'Oh my word – let's take a Cab!' or something like that, and repeat it until you had fully registered it. Or if you said that something was Identical with something else, he would say that So long as there wasn't a Dent in it, we would be all right. Or if you said that things looked rather Ominous, he would declare that So long as we weren't all run over by an Omnibus we would be all right. Or if you were so priggishly erudite as to allude to Metaphysics, he would first of all ask you, in a complaining tone, Met What? – and then add consolingly that So long as we Met it Half Way it would be all right. It was a kind of patter in the conditional. Similarly, in his own particular idiom, Martyrs were associated with Tomatoes, Waiters with Hot Potatoes, Cribbage with Cabbage, Salary with Celery (the entire vegetable world was ineffably droll), Suits with Suet, Fiascoes with Fiancées, and the popular wireless genius with Macaroni. He was, perhaps, practically off his head.

'Well, Bob, my boy,' he said, rallying, as he came in. 'How're you? B an' B, please, calgirl.'

He employed the popular abbreviation for Bitter and Button mixed, and Ella gave it him, primly and deprecatingly, and took his money.

'How're you, Mr Wall?' she said. 'We haven't seen you lately.'

'Oh, I'm all right. Wotyavin, Bob?'

'I won't have nothing to-night, thank you, Mr Wall.'

'What – You on the Wagon?'

'Pro Tem,' said Bob.

' 'Bout time he was,' said Ella.

At this the door creaked open, and Mr Sounder entered.

'Ah ha!' said Mr Sounder. 'The worthy Mr Wall!'

'Oh ho!' said Mr Wall. 'The good Mr Sounder!' But the two gentlemen looked at each other with a kind of glassy gleam which belied this broad and amicable opening. Indeed, these two were notoriously incapable of hitting it off, and the thwarted conde- scension of the one, together with the invulnerable impudence of the other, were features of 'The Midnight Bell' in the evening.

'Been writin' any more letters to those papers of yours, Mr Sounder?' asked Mr Wall.

'Not my papers – alas – Mr Wall. Bitter I think, please, Ella.'

'Wish I owned a paper, 'tanyrate,' said Ella, trying to keep the peace, and she gave him his beer.

'No . . .' said Mr Sounder. 'As a matter of Absolute Fact, within the last hour I have been in the Throes of Composition.'

'So long as it ain't a *false* position,' said Mr Wall. 'It's all right.'

Here both Bob and Ella were seized by that irritating and inexplicable desire to giggle, and showed it on their shamefaced faces: but Mr Sounder ignored the interruption.

'I have, in fact, brought forth a Sonnet,' he said.

'A Sonnet?' said Bob.

'Oh,' said Mr Wall. 'Didn't know you wore a Bonnet. Glad to hear it.'

'What's the subject?' asked Bob.

('You might lend it to me,' said Mr Wall.)

'The subject is Evensong in Westminster Abbey,' said Mr Sounder, suavely, and looked portentously at his beer. ✴

NOVEMBER 2004

BOOKS BOUGHT:
* *Deception* – Philip Roth
* *Wonder Boys* – Michael Chabon
* *The Essential Tales of Chekhov*
* *Ward No. 6 and Other Stories, 1892–1895* – Anton Chekhov
* *The Death of Ivan Ilyich and Other Stories* – Leo Tolstoy

BOOKS READ:
* *On and Off the Field* – Ed Smith
* *A Life in Letters* – Anton Chekhov
* *Reading Chekhov: A Critical Journey* – Janet Malcolm
* *Oh, Play That Thing* – Roddy Doyle

I have been meaning to read a book about cricket for a while, with the sole intention of annoying you all. I even toyed with the idea of reading only cricket books this entire month, but then I realized that this would make it too easy for you to skip the whole column; this way, you have to wade through the cricket to get to the Chekhov and the Roddy Doyle. I'm presuming here that very few of you have ever seen a cricket match, and if you have, you are almost certain to have been both mystified and stupefied: this, after all, is a game that, in its purest form (there are all sorts of cheap-thrills bastardized versions now), lasts for five days and very frequently ends in a draw: five days is not quite long enough to get through everything that needs doing in a cricket match, especially as you can't play in the rain.

The funny thing is that we actually do like cricket here in England – it's not some hey-nonny-no phoney heritage thing, like Morris dancing (horrific bearded men with sticks and bells) or cream teas. Thirty or forty years ago it was our equivalent of baseball, an all-consuming summer sport that drove football off the back pages of newspapers completely for three months; now Beckham and the rest of them get the headlines even when they're lying on Caribbean beaches. But big international matches still sell out, and every now and again the England team starts winning, and we renew our interest.

Ed Smith reminds traditionalists of a time when cricketers were divided into two camps, 'Gentlemen' and 'Players'; the former were private-school boys and university graduates from upper-middle-class backgrounds, the latter horny-handed professionals who weren't even allowed to share a dressing room with their social betters. Smith is a Cambridge graduate who reviews fiction for one of the broadsheet newspapers. He's also good-looking, well-spoken, articulate, and he has played for England, so perhaps not surprisingly, *On and Off the Field*, his diary of a season, attracted a fair bit of attention, all of it, as far as I can tell, admiring. Where's the fairness in that? You'd think that if critics had any use at all, it would be to give our golden boys and girls a fearsome bashing, but of course you can't even rely on them for that.

To be fair to the critics, Smith didn't give them much ammunition: *On and Off the Field* is terrific, exactly the sort of book you want from a professional sportsman but you never get: it's self-analytical (even if, after the self-analysis, he attributes some of his early-season failure to sheer bad luck), wry and honest. The sports memoir is such a debased form – George Best, the biggest football star of the sixties and seventies, has 'written' five autobiographies to date, and he hasn't kicked a ball for thirty-odd years – but *On and Off the Field* is different: the photo on the back depicts Smith slumped against a wall, the very epitome of defeated misery. Defeated misery is what all sport is about, eventually, if you follow the story for long enough; all sportsmen know this, but Smith is one of the very few capable not only of recognizing this bitter truth, but acknowledging it in print. I know you're not going to read it. But let's say I've read it on your behalf, and we've all enjoyed it.

To my surprise, I managed to read, in its entirety, one of the many books of collected letters I inexplicably bought last month. Why I read it, however, is almost as mysterious as why I bought it in the first place; or rather, I'm not sure why I felt I had to read every word of every letter. After a little while, you get the pattern: letters to his feckless brothers tend to be fiercely admonitory (and therefore fun); letters to his mother and sister tend to be purely domestic, functional and a little on the dull side ('Tell Arseny to water the birch tree once a week, and the eucalyptus'); letters to his wife, Olga Knipper, are embarrassingly slushy, and the letters he wrote to Alexey Suvorin, his publisher, are the letters I was hoping for when I started the book: they're the ones where you're most likely to find something about writing. I should have stuck to the Suvorin letters, but you get addicted to the (mostly sleepy) rhythms of Chekhov's quotidian life.

Chekhov, as you probably know (I don't know why, but I always think of you lot knowing everything, pretty much, apart from the rules of cricket), started life as a hack, a journalist who wrote short comic articles for various Russian periodicals while training and then practising as a doctor. And then, in 1886, when he was just beginning to take his writing more seriously, he received the sort of letter most young writers can only dream of getting. Dmitry Grigorovich, a respected older novelist, wrote out of the blue to tell him he was a genius, and he should stop pissing around.

I know from personal experience that these letters have a

galvanizing effect at first. But once you've had twenty or thirty of them, you start to chuck them straight into the bin once you've checked out the signature. I had a rule that I'd only take any notice if the correspondent had a Pulitzer or a Nobel; if you get involved with every two-bit literary legend who wants to be your friend, you'd never get any work done. Some of them can be a real pain. (Salinger? Reclusive? Yeah, I wish.) Anyway, Chekhov's reply to Grigorovich is every bit as humbled, as sweetly thunderstruck, as you'd want it to be.

'Everyone has seen a *Cherry Orchard* or an *Uncle Vanya*, while very few have even heard of "The Wife" or "In the Ravine",' says Janet Malcolm in her short, moving, clever book *Reading Chekhov*. Perhaps this isn't the right time to talk about what 'everyone' means here, although one is entitled to stop and wonder at the world in which our men and women of letters live – not 'everyone' has seen a football match or an episode of *Seinfeld*, let alone a nineteenth-century Russian play. But she's right, of course, to point out that his stories languish in relative obscurity. In his introduction to the *Essential Tales*, Richard Ford writes about tackling the stories before he was old enough to realize that their plainness was deceptive, and though I hate that 'writers' writer' stuff (after a lifetime of reading, I can officially confirm that readers' writers beat writers' writers every time), I can see what he means. When you're young and pretentious, you want your Greats to come with bells on, otherwise you can't see what the fuss is about, and there are no bells in those stories.

What's remarkable about the letters is that the drama hardly comes up at all. Every now and again, Chekhov tells someone that he's just written a rubbish new play, or that he's hopeless at the craft. 'Reading through my newly born play convinces me more than ever that I'm not a playwright,' he says when writing to Suvorin about *The Seagull*; *Three Sisters* is 'boring, sluggish and awkward'. He'd have been staggered at the way things have turned

THE COMPLETE POLYSYLLABIC SPREE

out. His working life was about prose – and money. He tells just
about anyone who'll listen how much he got for this, and how
much they could get for that.

The letters are full of useful advice – advice that holds good
even now. 'Sleeping with a whore, breathing right in her mouth,
endlessly listening to her pissing . . . where's the sense in that?
Civilized people don't simply obey their baser instincts. They
demand more from a woman than bed, horse sweat and the sound
of pissing.' He's right, of course. There's no sense in that, at all. But
that pissing sound is sort of addictive after a few years, isn't it? If
you haven't even started listening to it, then I can only urge you
never to do so.

Apart from the peculiar obsession with the sound of pissing,
there's a modern writing life described here. There's the money
thing, of course, but there's also gossip, and endless charitable
activity, and fame. (Chekhov was recognized everywhere he went.)
He's also the only genius I've come across who had no recognition of, or interest in, the immensity of his own talent.

As a special bonus, you also get some of those bad biopic
comedy moments thrown in. 'I went to see Lev Tolstoy the day
before yesterday,' he writes to Gorky. 'He was full of praise for you,
and said you were a "splendid writer". He likes your "The Fair"
and "In the Steppe", but not "Malva".' You just know that there's
only three words in this letter Gorky would have registered, and
that he spent the rest of the day too depressed to get out of bed.

This month, my bookshelves functioned exactly as they are
supposed to. I'd just finished the Chekhov and dimly remembered
buying Janet Malcom's book when it was first published. And then
I found it, and read it. And enjoyed it. You forget that the very best
literary critics are capable of being very clever about people and
life, as well as books: there's a brilliant passage here where Malcolm,
who is travelling around Russia visiting Chekhov's houses, links her
feelings over the return of a lost bag to her feelings about travel:

'[Our homes] are where the action is; they are where the riches of experience are distributed . . . Only when faced with one of the inevitable minor hardships of travel do we break out of the trance of tourism and once again feel the sharp savor of the real.' I can't understand, though, why she thinks that the letters between Chekhov and Olga Knipper 'make wonderful reading'. I've only read Chekhov's side, but she seems to have reduced the man to mush: 'My little doggie', 'my dear little dog', 'my darling doggie', 'Oh, doggie, doggie', 'my little dog', 'little ginger-haired doggie', 'my coltish little doggie', 'my lovely little mongrel doggie', 'my darling, my perch', 'my squiggly one', 'dearest little colt', 'my incomparable little horse', 'my dearest chaffinch' . . . For god's sake, pull yourself together, man! You're a major cultural figure!

Knipper and Chekhov were together only rarely in their short marriage (she was acting in St Petersburg, he was trying to keep warm in Yalta) and Malcolm seems to suggest rather sadly that famous men and women with more conventional relationships rob biographers of future source material, because they have no reason to write to each other. On the evidence here, all couples should be compelled by law to spend twenty-four hours a day together, three hundred and sixty-five days a year, just in case either partner is tempted to call the other a chaffinch, or a perch, or an aardvark, in writing.

Malcolm, however, is one of those people so sweetly devoted to her subject that she won't recognize flaws as flaws, but as strengths – or, at least, as *characteristics*. There's this pedestal – I don't know anyone who's even seen it, but it's there – and once you're up on it, people stop telling you that you can't do this, or you're useless at that, and start wondering why you have allowed something that *looks* like uselessness to appear in your work. Christopher Ricks did it in his recent book *Dylan's Visions of Sin*: he becomes very troubled by a ropy rhyme ('rob them'/'problem') in 'Positively Fourth Street', and then nags at it until the ropy rhyme becomes yet another example of Bob's genius: 'It must be granted that if these lines induce queasiness, they do make a point of saying "No, I do not feel that good." So an unsettling rhyme such as *problem/rob them* might rightly be hard to stomach . . .' The notion that Dylan might have just thought, 'Oh, fuck it, that'll do' never crosses Ricks's mind for a moment.

Malcolm does her own, perhaps more self-aware version of this when talking about the troublingly 'abrupt' and 'unmotivated' changes of character in Chekhov's stories: 'after enough time goes by, a great writer's innovations stop looking like mistakes'. See, I'm still at that early stage, where everything still looks like a mistake, so I would have liked Ms Malcolm to be a little more precise with the figures here. What's 'enough time'? Just, you know, roughly? Are we talking six months? Two years? I don't really want to have to wait much longer than that.

I've known Roddy Doyle for a while now. I read him before I met him, and the Barrytown trilogy was an important source of inspiration for me when I was starting out: who knew that books written with such warmth and simplicity could be so complex and intelligent? On this side of the Atlantic, at least, Doyle single-handedly redefined what we mean by 'literary' fiction. *Oh, Play That Thing* is the second part of the trilogy that began with *A Star Called Henry*; it's set in the United States during the twenties and thirties, and features Louis Armstrong as a central character, so I've been reading it while listening to *Hot Fives and Sevens* on my iPod.

Reading reviews and interviews with him over the last few weeks, one is reminded that there's nothing critics like less than a writer producing something that he hasn't done before – apart, that is, from a writer producing more of the same. One reviewer complained that Doyle used to write short books, and now they've gone fat; another that he used to write books set in Dublin, and he should have kept them there; another that he used to write with a child's-eye view, and now he's writing about adults. All of these criticisms, of course, could have been based on the catalogue copy, rather than on the book itself – a two-line synopsis and information about the number of pages would have received exactly the same treatment. You're half-expecting someone to point out that back in the day he used to write books that sold for a tenner, and now they've gone up to seventeen quid.

What he's doing, of course, is the only thing a writer can do: he's writing the books that he wants, in the way he wants to. He wants to write about different things, and to add something to the natural talent that produced those early books. I wouldn't want to read anyone who did anything else – apart from P. G. Wodehouse, who did exactly the same thing hundreds of times over. So where does that leave us? Pretty much back where we started, I suppose. That's the beauty of this column, even if I do say it myself. ✶

A *selection from*

A LIFE IN LETTERS
by ANTON CHEKHOV

You have only one fault. But in that fault lies the falseness of your position, your discontent and even the catarrh in your bowels. It is your complete lack of manners. Please forgive me, but *veritas magis amicitiae* ...The fact of the matter is that there are certain rules in life ...You will always feel uncomfortable among intelligent people, out of place and inadequate, unless you are equipped with the manners to cope ...Your talent has opened the door for you into this milieu, you should be perfectly at home in it, but at the same time something pulls you away from it and you find yourself having to perform a kind of balancing act between these cultivated circles on the one hand and the people you live among on the other. That telltale lower-class flesh of yours is all too apparent, the result of growing up with the rod, next to the wine cellar, and subsisting on handouts. It is hard to rise above that, terribly hard!

Civilized people must, I believe, satisfy the following criteria:

1) They respect human beings as individuals and are therefore always tolerant, gentle, courteous and amenable ...They do not create scenes over a hammer or a mislaid eraser; they do not make you feel they are conferring some great benefit on you when they live with you, and they don't make a scandal when they leave, saying 'it's impossible to live with you!' They put up with noise and cold, over-done meat, jokes, and the presence of strangers in the house ...

2) They have compassion for other people besides beggars and cats. Their hearts suffer the pain of what is hidden to the

naked eye. So for example, if Pyotr realized that his father and mother are turning grey from worry and depression and are lying awake at nights because they see him so seldom (and when they do, he's the worse for drink), he hastens to see them and cuts out the vodka. Civilized people lie awake worrying about how to help the Polevayevs, to pay for their brothers to go through University, to see their mother decently clothed . . .

3) They respect other people's property, and therefore pay their debts.

4) They are not devious, and they fear lies as they fear fire. They don't tell lies even in the most trivial matters. To lie to someone is to insult them, and the liar is diminished in the eyes of the person he lies to. Civilized people don't put on airs; they behave in the street as they would do at home, they don't show off to impress their juniors . . . They are discreet and don't broadcast unsolicited confidences . . . They mostly keep silence, from respect for others' ears.

5) They don't run themselves down in order to provoke the sympathy of others. They don't play on other people's heartstrings to be sighed over and cosseted. They don't say: 'No one understands me!' or 'I've wasted my talents on trivial doodlings! I'm a whore!!' because all that sort of thing is just cheap striving for effects, it's vulgar, old hat and false . . .

6) They are not vain. They don't waste time with the fake jewellery of hobnobbing with celebrities, being permitted to shake the hand of a drunken Plevako, the exaggerated bonhomie of the first person they meet at the Salon, being

the life and soul of the bar . . . They regard phrases like 'I am a representative of the Press!!' – the sort of thing one only hears from people like Rozdevich and Levenberg – as absurd. If they have done a brass farthing's work they don't pass it off as if it were 100 roubles' by swanking about with their portfolios, and they don't boast of being able to gain admission to places other people aren't allowed in . . . True talent always sits in the shade, mingles with the crowd, avoids the limelight . . . As Krylov said, the empty barrel makes more noise than the full one . . .

7) If they do possess talent, they value it. They will sacrifice people of mind, women, wine, and the bustle and vanity of the world for it . . . They take pride in it. So they don't go boozing with school teachers or with people who happen to have come to stay with Skvortsov; they know they have a responsibility to exert a civilizing influence on them rather than aimlessly hanging out with them. And they are fastidious in their habits . . .

8) They work at developing their aesthetic sensibility. They do not allow themselves to sleep in their clothes, stare at the bedbugs in the cracks in the walls, breathe foul air, walk on a floor covered in spit, cook their food on a paraffin stove. As far as possible they try to control and elevate their sex drive . . . Sleeping with a whore, breathing right in her mouth, endlessly listening to her pissing, putting up with her stupidity and never moving a step away from her – where's the sense in that? Civilized people don't simply obey their baser instincts. They demand more from a woman than bed, horse sweat and the sound of pissing and more in the way of intelligence than an ability to swell up with a phantom pregnancy; artists above all need freshness, refinement, humanity,

the capacity to be a mother, not just a hole . . . They don't continually swill vodka, they're aware they're not pigs so they don't root about sniffing in cupboards. They drink when they want to, as free men . . . For they require *mens sana in corpore sano*.

And so on. That's what civilized people are like . . . Reading *Pickwick* and learning a speech from *Faust* by heart is not enough if your aim is to become a truly civilized person and not to sink below the level of your surroundings. Taking a cab over to Yakimanka and then decamping a week later is not enough . . .

What you must do is work unceasingly, day and night, read constantly, study, exercise willpower . . . Every hour is precious . . .

Shuttling backwards and forwards to Yakimanka won't help. You must roll up your sleeves and make a clean break, once and for all . . . Come back to us, smash the vodka bottle and settle down to read . . . even if it's just Turgenev whom you've never read . . .

You've got to get over your fucking vanity, you're not a child any more . . . you'll soon be thirty! Time to grow up!

I'm expecting you . . . We all are . . .

Your

A. Chekhov ✶

FEBRUARY 2005

The story so far: I have been writing a column in this magazine for the last fifteen months. And though I have had frequent battles with the Polysyllabic Spree – the fifty-five disturbingly rapturous and rapturously disturbing young men and women who edit the *Believer* – I honestly thought that things had got better recently. We seemed to have come to some kind of understanding, a truce. True, we still have our differences of opinion: they have never really approved of me reading anything about sport, and nor do they like me referring to books wherein people eat meat or farmed fish. (There are a whole host of other rules too ridiculous to mention – for example, you try finding 'novels which express no negative and/or strong emotion, either directly or indirectly' – but I won't go into them here.) Anyway, I was stupid enough to try to accommodate their whims, and you can't negotiate with moral terrorists. In my last column, I wrote a little about cricket, and I made a slightly off-colour joke about Chekhov, and that was it: I was banned from the magazine, sine die, which is why my column was mysteriously absent from the last issue and replaced by a whole load of pictures. Pictures! This is how they announce my death! It's like a kind of happy-clappy North Korea round here.

I have no idea whether you'll ever get to read these words, but my plan is this: not all the fifty-five members of the Spree are equally sharp, frankly speaking, and they've got this pretty dozy woman on sentry duty down at the *Believer* presses. (Sweet girl, loves her books, but you wouldn't want her doing the Harold Bloom interview, if you know what I mean.) Anyway, we went out a couple of times, and I've told her that I've got the original, unedited, 600-page manuscript of *Jonathan Livingston Seagull*, her favourite novel. I've also told her she can have it if she leaves me unsupervised for thirty minutes while I work out a way of getting 'Stuff I've Been Reading' into the magazine. If you're reading these words, you'll know it all came off. This is guerrilla column-writing, man. We're in uncharted territory here.

They couldn't have picked a worse time to ban me, because I read my ass off last month. *Gravity's Rainbow*, *Daniel Deronda*, Barthes's *S/Z*, an enormous biography of some poet or another that was lying around . . . It was insane, what I got through. And it was all for nothing. This month I read what I wanted to read, rather than what I thought the Spree might want me to read, and there was nothing I wanted to read more than *Chronicles* and *The Plot Against America*.

I'm not a Dylanologist – to me he's your common-or-garden great artist, prone to the same peaks and troughs as anyone else and with nothing of any interest in his trash can. Even so, when I first heard about a forthcoming Dylan autobiography, I still found it hard to imagine what it would look like. Would it have a corny title – *My Back Pages*, say, or *The Times, They Have A-Changed*? Would it have photos with captions written by the author? You know the sort of thing: 'The eyeliner years. What was *that* all about?!!?' Or, 'Mary Tyler Moore and I, Malibu, 1973. Not many people know that our break-up inspired *Blood On The Tracks*.' Would he come clean about who those Five Believers really were, and what was so obvious about them? Even if you don't have much time for the myth of Dylan, it's still hard to imagine that he'd ever be able to make himself prosaic enough to write autobiographical prose.

Chronicles ends up managing to inform without damaging the mystique, which is some feat. In fact, after reading the book, you end up realizing that Dylan isn't wilfully obtuse or artful in any way – it's just who he is and how his mind works. And this realization in turn has the effect of contextualizing his genius – maybe even diminishing it, if you had a lot invested in his genius being the product of superhuman effort. He thinks in apocalyptic metaphors and ellipses, and clearly sees jokers and thieves and five (or more) believers everywhere he looks, so writing about them is, as far as he is concerned, no big deal. Here he is describing the difference a change in his technique made to him: 'It was like parts of my psyche were being communicated to by angels. There was a big fire in the fireplace and the wind was making it roar. The veil had lifted. A tornado had come into the place at Christmastime, pushed away all the fake Santa Clauses aside and swept away the rubble . . .' The boy can't help it. (My favourite little enigmatic moment comes when Dylan tells us how he arrived at his new surname, an anecdote that includes a reference to 'unexpectedly' coming across a book of Dylan Thomas's poems. Where did the element of surprise come in, do you think? Did it land on his head? Did he find it under his pillow one morning?)

What's so impressive about *Chronicles* is the seriousness with which Dylan has approached the task of explaining what it's like to be him and how he got to be that way. He doesn't do that by telling you about his childhood or about the bath he was running when he started humming 'Mr Tambourine Man' to himself for the first time; *Chronicles* is non-linear and concentrates on tiny moments in a momentous life – an afternoon in a friend's apartment in New York in 1961, a couple of days in New Orleans in 1989, recording *Oh Mercy* with Daniel Lanois. But he uses these moments like torches, to throw light backwards and forwards, and by the end of the book he has illuminated great swathes of his interior life – the very part one had no real hope of ever being able to see.

And *Chronicles* is a lot humbler than anyone might have anticipated, because it's about wolfing down other people's stuff as much as it's about spewing out your own. Here is a random selection of names taken from the second chapter: The Kingston Trio, Roy Orbison, George Jones, Greil Marcus, Tacitus, Pericles, Thucydides, Gogol, Dante, Ovid, Dickens, Rousseau, Faulkner, Leopardi, Freud, Pushkin, Robert Graves, Clausewitz, Balzac, Miles Davis, Dizzy Gillespie, Leadbelly, Judy Garland, Hank Williams, Woody Guthrie . . . Many of the writers on this list were apparently encountered for the first time on a bookshelf in that NYC apartment. I have no idea whether the shelf, or the apartment, or even the friend actually existed, or whether it's all an extended metaphor; and nor do I care, because this is a beautiful, remarkable book, better than anyone had any right to expect, and one of the best and most scrupulous I can remember reading about the process of creativity. You don't even have to love the guy to get something out of it; you just have to love people who create any art at all.

For a brief moment, as I put down *Chronicles* and picked up *The Plot Against America*, neither of them published for longer than a fortnight, I felt like some kind of mythical reader, dutifully ploughing through the 'new and noteworthy' list. I knew almost enough about what's *au courant* to throw one of those dinner parties that the newspaper columnists in England are always sneering at. They're invariably referred to as 'Islington dinner parties' in the English press, because that's where the 'liberal intelligentsia' – aka the 'chattering classes' – are supposed to live, and where they talk about the new Roth and eat focaccia, which is a type of bread that the 'chattering classes' really, really like, apparently. Well, I live in Islington (there's no entrance exam, obviously), and I've never been to a dinner party like that, and this could have been my moment to start a salon. I could have bought that bread and said to people, 'Have you read the new Roth?' as they were taking off their coats. And they'd have gone, like, 'What the fuck?' if they were my friends, or 'Yes, isn't it marvellous?', if they were people I didn't know. Anyway, it's too late now. The books have been out for ages. It's too late for the dinner party, and it's too late even to impress readers of this column. The Spree took care of that with their pictures. This was the one chance I had to show off, and they ruined it, like they ruin everything.

What's even more galling is that I had something to say about *The Plot Against America*, and that almost never happens. The truest and wisest words ever written about reviewing were spoken by Sarah Vowell in her book *Take the Cannoli*. Asked by a magazine to review a Tom Waits album, she concludes that she 'quite likes the ballads', and writes that down; now all she needs is another eight-hundred-odd words restating this one blinding aperçu. That's pretty much how I feel about a lot of things I read and hear, so the realization that I actually had a point to make about Roth's novel came as something of a shock to me. You'll have heard my point a million times by now, but tough – I don't have them often enough to just let them float off.

Actually, if I put it this way, my point will have the virtue of novelty and freshness: in my humble and partial opinion, my brother-in-law's alternative-history novel *Fatherland* was more successful as a work of fiction. (You've never heard anyone say that, right? Because even if you've heard someone compare Roth's book to *Fatherland*, they won't have begun the sentence with 'My brother-in-law . . .' My brother could have said it, but I'll bet you any money you like, he hasn't read the Roth. He probably lied about having read *Fatherland*, come to think of it.) *The Plot Against America* is a brilliant, brilliantly argued and chilling thesis about America in the twentieth century, but I'm not sure it works as a novel, simply because one is constantly reminded that it is a novel – and not in a fun, postmodern way, but in a strange, slightly distracting way. As you will know, *The Plot Against America* is about what happened to the US after the fascist-sympathizer Charles Lindbergh won the 1940 presidential election, but for large chunks of the book, this is *precisely* what it's about: the alternative history drives the narrative, and as a consequence, you find yourself wondering why we're being told these things. Because if Lindbergh became US president in 1940 – and this book asks us to believe that he did, asks us to inhabit a world wherein this was a part of our history – then surely we know it all already? Surely we know about the rampant anti-semitism and the ensuing riots, the heroic role that Mayor LaGuardia played, and Lindbergh's eventual fate? We read on, of course, because we don't know, and we want to know; but it's an uncomfortable compulsion, working as it does against the novel's easy naturalism. When Roth writes, for example, that 'the November election hadn't even been close . . . Lindbergh got 57 percent of the popular vote', the only thing the sentence is doing is providing us with information we don't have; yet at the same time, we are invited to imagine that we do have it – in which case, why are we being given it again?

In *Fatherland*, my brother-in-law – Harris, as I suppose I

should call him here – takes the view that in an alternative-history novel, he must imagine not only the alternative history, but the historical consciousness of his reader; in other words, the alternative history belongs in the background, and the information we need to understand what has taken place (in *Fatherland*, the Nazis have won WWII) is given out piecemeal, obliquely, while the author gets on with his thriller plot. Roth chooses to place his what-if at the centre of his book, and so *The Plot Against America* ends up feeling like an extended essay.

The thing is, I don't even know if I care. Did any of this really spoil my enjoyment of *The Plot Against America*? Answer: no. I could see it, but I didn't feel it. Who wouldn't want to read an extended essay by Philip Roth? It's only on the books pages of newspapers that perceived flaws of this kind inhibit enjoyment, and that's because book reviewers are not allowed to say 'I quite like the ballads.'

I now see that just about everything I read was relatively new: Tom Perrotta's absorbing and brave satire *Little Children*, Tony Hendra's mostly lovable *Father Joe* . . . *Soldiers of Salamis* is, I think, the first translated novel I've read since I began this column. Is that shameful? I suppose so, but once again, I don't feel it. When you're as ill-read as I am, routinely ignoring the literature of the entire non-English-speaking world seems like a minor infraction.

In Scottish poet Don Paterson's clever, funny and maddeningly addictive new book of epigrams, *The Book of Shadows*, he writes that 'nearly all translators of poetry . . . fail to understand the poem's incarnation in its tongue is *all there is of it*, as a painting is its paint'. I suppose this can't be true for novels, but there is always the sense that you're missing something. *Soldiers of Salamis* is moving and informative and worthwhile and well translated and blah blah, and on just about every page I felt as though I were listening to a radio that hadn't quite been tuned in properly. You don't need to write in to express your disgust and disappointment. I'm disappointed enough in myself.

The Book of Shadows, though, came through loud and clear – FM through Linn speakers. Thought for the day: 'Anal sex has one serious advantage: there are few cinematic precedents that instruct either party how they should *look*.' Your bathroom needs this book badly. ✳

MARCH 2005

So this last month was, as I believe you people say, a bust. I had high hopes for it, too; it was Christmastime in England, and I was intending to do a little holiday comfort reading – *David Copperfield* and a couple of John Buchan novels, say, while sipping an eggnog and . . . wait a minute! I only just read *David Copperfield*! What the hell's going on here?

Aha. I see what's happened. In hoping to save myself some time by copying out the sentence that began this column a year ago, I neglected to change anything at all. If I'd substituted *Barnaby Rudge* for *David Copperfield*, say, I might have got away with it, but I couldn't be bothered, and now I'm paying the price.

A few months ago – back in the days when the Polysyllabic Spree used to tell me, repeatedly and cruelly, that they had commissioned research showing I had zero readers – I could have got away with repeating whole columns. But then, gloriously and unexpectedly, a reader wrote in ['Dear the Believer', November 2004] and the Spree had to eat their weasel words. My reader's name is Caroline, and she actually ploughed through *Copperfield* at my suggestion, and I love her with all my heart. I think it's time to throw the question back at the Spree: so how many readers do you have, then?

Anyway, Caroline also responded to my recent plea for a list of thrillers that might make me walk into lamp-posts, which is how come I read Laura Lippman's *Every Secret Thing*. I really liked it, although at the risk of alienating my reader at a very early stage in our relationship, I have to say that it didn't make me walk into a lamp-post. I'm not sure that it's intended to be that propulsive: it's gripping in a quiet, thoughtful way, and the motor it's powered with equips the author to putter around the inside of her characters' damaged minds, rather than to smash her reader headlong into an inert object. On Lippman's thoughtful and engaging website – and there are two adjectives you don't see attached to that particular noun very often – a reviewer compares *Every Secret Thing* to a Patricia Highsmith novel, and the comparison made sense to me: like Lippman, Highsmith wants to mess with your head without actually fracturing your skull. *Every Secret Thing* is an American-cheeseburger version of Highsmith's bloody filet mignon, and that suited me fine.

Like many parents, I no longer have a lot of desire to read books in which children are harmed. My imagination is deficient and puny in every area except this one, where it works unstoppably for eighteen or twenty hours a day; I really don't need any help from no thriller. *Every Secret Thing* opens with the release from prison of two girls jailed for the death of a baby, and no sooner are they freed than another child disappears. 'It's not incidental that a childless woman wrote *Every Secret Thing*, and I was *very* worried about how readers would react,' Lippman said in an interview with the crime writer Jeff Abbott, but I suspect that it's precisely *because* Lippman is childless that she doesn't allow her novel to be pulled out of shape by the narrative events within it. I recently saw *Jaws* again, for the first time since it was in the cinema, and I'd forgotten that a small boy is one of the shark's first victims; what's striking about the movie now is that the boy is chomped and then pretty much forgotten about. In the last thirty years, we've sentimentalized kids and childhood to the extent that if *Jaws* were made now, it would have to be about the boy's death in some way, and it would be the shark that got forgotten about. *Every Secret Thing* is suitably grave in all the right places, but it's not hysterical, and it's also morally complicated in ways that one might not have expected: the mother who lost a child in the original crime is unattractively vengeful, for example, and it's her bitterness that is allowed to drive some of Lippman's narrative. My reader, huh? She shoots, she scores.

Assassination Vacation is the first of the inevitable *Incredibles* cash-ins — Sarah Vowell, as some of you may know, provided the voice of Violet Incredible, and has chosen to exploit the new part of her fame by writing a book about the murders of Presidents Lincoln, Garfield and McKinley. See, I don't know how good an idea this is, from the cash-in angle. Obviously I'm over here in London, and I can't really judge the appetite for fascinating facts about the Garfield presidency among America's pre-teens, but I reckon Vowell might have done better with something more contemporary — a book about the Fair Deal, say, or an analysis of what actually happened at Yalta.

I should own up here and say that Sarah Vowell used to be a friend, back in the days when she still spoke to people who weren't sufficiently famous to warrant animation. She even knows some of the Spree, although obviously she's been cast out into the wilderness since she started bathing in asses' milk etc. Anyway, I make a walk-on appearance in *Assassination Vacation* – I am, enigmatically, a smoker from London called Nick – and Vowell writes of the four hours we spent sitting on a bench in a cold Gramercy Park staring at a statue of John Wilkes Booth's brother. (This was her idea of a good time, not mine.)

Being reminded of that day made me realize how much I will miss her, because, incredibly, ha ha, she made those four hours actually interesting. Did you know that John Wilkes came from this prestigious acting family, a sort of nineteenth-century Baldwin clan? Hence the Booth Theatre in NYC, and hence the statue in the park? There's loads more of this sort of stuff in *Assassination Vacation*: she trawls round museums examining bullets and brains and bits of Lincoln's skull, and hangs out in mausoleums, and generally tracks down all sorts of weird, and weirdly resonant, artefacts and anecdotes. If any other of my friends had told me that they were writing a book on this subject, I'd probably have moved house just so that they wouldn't have had a mailing address for the advance copy. But Vowell's mind is so singular, and her prose is so easy, and her instinct for what we might want to know so true, that I was actually looking forward to this book, and I wasn't disappointed. It's sad, because she does such a good job of bringing these people back to life before bumping them off again, and it's witty, of course (Garfield's assassin Charles Guiteau was a hoot, if you overlook the murderous bit), and, in the current political climate, it's oddly necessary – not least because it helps you to remember that all presidencies and all historical eras end. I hope her new friends, Angelina and Drew and Buzz and Woody and the rest, value Sarah Vowell as much as we all did.

Those of you who like to imagine that the literary world is a vast conspiracy run by a tiny yet elite cabal will not be surprised to learn that I read Rodney Rothman's book because Sarah recommended it, and she happened to have an advance copy because Rothman is a friend of hers. So, to recap: a friend of mine who's just written a book which I read and loved and have written about gives me a book by a friend of hers which she loved, so I read it and then I write about it. See how it works? Oh, you've got no chance if you have no connection with One of Us. Tom Wolfe, Patricia Cornwell, Ian McEwan, Michael Frayn, Ann Rivers Siddons . . . You're doomed to poverty and obscurity, all of you. Anyway, Rothman's book is the story of how he went to live in a retirement community in Florida for a few months, and it's very sweet and very funny. If you're wondering why a man in his late twenties went to live in a retirement community in Florida, then I can provide alternative explanations. Rothman's explanation is that he wanted to practise being old, which is a good one; mine is that he had a terrific idea for a non-fiction book, which in some ways is even better, even if it's not the sort of thing you're allowed to own up to. Travel writers don't have to give some bullshit reason why they put on their kayaks and climb mountains – they do it because that's what they do, and the idea of voluntarily choosing to eat at 5 p.m. and play shuffleboard for half a year simply because there might be some good jokes in it is, I would argue, both heroic and entirely laudable.

In *Early Bird*, Rothman discovers that he's hopeless at both shuffleboard and bingo, and that it's perfectly possible to find septuagenarians sexually attractive. He gets his ass kicked at softball by a bunch of tough old geezers, and he tries to resuscitate the career of a smutty ninety-three-year-old stand-up comic with the catchphrase 'But what the hell, my legs still spread.' There are very few jokes about Alzheimer's and prune juice, and lots of stereotype-defying diversions. And Rothman allows the sadness that must, of course, attach itself to the end of our lives to seep through slowly, surely and entirely without sentiment.

So this last month was, as I believe you people say . . . oh.

Right. Sorry. What I'm trying to say here is that, once again, I didn't read as much as I'd hoped over the festive season, and one of the chief reasons for that was a book. This book is called *The Man on the Moon*, and I bought it for my two-year-old son for Christmas, and I swear that I've read it to him fifty or sixty times over the last couple of weeks. Let's say that it's, what, two thousand words long? So that's one-hundred-and-twenty-thousand-odd words – longer than the Alan Hollinghurst novel I still haven't read. And given I haven't got many other books to tell you about, I am reduced to discussing the salient points of this one, which has, after all, defined my reading month.

I bought *The Man on the Moon* after reading a review of it in a newspaper. I don't normally read reviews of children's books, mostly because I can't be bothered, and because kids – my kids, anyway – are not interested in what the *Guardian* thinks they might enjoy. One of my two-year-old's favourite pieces of night-time reading, for example, is the promotional flyer advertising the *Incredibles* that I was sent (I don't wish to show off, but I know one of the stars of the film personally), a flyer outlining some of the marketing plans for the film. If you end up having to read that out loud every night, you soon give up on the idea of seeking out improving literature sanctioned by the liberal broadsheets. I had a hunch, however, that what with the Buzz Lightyear obsession and the insistence on what he calls Buzz Rocket pyjamas, he might enjoy a picture book about an astronaut who commutes to the moon every day to tidy it up. I dutifully sought the book out – and it wasn't easy to find, you know, just before Christmas – only to be repaid with a soul-crushing enthusiasm, when I would have infinitely preferred a polite, mild and temporary interest. Needless to say, I won't be taking that sort of trouble again.

After his busy day on the moon, Bob the astronaut, we're told, has a nice hot bath, because working on the moon can make you pretty 'grubby'. And as my son doesn't know the word 'grubby',

I substitute the word 'dirty', when I remember. Except I don't always remember, at which point he interrupts – somewhat tetchily – with the exhortation 'Do "dirty"!' And I'll tell you, that's a pretty disconcerting phrase coming from the mouth of a two-year-old, especially when it's aimed at his father. He says it to his mum, too, but I find that more acceptable. She's a very attractive woman.

Amos Oz's *Help Us to Divorce* isn't really a book – it's two little essays published between tiny soft covers. But as you can see, I'm desperate, so I have to include it here. Luckily, it's also completely brilliant: the first essay, 'Between Right and Right', is a clear-eyed, calm, bleakly optimistic view of the Palestinian crisis, so sensible and yet so smart. 'The Palestinians want the land they call Palestine. They have very strong reasons to want it. The Israeli Jews want exactly the same land for exactly the same reasons, which provides for a perfect understanding between the parties, and for a terrible tragedy,' says Oz, in response to repeated invitations from well-meaning bodies convinced that the whole conflict could be solved if only the relevant parties got to know each other better. I wanted Oz's pamphlet to provide me with quick and easy mental nutrition at a distressingly mindless time of year; it worked a treat. He kicked Bob the astronaut's ass right into orbit. ✶

ASSASSINATION VACATION
by SARAH VOWELL

★ ★ ★

I live six blocks down Twenty-first Street from Gramercy Park and even though I walk by it every other day, I have been inside it precisely once, when my friend Nick, a Londoner, came to town and stayed at the Gramercy Park Hotel. How fitting that I cannot enter a park on my street without the escort of a subject of the British crown.

Nick gets the hotel's bellman to unlock the gate for us. Then the bellman asks how long we would like to stay. Why does he care? Because he has to know when to come back and *un*lock the gate. Unbelievable.

Nick seems to like the park, but then he likes any place in America where he can smoke. We mosey toward Edwin's behind. A life-size bronze in Elizabethan garb, his head's bowed, as if he's about to ask Hamlet's that-is-the-question question. Like the Prince of Denmark, Edwin could have come up with at least three reasons not to be. For starters, little brother going down in history as the president's killer was a cringing, galling shame. Before that, as a boy on the road with his drunken actor father, Junius Brutus Booth, when Edwin finally chose his own stage career over being Junius's babysitter, the elder Booth only lasted a few days without him, drinking rancid river water and dying, sick, on the Mississippi. Though it's hard to blame a kid for wanting more out of life than holding back his father's hair every night as he vomited up his Shakespearean pay, Edwin felt responsible for Junius's demise. Not that this guilt kept Edwin off the bottle. When Mary, his first and favorite wife, was lying on her deathbed in Boston, Edwin was in New York, too smashed to make the last train north. She was dead when he got there. He kicked himself for the rest of his life.

'So who was he?' Nick asks, pointing at Edwin's statue.

'Only the greatest Shakespearean actor of the nineteenth century.'

Says the English accent, 'You mean, in America?'

Whatever. I let that slide. I've been dying to get inside this park for years, but eventually, I'm going to need Nick and his bellman to get me out.

I tell him how Edwin was known as *the* Hamlet of his day; how his father, Junius Brutus, was the greatest Shakespearean actor in England, until 1821, when he emigrated to Maryland, at which point he became the greatest Shakespearean actor in America; how three of Junius's children became actors themselves – Edwin, John Wilkes, and Junius Brutus Jr; how the three brothers appeared onstage together only once, in *Julius Caesar* here in New York in 1864 as a benefit performance for the Shakespeare statue in Central Park; how their performance was interrupted because that was the night that Confederate terrorists set fires in hotels up and down Broadway and Edwin, who was playing Brutus, interrupted the play to reassure the audience; how the next morning Edwin informed John at breakfast that he had voted for Lincoln's re-election and they got into one of the arguments they were always having about North versus South; how Edwin retired from acting out of shame when he heard his brother was the president's assassin, but that nine months later, broke, he returned to the stage here in New York, as Hamlet, to a standing ovation; how he bought the house on Gramercy Park South and turned it into the Players Club, a social club for his fellow thespians and others, including Mark Twain and General Sherman; how he built his own theatre, the Booth, on Twenty-third and Sixth, where Sarah Bernhardt made her American debut; and how, in the middle of the Civil War, on a train platform in Jersey City, he rescued a young man who had fallen onto the tracks and that man was Robert Todd Lincoln, the president's son, so he's the Booth who saved a Lincoln's life.

It is remarkable that Edwin earned back the public's affection after his brother had committed such a crime. It says something about his talent and his poise that he could pull this off. I have a recording of Edwin, performing Othello, from an 1890 wax cylinder. It sounds like a voice from the grave, so thick with static the only phrase I can understand is 'little shall I'. Though I cannot make out most of the words, something of Edwin's gentleness comes across, a kind of wispy melancholy I can imagine inspiring more sympathy than scorn.

Perhaps this is the approach Dr Mudd's grandson Richard should have taken. Instead of spending his very long life pestering state legislatures to pass resolutions recognizing his grandfather's innocence, if he really wanted to get the country behind his family name, he should have recorded a hit song or come up with a dance craze or something.

In Bel Air, the Booths' hometown in Maryland, Edwin is a local hero. The Edwin Booth Memorial Fountain stands in front of the courthouse, next to a sign announcing that Edwin made his theatrical debut in the building. A WPA mural in the post office depicts the scene: a gangly teenager in tails leans pompously toward the assembled audience, half of whom have their heads in their hands they look so bored. A roadside historical marker at Tudor Hall reads, 'The home of the noted actor Junius Brutus Booth, the Elder. Birthplace of his children. His son Edwin Booth was born here November 13, 1833.' That's the whole sign. No mention of John Wilkes unless you count that cryptic reference to 'his children'.

Edwin's Players Club still exists in Gramercy Park. It remains the club Edwin envisioned, a fancy place for actors and their friends to get together. Edwin, the illegitimate son of a drunk, the heartbroken brother of an assassin, longed for propriety and elegance. He was an actor back when the theatre was one of the trashier professions. His actor brother offing the president in a theatre didn't improve his profession's profile. Thus did Edwin establish the Players. It's a beautiful house. I've been inside a few times, mostly for literary events. The last time I went, after wandering around and admiring the Edwin memorabilia on display – the John Singer Sargent portrait of Edwin hanging over the fireplace, the helmet he wore as Brutus in *Julius Caesar* – I listened to a novelist confess that his childhood sexual awakening occurred while watching a Porky Pig cartoon in which Porky dressed up in high heels.

Edwin would have loved his statue in Gramercy Park – the first statue of an actor in the city. He warranted a stained-glass window too – a multicolored Shakespearean portrait in the Church of the Transfiguration on Twenty-ninth. Known as the Little Church Around the Corner, it became an actors' church in the nineteenth century because it was the one church in town where actors would be granted a proper funeral.

The church hosted Edwin's funeral on June 9, 1893. Just as his pallbearers were carrying his coffin out the door in New York, in Washington, three floors of Ford's Theatre collapsed. The building has been turned into a government office building after the Lincoln assassination. Twenty-two federal employees died.

APRIL 2005

A few years ago, I was having my head shaved in a local barbers' when the guy doing the shaving turned to the young woman working next to him and said, 'This bloke's famous.'

I winced. This wasn't going to end well, I could tell. Any fame that you can achieve as an author isn't what most people regard as real fame, or even fake fame. It's not just that nobody recognizes you; most people have never heard of you, either. It's that anonymous sort of fame.

The young woman looked at me and shrugged.

'Yeah,' said the barber. 'He's a famous writer.'

'Well, I've never heard of him,' said the young woman.

'I never even told you his name,' said the barber.

The young woman shrugged again.

'Yeah, well,' said the barber. 'You've never heard of any writers, have you?'

The young woman blushed. I was dying. How long did it take to shave a head, anyway?

'Name one author. Name one author ever.'

I didn't intercede on the poor girl's behalf because it didn't seem to be that hard a question, and I thought she'd come through. I was wrong. There was a long pause, and eventually she said, 'Ednit.'

'Ednit?' said her boss. 'Ednit? Who the fuck's Ednit?'

'Well, what's her name, then?'

'Who?'

'Ednit.'

Eventually, after another two or three excruciating minutes, we discovered that 'Ednit' was Enid Blyton, the enormously popular English children's author of the 1940s and 1950s. In other words, the young woman had been unable to name any writer in the history of the world – not Shakespeare, not Dickens, not even Michel Houellebecq. And she's not alone. A survey conducted by W.H. Smith in 2000 found that 43 per cent of adults questioned were unable to name a favourite book, and 45 per cent failed to come up with a favourite author. (This could be because those questioned were unable to decide between Roth and Bellow, but let's presume not.) Forty per cent of Britons and 43 per cent of Americans never read any books at all, of any kind. Over the past twenty years, the proportion of Americans aged 18–34 who read literature (and literature is defined as poems, plays or narrative fiction) has fallen by 28 per cent. The 18–34 age group, incidentally, used to be the one most likely to read a novel; it has now become the least likely.

And meanwhile, the world of books seems to be getting more bookish. Anita Brookner's new novel is about a novelist. David

Lodge and Colm Tóibín wrote novels about Henry James. In *The Line of Beauty*, Alan Hollinghurst wrote about a guy writing a thesis on Henry James. And in Ian McEwan's *Saturday*, the central character's father-in-law and daughter are both serious published poets and past winners of Oxford University's Newdigate Prize for undergraduate poetry. And though nobody should ever tell a writer what to write about . . . Actually, forget that. Maybe somebody should. I have called for quotas in these pages before – I would have been great on some Politburo cultural committee – and I must call for them again. Nobody listens anyway. Sort it out, guys! You can't all write literature about literature! One book a year, maybe, between you – but all of the above titles were published in the last six months.

There are, I think, two reasons to be a little queasy about this trend. The first is, quite simply, that it excludes readers; the woman in the barbers' is not the only one who wouldn't want to read about the Newdigate Prize. And yes, maybe great art shouldn't be afraid of being elitist, but there's plenty of great art that isn't, and I don't want bright people who don't happen to have a degree in literature to give up on the contemporary novel; I want them to believe there's a point to it all, that fiction has a purpose visible to anyone capable of reading a book intended for grown-ups. Taken as a group, these novels seem to raise the white flag: we give in! It's hopeless! We don't know what those people out there want! Pull up the drawbridge!

And the second cause for concern is that writing exclusively about highly articulate people . . . Well, isn't it cheating a little? McEwan's hero, Henry Perowne, the father and son-in-law of the poets, is a neurosurgeon, and his wife is a corporate lawyer; like many highly educated middle-class people, they have access to and a facility with language, a facility that enables them to speak very directly and lucidly about their lives (Perowne is 'an habitual observer of his own moods'), and there's a sense in which McEwan is wasted on them. They don't need his help. What I've always loved about fiction is its ability to be smart about people who aren't themselves smart, or at least don't necessarily have the resources to describe their own emotional states. That was the way Twain was smart, and Dickens; and that is surely one of the reasons why Roddy Doyle is adored by all sorts of people, many of whom are infrequent book-buyers. It seems to me to be a more remarkable gift than the ability to let extremely literate people say extremely literate things.

It goes without saying that *Saturday* is a very good novel. It's humane and wise and gripping, just like *Atonement* and *Black Dogs* and just about everything McEwan has written. Set entirely on the day of the anti-war march in February 2003, it's about pretty much everything – family, uxoriousness, contemporary paranoia, the value of literature, liberalism, the workings of the human brain – and readers of this magazine will find much with which they identify. I spent too much time wondering about Henry Perowne's age, however. McEwan tells us that he's forty-eight years old, and though of course it's possible and plausible for a forty-eight-year-old man to have a daughter in her early twenties, it's by no means typical of highly qualified professional people who must have spent a good deal of their twenties studying; at the end of the book (SKIP TO THE NEXT SENTENCE IF YOU DON'T WANT TO KNOW), Perowne learns that he is about to become a grandfather, and this too bucks a few demographic trends. I belong to Henry Perowne's generation, and my friends typically have kids who are now in their early-to-mid-teens. On top of that, I'm not sure that I am as consumed by thoughts of my own mortality as Perowne, although to be fair I'm a lot dimmer than he is, and as a consequence it may take me longer to get there. McEwan himself is fifty-six, and it felt to me like Perowne might have been, too. It doesn't matter much, of course, but the author's decision perhaps inevitably invites attempts at psychoanalysis.

It made me sad, thinking back to the day of the anti-war

march. All that hope! All that confidence! And now it's dwindled to nothing! I should explain that Arsenal beat Man Utd 2–0 that afternoon in an FA Cup match – my passionate opposition to the war was conquered by my passionate desire to watch the TV – and it looked as though we would beat them for ever. In fact, we haven't beaten them since, and I finished *Saturday* in the very week that they thumped us 4-2 at Highbury to end all championship aspirations for the season.

Usually, when I read a novel I'm enjoying, I just lie there with my mouth open, occasionally muttering things like, 'Oh, no! Don't go in there!' or, 'You could still get back together, right? You love each other.' But both *Saturday* and Kate Atkinson's novel *Case Histories* contain detailed descriptions of places where I used to live and work, and as a consequence there were moments when I forgot to maintain even that level of critical engagement. Whenever Kate Atkinson mentioned Parkside, a street in Cambridge, I exclaimed – out loud, the first few dozen times, and internally thereafter – 'Parkside!' (I used to teach at Parkside Community College, you see, so that was weird.) And then whenever Ian McEwan mentioned Warren Street, or the Indian restaurants on Cleveland Street, the same thing happened: 'Ha! Warren Street!' Or, 'Ha! The Indian restaurants!' And if someone was in the room with me while I was reading, I'd say, 'This book's set around Warren Street! Where I used to live!' (It's not a residential area, you see, so that was weird, too.) It felt entirely right that I should read these books back-to-back, and then I was sent a copy of John Harris's *So Now Who Do We Vote For?*, and I felt for a moment as though certain books were stalking me or something. Until someone writes a book called *I Know Where You Put Your House Keys Last Night*, I can't imagine a title more perfectly designed to capture my attention.

I am sorry if the following lesson in UK politics is redundant, but I'm going to give it anyway: our Democrats are already in office. We voted the right way in 1997, and we have had a Labour government ever since, and at the time of writing it is absolutely certain that we will have one for the next five years: there will be an election some time in 2005, and Blair will walk it. As you may have noticed, the only problem is that the Labour government turned out not to be a Labour government at all. It's not just that Blair helped to bomb Iraq; he's also introducing the profit motive into our once-glorious National Health Service, and allowing some pretty dodgy people to invest in the education of our children. Sir Peter Vardy, an evangelical Christian car-dealer, wants creationism taught alongside theories of evolution, and in return for two million pounds per new school he can do pretty much whatever he wants. He already controls a couple of schools in the North of England.

I waited for this government all my voting life, and Harris's title perfectly captures the disillusionment of several generations of people who thought that when the Tories went, all would be right with the world. Disappointingly, Harris tells me that I should carry on doing what I've been doing: my local MP (and we don't elect leaders, just local representatives of political parties) has voted against everything I would want him to vote against, so it seems unfair to castigate him for Blair's crimes and misdemeanours. I wanted to be told that the Liberal Democrats, our third party, or the Greens, or the vaguely nutty Respect Coalition were viable alternatives, but they're not, so we're stuffed. *So Now Who Do We Vote For?* is a useful and impassioned book nevertheless; it's a brave book, too – nobody wants to write anything that will self-destruct at a given point in its publication year, and I don't think he's going to pick up many foreign sales, either. John Harris, we salute you.

Another Bullshit Night in Suck City wasn't one of the stalker books, but after a couple of recommendations, I wanted to read it anyway. Nick Flynn's dark, delirious memoir describes his father's journey from employment, marriage and a putative writing career to vagrancy and alcoholism. (The ambition to write, incidentally, is never abandoned, which might give a few of us pause for thought.)

THE COMPLETE POLYSYLLABIC SPREE

Nick loses touch with his dad; lives, not entirely companionably, with a few demons of his own; and then ends up working in a homeless shelter. And guess who turns up? One image in *Another Bullshit Night in Suck City*, of a homeless man sitting in the street in an armchair, watching a TV he has managed to hook up to a street lamp, is reminiscent of Beckett; readers will find themselves grateful that Flynn is a real writer, stonily indifferent to the opportunities for shameless manipulation such an experience might provide.

I bought Michael Frayn's *Towards the End of the Morning* from one of Amazon's 'Marketplace Sellers' for 25p. I could have had it for 1p, but I was, perhaps understandably, deterred rather than attracted by the price: What can you get for a penny these days? Would I be able to read it, or would all the pages have been masticated by the previous owner's dog? It wasn't as if I was entirely reassured by the higher price, but a few days later, a perfectly preserved, possibly unread 1970 paperback turned up in the post, sent by a lady in Scotland. Does anyone understand this Marketplace thing? Why does anyone want to sell a book for a penny? Or even twenty-five pennies? What's in it for anyone, apart from us? I'm still suspicious. It's a wonderful novel, though, urbane and funny and disarmingly gentle, and I might send the lady in Scotland some more money anyway. Or is that the scam? That's clever.

'If Frayn is about to step into anybody's shoes, they aren't Evelyn Waugh's, but Gogol's,' says the blurb on the front of my thirty-five-year-old paperback. Is that how you sold books back then? And how would it have worked? As far as I can work out, the quote is a stern warning to fans of elegant English comic writing that this elegant English comic novel won't interest them in the slightest. It was a daring tactic, certainly; the penny copies lead one to suspect that it didn't quite come off. ✶

MAY 2005

Earlier today I was in a bookstore, and I picked up a new book about the migration patterns of the peregrine falcon. For a moment, I ached to buy it – or rather, I ached to be the kind of person who would buy it, read it, and learn something from it. I mean, obviously I could have bought it, but I could also have taken the fifteen pounds from my pocket and eaten it, right in the middle of Borders, and there seemed just as much point in the latter course of action as the former. (And before anyone gets on at me about Borders, I should point out that the last independent bookshop in Islington, home of the chattering literary classes, closed down a couple of weeks ago.)

I don't know what it was about, the peregrine falcon thing. That's some kind of bird, right? Well, I've only read one book about a bird before, Barry Hines's heartbreaking *A Kestrel for a Knave*, later retitled *Kes* to tie in with Ken Loach's film adaptation of that name. (You, dear reader, are much more likely to have read *Jonathan Livingston Seagull* than *Kes*, I suspect, and our respective tastes in bird books reveal something fundamental about our cultures. An Amazon reviewer describes *Jonathan Livingston Seagull* as 'a charming allegory with a very pertinent message: DON'T ABANDON YOUR DREAMS.' I would not be traducing the message of *Kes* if I were to summarize it thus: ABANDON YOUR DREAMS. In fact, 'ABANDON YOUR DREAMS' is a pretty handy summary of the whole of contemporary English culture – of the country itself, even. It would be great to be you, sometimes. I mean, obviously our motto is more truthful than yours, and ultimately more useful, but there used to be great piles of *Kes* in every high-school stock room. You'd think they'd let us reach the age of sixteen or so before telling us that life is shit. I read Hines's book because it was a work of literature, however, not because it was a book about a bird. And maybe this book will turn out to be a work of literature, too, and a million people will tell me to read it, and it will win tons of prizes, and eventually I'll succumb, but by then, it will have lost the allure it seemed to have this afternoon when it promised to be the kind of book I don't usually open. I'm always reading works of bloody literature; I'm never reading about migration patterns.

   This month, my taste in books seems to have soured on me: every book I pick up seems to be exactly the sort of book I always pick up. On the way home from the bookstore, as I was pondering the unexpectedly seductive lure of the peregrine falcon, I tried to name the book least likely to appeal to me that I have actually read all the way through, and I was struggling for an answer. Isn't that ridiculous? You'd have thought that there'd been something, somewhere – an apparently ill-advised dalliance with a book about mathematics or physics, say, or a history of some country that I didn't know anything about, but there's nothing. I read a biography of Margaret Thatcher's press secretary once, but my brother-in-law wrote it, so that doesn't really count. And I did struggle through Roy Jenkins's enormous *Gladstone*, which reduced me to tears of boredom on several occasions, but that was because I was judging a non-fiction prize. I would like my personal reading map to resemble a map of the British Empire *circa* 1900; I'd like people to look at it and think, How the hell did he end up right over there? As it is, I make only tiny little incursions into the territory of my own ignorance – every year, another classic novel conquered here, a couple of new literary biographies beaten down there. To be honest, I'm not sure that I can spare the troops for conquests further afield: they're needed to quell all the rebellions and escape attempts at home. But that's not the attitude. When you turn to these pages next month, I swear you'll be reading about peregrine falcons, or Robert the Bruce, or the combustion engine. I'm sorry that the four books I read these last few weeks seem to have brought all this on, because I loved them all. But look at them: a cute, sad literary novel, a couple of elegant true-crime stories, and a book about Dylan by one of America's cleverest cultural commentators – chips off the old block, every one of them. I can hardly claim to have pushed back any personal frontiers with any of these.

Recently the Polysyllabic Spree, the fifteen horrifically enthusiastic young men and women who control the minds of everyone who writes for this magazine, sent an emissary to London, and the young man in question handed me, without explanation, a copy of Philip Gourevitch's *A Cold Case*. I felt duty-bound to read it, not least because the Spree frequently chooses enigmatic methods of communication, and I presumed that the book would contain some kind of coded message. In fact, the purpose of the gift was

NICK HORNBY

straightforwardly cruel: the security tag was still attached to it, and
as a consequence I was humiliated by store detectives whenever I
tried to enter a shop with the book in my bag. I don't really know
why the Spree wanted to do this to me. I suspect it's something to
do with the recent discovery that I have one reader (a charming
and extremely intelligent woman called Caroline – see the March
issue) whereas there is still no evidence that they have any at all. I've
tried not to be triumphalist, but even so, they haven't reacted with
great magnanimity, I'm afraid.

A Cold Case is a short, simple and engrossing account of a
detective's attempt to solve a twenty-seven-year-old double homi-
cide – or rather, to find out whether the prime suspect is still alive.
The detective's renewed interest in the case seems almost alarmingly whimsical (he happens to drive past a bar which reminds
him of the night in question), but his rigour and probity are
unquestionable, and one of the joys of the book is that its characters – upright, determined detective, psychotic but undeniably
magnetic villain – seem to refer back to the older, simpler and
more dangerous New York City. In one of my favourite passages,
Gourevitch reports verbatim the conversations he overhears in the
office of a colourful lawyer with a lot of Italian-American clients:

> [*Enter Rocco, a burly man with a voice like a cement mixer*]
> RICHMAN: Your father and I grew up together . . . Your mother
> is a beautiful lady.
> ROCCO: She sure is . . .
> RICHMAN: Your uncle – the first time I had him, he was thirteen
> years old.
> ROCCO: Yup.
> RICHMAN: I represented Nicole when she killed her mother,
> when she cut her mother's throat.
> ROCCO: Yes, yes, I remember that.

The end of this exchange raises the alarming possibility of an alternative version, wherein Rocco had forgotten all about Nicole cutting her mother's throat. And though I do not wish to generalize about the people or person who reads this magazine, I'm sure I speak for all of us when I say that we would have retained at least the vaguest memory of an equivalent occasion in our own lives.

I was shamed into reading *In Cold Blood* at one of Violet Incredible's London literary soirées. I think I may have mentioned before that I know Violet Incredible of *The Incredibles* personally. Anyway, ever since the success of that film, she has taken to gathering groups of writers around her, presumably in the hope that she becomes more literary (and, let's face it, less animated) by osmosis. I don't know why we all turn out. I suppose the truth is that we are none of us as immune to the tawdry glitter of Hollywood as we like to pretend. At the most recent of these events, most of the writers present suddenly started enthusing about Truman Capote's 1965 non-fiction classic. And though it goes without saying that I joined in, for fear of incurring Violet's disapproval, I've never actually read the thing.

It makes a lot of sense reading it immediately after *A Cold Case*, and not just because they belong in the same genre. Philip Gourevitch thanks David Remnick in his acknowledgements, and Truman Capote thanks William Shawn; this is *New Yorker* true crime, then and now (ish), and the comparison is instructive. Capote's book is much wordier, and researched almost to within an inch of its life, to the extent that one becomes acutely aware of the information that is being concealed from the reader. (If he knows *this* much, you keep thinking, then he must know the rest, too. And of course anyone constructing a narrative out of real events knows more than they're letting on, but it's not helpful to be reminded so forcefully of the writer's omniscience.) Gourevitch's book is short, understated, selective. And though *A Cold Case* doesn't quite attain the heights that *In Cold Blood* reaches in its bravura, vertiginously tense, unbearably ominous opening section, Gourevitch clearly reaps the benefits of Capote's groundbreaking work. *In Cold Blood* is one of the most influential books of the last fifty years, and as far as I can tell, just about every work of novelistic non-fiction published since the 1960s owes it something or another. But the trouble with influential books is that if you have absorbed the influence without ever reading the original, then it can sometimes be hard to appreciate the magnitude of its achievement. I loved *In Cold Blood*, but at the same time I could feel it slipping away from me as a Major Literary Experience – *A Cold Case* seemed to me simultaneously less ambitious and more sure-footed. I mean, I'm sure my impression is, you know, *wrong*. But what can I do?

I read Amanda Eyre Ward's lovely *How To Be Lost* after a warm recommendation from a friend, and it's got the mucus, as P. G. Wodehouse would and did say. ('The mucus' was to Wodehouse's way of thinking a desirable attribute, lest people think this is some kind of snotty snark.) *How To Be Lost* isn't one of those irritatingly perfect novels that people sometimes write; it has a slightly ungainly, gawky shape to it, and slightly more plot than it can swallow without giving itself heartburn. But it has that lovely tone that only American women writers seem to be able to achieve: melancholic, wry, apparently (but only apparently) artless, perched on the balls of its feet and ready to jump either towards humour or towards heartbreak, with no run-up and no effort. *How To Be Lost* has a great set-up, too. Narrator Caroline, a New Orleans barmaid with a drinking habit, has/had a sister who disappeared without trace when she was a little girl. Just as Caroline's family is about to declare Ellie dead, Caroline spots a photo in a magazine of a woman in a crowd whose face contains an unmistakeable trace of the child she knew, and she sets off to track the woman down. Good, no?

How To Be Lost is about all the usual stuff you read in literary novels: grief and families and disappointment and so on, and I was interested in what Ward had to say about all of these things. But as far as I was concerned, she'd earned the right to sound off because she'd lured me into her book with an intriguing narrative idea. It doesn't hurt, that's all I'm saying. The Kate Atkinson novel I read a few weeks back had a long-time absent little sister in it, too. But where *Case Histories* (and Atkinson is English) differs from *How To Be Lost* is . . . Are you going to read either of these? Perhaps you will. Well, remember the bird books, and choose accordingly.

The last book I read that contained the wealth and range of cultural references on show in Greil Marcus's *Like A Rolling Stone* was Bob Dylan's *Chronicles*. Those of you who've read Dylan's breathtakingly good memoir might remember that one of the many, many names (of writers, artists, historians, musicians) in there was that of Marcus himself, and there is no reason why Marcus shouldn't have helped Dylan to think about culture in the same way that he's helped many of us think about culture.

For the second time this month I found myself envying the advantages that being an American can bring, although on this occasion I envied only those who live and think in America; you can't envy those who live in America and don't think (although you could argue that those who don't think aren't really living anyway). One of the things that Marcus's book is about is the slipperiness of meaning in the US; any major American artist, in any idiom, can change the way the country perceives itself. I'm not sure this is possible here in England, where our culture appears so monolithic, and our mouthiest cultural critics so insanely and maddeningly sure of what has value and what doesn't. If we have never produced a Dylan, it is partly because he would have been patronized back into obscurity: we know what art is, pal, and it's nothing you'd ever have heard on top 40 radio. I didn't always understand *Like a Rolling Stone* (and I can't for the life of me hear the things that Marcus can in the Pet Shop Boys' version of 'Go

West'), but my sporadic bafflement didn't matter to me in the least. Just to live in the world of this book, a world of intellectual excitement and curiosity and rocket-fuelled enthusiasm, was a treat.

STOP PRESS: Since I began this column, a friend has had an idea for a literary genre I'd never touch in a million years: SF/Fantasy, of the non-literary, nerdy-boys-on-websites variety. He's right, and already my heart is sinking in a gratifying way. Do I have to? I'm already wishing I'd shelled out for the peregrine falcon book. ✶

JUNE/JULY 2005

BOOKS BOUGHT:
* *Little Scarlet* – Walter Mosley
* *Out of the Silent Planet* – C. S. Lewis·
* *Voyage to Venus* – C. S. Lewis·
* *Maxton* – Gordon Brown·
* *Nelson And His Captains* – Ludovic Kennedy·
* *Excession* – Iain M. Banks

· Don't worry. These books were bought for one pound or less at the Friends of Kenwood House Book Sale.

BOOKS READ:
* *Excession* – Iain M. Banks (abandoned)
* *The Men Who Stare at Goats* – Jon Ronson
* *Adrian Mole and the Weapons of Mass Destruction* – Sue Townsend
* *The Wonder Spot* – Melissa Bank
* *Stuart: A Life Backwards* – Alexander Masters

The story so far: suddenly sick of my taste in books, I vowed in these pages last month to read something I wouldn't normally pick up. After much deliberation (and the bulk of the otherwise inexplicable Books Bought can be explained by this brief but actually rather exhilarating period), I decided that my friend Harry was right, and that in the normal course of events I'd never read an SF/Fantasy novel in a million years. Now read on, if you can be bothered.

Even buying Iain M. Banks's *Excession* was excruciating. Queuing up behind me at the cash desk was a very attractive young woman clutching some kind of groovy art magazine, and I felt obscurely compelled to tell her that the reason I was buying this purple book with a spacecraft on the cover was because of the *Believer*, and the *Believer* was every bit as groovy as her art magazine. In a rare moment of maturity, however, I resisted the compulsion. She could, I decided, think whatever the hell she wanted. It wasn't a relationship that was ever going to go anywhere anyway. I'm with someone, she's probably with someone, she was twenty-five years younger than me, and – let's face it – the *Believer* isn't as groovy as all that. If we had got together, that would have been only the first of many disappointing discoveries she'd make.

When I actually tried to read *Excession*, embarrassment was swiftly replaced by trauma. Iain M. Banks is a highly rated Scottish novelist who has written twenty-odd novels, half of them (the non-SF half) under the name Iain Banks, and though I'd never previously read him, everyone I know who is familiar with his work loves him. And nothing in the twenty-odd pages I managed of *Excession* was in any way bad; it's just that I didn't understand a word. I didn't even understand the blurb on the back of the book: 'Two and a half millennia ago, the artifact appeared in a remote corner of space, beside a trillion-year-old dying sun from a different universe. It was a perfect black-body sphere, and it did nothing. Then it disappeared. Now it is back.' This is clearly intended to entice us into the novel – that's what blurbs do, right? But this blurb just made me scared. An artifact – that's something you normally find in a museum, isn't it? Well, what's a museum exhibit doing floating around in space? So what if it did nothing? What are museum exhibits supposed to do? And this dying sun – how come it's switched universes? Can dying suns do that?

The urge to weep tears of frustration was already upon me even before I read the short prologue, which seemed to describe some kind of androgynous avatar visiting a woman who has been pregnant for forty years and who lives on her own in the tower of a giant spaceship. (Is this the artifact? Or the dying sun? Can a dying sun be a spaceship? Probably.) By the time I got to the first chapter, which is entitled 'Outside Context Problem' and begins '(*CGU Grey Area* signal sequence file #n428857/119)', I was crying so hard that I could no longer see the page in front of my face, at which point I abandoned the entire ill-conceived experiment altogether. I haven't felt so stupid since I stopped attending physics lessons aged fourteen. 'It's not *stupidity*,' my friend Harry said when I told him I'd had to pack it in. 'Think of all the heavy metal fans who devour this stuff. You think you're dimmer than them?' I know that he was being rhetorical, but the answer is: yes, I do. In fact, I'm now pretty sure that I've never really liked metal because I don't understand that properly, either. Maybe that's where I should start. I'll listen to Slayer or someone for a few years, until I've grasped what they're saying, and then I'll have another go at SF. In the meantime, I have come to terms with myself and my limitations, and the books I love have never seemed more attractive to me. Look at them: smart and funny novels, non-fiction books about military intelligence and homeless people . . . It's a balanced, healthy diet. I wasn't short of any vitamins. I was looking for the literary equivalent of grilled kangaroo, or chocolate-covered ants, not spinach, and as I am never drawn to the kangaroo section of a menu in a restaurant, it's hardly surprising that I couldn't swallow it in book form.

Stupidity has been the theme of the month. There's a lot of it in Jon Ronson's mind-boggling book about US military intelligence, *The Men Who Stare at Goats*; plenty of people (although admittedly none of us is likely to spend much time with them) would describe the behaviour of the tragic and berserk Stuart in Alexander Masters's brilliant book as stupid beyond belief. And Sue Townsend's comic anti-hero Adrian Mole, who by his own admission isn't too bright, has unwittingly contributed to the post-

Excession debate I've been having with myself about my own intelligence.

Adrian Mole is one of the many cultural phenomena that has passed me by until now, but my friend Harry – yes, the same one, and no, I don't have any other friends, thank you for asking – suddenly declared Townsend's creation to be a work of comic genius, and insisted I should read *Adrian Mole and the Weapons of Mass Destruction* immediately. He pointed out helpfully that I'd understand quite a lot of it, too, and as I needed the boost in confidence, I decided to take his advice.

Adrian Mole, who famously began his fictional life aged thirteen and three-quarters, is now thirty-four, penniless, becalmed in an antiquarian bookshop, and devoted to our Prime Minister. One of the many unexpected pleasures of this book was the acerbity of its satire. There is real anger in here, particularly about the war in Iraq, and the way Townsend manages to accommodate her dismay within the tight confines of light comedy is a sort of object lesson in what can be done with mainstream fiction. There's a great running gag about Blair's ludicrous claim that Saddam could hit Cyprus with some of the nasty missiles at his disposal: Adrian Mole has booked a holiday on that very island, and spends much of the book trying to reclaim his deposit from the travel agent.

I do wish that comic writing took itself more seriously, though. I don't mean I want fewer jokes; I simply mean that the cumulative effect of those jokes would be funnier if they helped maintain the internal logic of the book. Mole has a blind friend, Nigel, to whom he reads books and newspapers, and at one point Nigel accuses him of not understanding much of what he's reading. 'I had to admit that I didn't,' Mole says, before, just a few pages later, making an admittedly inappropriate allusion to Antony Beevor's *Stalingrad*. It might seem pedantic to point out that anyone who's ploughed their way through *Stalingrad* is probably capable of grasping the essence of a newspaper article (if not the opening of an Iain M. Banks novel) – just as it's probably literal-minded to wonder how an unattractive man with a spectacularly unenviable romantic history gets repeatedly lucky with an extremely attractive woman. But moments like this tend to wobble the character around a little bit, and I found myself having occasionally to recreate him in my head, almost from scratch. I'm sure that Mole has a fixed identity for those who have read the entire series, and he remains a fantastic, and fantastically English, comic creation: upright and self-righteous, bewildered, snobby, self-hating, provincial and peculiarly lovable. We all are, here.

Jon Ronson's *The Men Who Stare at Goats* is one of the most disorienting books I have ever read. While reading it, I started feeling like the victim of one of the extremely peculiar mindfuck experiments that Ronson describes in his inimitable perplexed tones. Here's his thesis: after the rout in Vietnam, the US military started investigating different ways to fight wars, and as a consequence co-opted several somewhat eccentric New Age thinkers and practitioners who, your generals felt, might point them towards a weaponless future, one full of warriors capable of neutralizing the enemy with a single glance. And the first half of the book is uproarious, as Ronson endeavours to discover, for example, whether the actress Kristy McNichol (who appeared in *The Love Boat 2* and the cheesy soft porn movie *Two Moon Junction*) had ever been called upon to help find Manuel Noriega. (A US Sergeant called Lyn Buchanan, who was part of a secret unit engaged in a 'supernatural war' against Noriega, had repeatedly written her name down while in a self-induced trance, and became convinced that the actress knew something.) Gradually Ronson builds a crazy-paving path that leads to Abu Ghraib, and both the book and its characters become darker and more disturbing.

You have probably read those stories of how people in Iraq

and Afghanistan were tortured by having American pop music blasted at them day and night. And you have probably read or heard many of the jokes made as a consequence of these stories – people writing in to newspapers to say that if you have a teenager who listens to 50 Cent or Slipknot all day then you know how those Iraqi prisoners feel, etc. and so on. (Even the *Guardian* made lots of musical torture jokes for a while.) Ronson floats the intriguing notion that the jokes were an integral part of the strategy: in other words, if you can induce your citizens to laugh at torture, then outrage will be much harder to muster. Stupidity is, despite all appearances to the contrary, a complicated state of mind. Who's stupid, in the end – them or us?

This month's Book by a Friend was Melissa Bank's *The Wonder Spot*, and this paragraph must be parenthetical, because neither the novel nor the friend can be shoehorned into the stupid theme. It's been a long time since *The Girl's Guide to Hunting and Fishing*, and some of us – including the author herself – were wondering whether she'd ever get around to a second book. But she has, finally, and it's a lovely thing, sweet-natured, witty, lots of texture. It's hard to write, as Bank does here, about growing up, and about contemporary adult urban romance: it's such an apparently overpopulated corner of our world that she must have been tempted, at least for a moment, by artifacts and dying suns and women who are pregnant for decades. We need someone who's really, really good at that stuff, though, because it still matters to us, no matter how many millions of words are written on the subject. In fact – and once again in these pages I'm calling for Soviet-style intervention into the world of literature – it would be much easier for everyone if Melissa Bank and maybe two or three other people in the world were given an official government licence, and you could no more appoint yourself as chronicler of contemporary adult urban romance than you could set yourself up as a neurosurgeon. In

THE COMPLETE POLYSYLLABIC SPREE

this Utopia, Melissa Bank would be . . . well, you'll have to insert the name of your own top neurosurgeon here. I don't know any. Obviously. I'm too dim. Damn that Iain M. Banks. He's wrecked my confidence.

Here's an unlikely new subgenre: biographical studies of vagrants. Alexander Masters's *Stuart: A Life Backwards* is, after *Another Bullshit Night in Suck City*, the second one I've read recently, and if these two are as successful as they should be, then on top of everything else, down-and-outs may have to contend with the unwanted attentions of hungry non-fiction writers. At the moment, there's still plenty of room in the field for tonal contrast; where Nick Flynn's book about his homeless, alcoholic father was poetic, as deep and dark and languid as a river, *Stuart* is quick, bright, angry, funny and sarcastic – Masters finds himself occasionally frustrated by Stuart's inexplicable and self-destructive urge to punch, stab, self-lacerate, incinerate and cause general mayhem. ('I headbutted the bloke,' Stuart explains when Masters asks him what happened to a particular employer and job. 'Excellent. Of course you did. Just the thing,' Masters finds himself thinking.)

The story is told backwards at Stuart's suggestion, after he'd told Masters that his first draft was 'bollocks boring'; he thinks the narrative structure will pep it up a little, turn it into something 'like what Tom Clancy writes'. It feels instead like a doomed search for hope and innocence; as Masters trudges back through three decades of illness and drug abuse and alcohol abuse and self-abuse and the shocking, sickening abuse perpetrated by Stuart's teachers and family members, he and we come to see that there never was any. This is an important and original book, and it doesn't even feel as though you should read it. You'll want to, however much good it's doing you.

I'm certain that I read five books all the way through in the last month, and yet I've written about only four of them. This means that I've forgotten about the other one completely, the first time that's happened since I began writing this column. I'm sorry, whoever you are, but I think you've got to take some of the blame. Your book was . . . well, it was good, obviously, because we are forced by the Polysyllabic Spree, the sixty-three white-robed literary maniacs who run this magazine, to describe every book as good. But clearly it could have been better. Try a joke next time, or maybe a plot. ★

AUGUST 2005

A few months ago, I heard a pompous twit on a radio programme objecting, bitterly and at some length, to Martin Amis's *Money* being republished in the Penguin Modern Classics series. It couldn't possibly be a classic, said the pompous twit, because we need fifty years to judge whether a book is a classic or not. It seemed to me that the twit's argument could be summarized succinctly thus: 'I don't like Martin Amis's *Money* very much', because nothing else made much sense. (Presumably we're not allowed to use the phrase 'modern classic' about anything at all unless we wish to appear oxymoronic, even though in this context the word 'classic' means, simply, 'of the highest class'. The pompous twit

183

seemed to be labouring under the misapprehension that a 'classic' book is somehow related to classical music, and therefore has to be a bit old and a bit posh before it qualifies.) Do you have Penguin Modern Classics in your country? Over here, they used to mean a lot to young and pretentious lovers of literature. My friends and I used to make sure we had a PMC, with its distinctive light green spine, about our persons at all times, as an indication both of our intellectual seriousness and of our desire/willingness to sleep with girls who also liked books. It never worked, of course, but we lived in hope. Anyway, *L'Étranger* was a Penguin Modern Classic; I probably read it in 1974, thirty-odd years after it was published. And when I was talking embarrassing rubbish about Sartre to fellow seventeen-year-olds, *La Nausée* – another light green 'un – had been around for less than forty years. If the pompous twit's fifty-year rule had been enforced when I was a teenager, I'd never have read either of them – we needed that green spine for validation – and as a consequence I'd be even more ill-educated than I am now.

Anyway, Marilynne Robinson's *Gilead* is clearly a modern classic, and it hasn't even been in print for five minutes. It's a beautiful, rich, unforgettable work of high seriousness, and you don't need to know that the book has already won the Pulitzer Prize to see that Robinson isn't messing around. I didn't even mind that it's essentially a book about Christianity, narrated by a Christian; in fact, for the first time I understood the point of Christianity – or at least, I understood how it might be used to assist thought. I am an atheist living in a godless country (7 per cent of us attend church on a regular basis), so the version of Christianity I am exposed to most frequently is the evangelical US version. We are a broad church here at the *Believer*, and I don't wish to alienate any of our subscribers who believe that gays will burn in hell for all eternity and so on, but your far-right evangelism has never struck me as being terribly conducive to thought – rather the opposite, if anything. I had to reread passages from *Gilead* several times – beautiful, luminous passages about grace, and debt, and baptism – before I half-understood them, however: there are complicated and striking ideas on every single page.

Gilead is narrated by a dying pastor, the Reverend John Ames, and takes the form of a long letter to his young son; the agony of impending loss informs every word of the book, although this agony has been distilled into a kind of wide-eyed and scrupulously unsentimental wonder at the beauty of the world. It's true that the book contains very little in the way of forward momentum, and one reads it rather as one might read a collection of poetry; it's only two hundred and fifty pages long, but it took me weeks to get through. (I kept worrying, in fact, about reading *Gilead* in the wrong way. I didn't want it to go by in dribs and drabs, but it seemed equally inappropriate to scoff something containing this amount of calories down in a few gulps.) This column has frequently suggested that a novel without forward momentum isn't really worth bothering with, but that theory, like so many others, turned out not to be worth the (admittedly very expensive) paper it was printed on: *Gilead* has turned me into a wiser and better person. In fact, I am writing these words in a theological college somewhere in England, where I will spend the next several years. I'll miss my kids, my partner and my football team, but when God comes knocking, you don't shut the door in His face, do you? All this only goes to show that you never know how a novel's going to affect you.

We all of us know that the circumstances surrounding the reading of a book are probably every bit as important as the book itself, and I read *Gilead* at a weird time. I was on book tour in the UK, and I was sick of myself and of the sound of my own voice, and of appearing on daft radio shows, where I found that it was surprisingly easy to reduce my own intricately wrought novel to idiotic sound bites: if anyone were ever in need of the astonishing hush that Marilynne Robinson achieves in her book – how do

---

you do that, in something crafted out of words? – it was I. *Caveat emptor*, but if you don't like it, then you have no soul.

So *Gilead* is one of the most striking novels I have ever read, and it won the Pulitzer Prize, and it's a modern classic, but it doesn't win the coveted 'Stuff I've Been Reading' book-of-the-month award. It didn't even come close, incredibly. That honour goes to my sister Gill's *Jane Austen: The Girl With the Magic Pen*, a biography intended for children but strongly recommended to anyone of any age. If you want me to be definitive about it, then I would say that whereas *Gilead* is one of the best new novels I've read for years, Hornby's biography is undoubtedly the best book of all time. Strong words, I know, but: it's ninety pages long! It's about Jane Austen, who was great, right? I rest my case.

My sister's work is, however, quite clearly, underneath it all, both about and aimed at me. Listen to this: 'Jane's eldest brother, James, was busy trotting out lofty verse, in a manner befitting the vicar he was soon to become ... There was no doubt, they all said, who was the writer in the family – and James readily (and a little smugly) agreed!' I think we can all read the subtext here, can't we? James Austen = NH. Jane Austen = GH. (Weirdly, my sister didn't even know about my recent decision to become a man of the cloth when she wrote those lines.) And what about this? 'Families are funny things, and often cannot see what is under their noses.' Hey, no need to beat around the bush! Just come out and say what's on your mind, Oh Great One! As if Mum ever allowed me to forget that you were the really clever member of the family. As if Mum didn't always love you more than me anyway ... Sorry. This probably isn't the most appropriate forum in which to air grievances of this kind, however justifiable. And in any case, if you're too dim to understand the book properly, to see it for what it really is – namely, a rage-fuelled, ninety-page poison-pen letter to the author's brother – you'll find much to enjoy on the superficial level. She had to pretend at least that she was writing about Austen, and that stuff is great, lively and informative. See? If I can be generous about your work, how come you can't bring yourself to . . . Sorry again. I'm just going out for a cigarette and a walk. I'll be right back.

A whole bunch of these books I read for work. You can't just go on the radio and say, 'Buy my new novel. It's great.' Oh, no. That's not how it works. You have to go on the radio and say, 'Buy *his* new novel. It's great.' And then, according to the publicity departments at my publishers, the listening public is so seduced by the sound of your voice that it ignores what you're actually telling them, and goes out to buy your book anyway. We have this show called *A Good Read*, on which a couple of guests talk with the show's presenter about a book they love, and I chose Michael Frayn's *Spies*, which is a wonderful, complicated, simple novel about childhood, suburbia and the Second World War. My fellow guest chose Nancy Mitford's *Noblesse Oblige*, which was published in the 1950s, and discusses the upper classes and their use of language – they say 'lavatory', we say 'toilet', that kind of thing. My fellow guest wasn't so keen on *Spies*, which was kind of hilarious, considering that he'd just made us plough through all this stuff about 'napkin' versus 'serviette'. I won't say any more about *Noblesse Oblige*, as otherwise the Polysyllabic Spree will ban me for yet another issue, and I'm spending more time out than in as it is.

Our host, meanwhile, chose Anne Tyler's *The Amateur Marriage*, and both the choice and the novel itself made me very happy. Anne Tyler is the person who first made me want to write: I picked up *Dinner at the Homesick Restaurant* in a bookshop, started to read it there and then, bought it, took it home, finished it, and suddenly I had an ambition, for about the first time in my life. I was worried that *The Amateur Marriage* was going to be a little schematic: Tyler tells the story of a relationship over the decades, and the early part of the book is perhaps too tidy. In the '50s, the couple are living out America's postwar suburban dream, in the '60s they're on the receiving end of the countercultural revolution, and so on. But the cumulative details of the marriage eventually sprawl all over the novel's straight, tight lines as if Tyler were creating a garden; as it turns out, in those first chapters, she's saying, 'Just wait for spring – I know what I'm doing.' And she does, of course. Before too long, *The Amateur Marriage* is teeming with life and artfully created mess, and when it's all over, you mourn both the passing of Tyler's creation and the approaching end of her characters' lives.

My ongoing disciplinary troubles with the Polysyllabic Spree, the four hundred and thirty white-robed and utterly psychotic young men and women who control both the *Believer* and the minds of everyone who contributes to it, mean that I have to cram two months' worth of reading into one column. (I no longer have any sense of where I'm going wrong, by the way. I've given up. I think I may have passed on some admittedly baseless gossip about the Gawain poet at the monthly editorial conference, and it didn't go down well, but who knows, really?) So, in brief: Jeremy Lewis's biography of Allen Lane, the founder of Penguin, is a tremendous piece of social history, which I have already written about in *Time Out*. (It was the same deal as with *Spies* – I recommend someone else's book, this time in print, and everyone rushes out to buy mine. See how it works? You've got to hand it to the people who think this stuff up.) And Walter Mosley's *Little Scarlett* comprehensively rubbishes yet another theory this column has previously and unwisely expounded – that crime novels in a series are always inferior to what I believe the trade calls 'stand-alones'. Easy Rawlins is one of probably scores of exceptions to the rule, possibly because one of Mosley's aims in the Rawlins books is to write about race in twentieth-century America. *Little Scarlett* is set in LA during the Watts riots of 1965, and you never get the sense that you're whiling away the time; the stakes are high, and both detective and book demonstrate a moral seriousness that you don't find in many literary novels, never mind generic thrillers.

Seth Mnookin is yet another member of Violet Incredible's

literary set. So those of us who pretend we still know her since she went all Hollywood animated have dutifully read his book about Jayson Blair and the *New York Times*, even though the subject has nothing to do with us, for fear that we'll be cast into the darkness, far away from the warm glow of celebrity. Luckily, Mnookin's book is completely riveting: I doubt I'll read much else about US newspaper culture, so it's just as well that this one is definitive. Mnookin's thoroughness – he explains with clarity and rigour how Blair and the *NYT* was an accident waiting to happen – could have resulted in desiccation, but it's actually pretty juicy in all the right places. None of the outrage Blair caused makes much sense to us in England – you can make up whatever you want here, and you'll never hear from a fact-checker or even an editor – so reading *Hard News* was like reading an Austen novel. You have to understand the context, the parameters of decency in an alien environment, to make any sense of it.

So I'm off on a book tour of the US now, and I'm thinking of taking *Barnaby Rudge* with me. It'll last me the entire three weeks, and it's about the Gordon riots, apparently. I'll bet you can't wait for the next column. ✶

SEPTEMBER 2005

BOOKS BOUGHT:
* *The Diary of a Country Priest* – Georges Bernanos
* *A Complicated Kindness* – Miriam Toews
* *Blood Done Sign My Name* – Timothy B. Tyson
* *Over Tumbled Graves* – Jess Walter
* *Becoming Strangers* – Louise Dean

BOOKS READ:
* *Citizen Vince* – Jess Walter
* *A Complicated Kindness* – Miriam Toews

On my recent book tour of the US I met a suspiciously large number of people who claimed to be *Believer* readers; some of the people who came to the signings even told me that they had read and enjoyed this column, although I can see that if you're standing in front of someone waiting for a signature, you might as well say something, even if what you end up saying is patently and laughably untrue. Anyway, having met and talked to some of you, I now realize that the descriptions I occasionally provide of the Polysyllabic Spree, the eighty horribly brainwashed young men and women who control this magazine (and who may in turn, I am beginning to realize, be controlled by someone else), have been misleading. There are some misconceptions out there, and I feel it's only fair, both to you and to the Spree, to clear a few things up.

Numbers. The Spree consists of sixty-four people. You can safely ignore any other figure you may come across, either here or in the national media. Sometimes I have inflated or deflated the numbers, for comic purposes – because the joke of saying, for example, forty or eighty when really it's sixty-four is always funny, right? Or it could have been funny, if people weren't so literal-minded. My recent conversations have left me with the feeling that this particular witticism, along with several others (see below), may have fallen flat.

Robes. The trademark, tell-tale Spree white robes are only worn in certain circumstances, namely during editorial meetings, major sporting events (as a protest against their existence) and morning 'prayers', wherein the Spree shout out the names of literary figures. (I can't tell you how disconcerting it is to hear otherwise attractive and frequently naked young women yelling out 'SYBILLE BEDFORD!' in a banshee wail.) I'm sorry if I have somehow given the impression that they wear white robes all the time. They don't. In fact, given the propensity for nudity up at Believer Towers, I wish they'd put them on more often.

Free copies of the *Believer*. A while back I remarked in passing that I didn't ever see this magazine because the Spree refused to send me free copies. I can't say too much about this, because, sadly, it's all *sub judice*, and my lawyers have told me to be careful about how I address the matter in print. In brief: I have discovered that the magazine and its new publishing venture is not, as I had been assured previously, a vanity publishing outfit, and that therefore I should not have been paying the company to have my columns and my book *The Polysyllabic Spree* published. In a desperate attempt to avoid having their asses sued off, the Spree have started lavishing subscriptions and T-shirts upon me. It won't do them any good. Things have gone too far.

Suspensions. Similarly, I have in the past complained bitterly about my suspension from these pages after having ignored one of the Spree's many unfathomable and apparently random edicts. The truth is that I haven't been suspended by the Spree nearly as often as I've claimed; I made some of those stories up, usually to excuse my own indolence and/or temporary disappearances, usually prompted by the investigations of the relentless Child Support Agency here in the UK.

I hope that's cleared a few things up and we can now all make a fresh start.

As you were probably beginning to suspect, the preceding nonsense was a crude attempt to deflect attention away from the dismal brevity of this month's 'Books Read' list: for the first time since I began writing for this magazine, I have completely lost my appetite for books. I have half-read several, and intend to finish all of them, but at the moment I find it impossible to concentrate on what anyone has to say about more or less any subject. This seems, in part, to be something to do with my book tour – it's unfair, I know, but I seem to be sick of the sound of everyone's voice, not just my own. Plus, at the time of this writing, I live in a city which seems to be exploding about our ears, and this has done nothing at all for my interest in contemporary literature. It all seems a bit beside the point at the moment. I'm sure that's an error in my thinking, and that my unwillingness to engage with sensitive first novels about coming out on a sheep farm in North Dakota in the 1950s – I made this book up, by the way, and if you wrote it, I mean no offence – proves that the terrorists have won, to use the phrase that seems to end every sentence here at the moment. ('It means they've won' is applied indiscriminately to anyone's failure to do anything at all that they usually do. If you don't feel like getting on a tube or a bus, going into the centre of the city, reading a book, getting drunk, or punching someone on the nose, it means you're a scaredy-cat, not British, etc.) Instead of reading, I play endless games of solitaire on my mobile phone, watch twenty-four-hour news channels, and try to find newspaper articles written by experts on fundamentalism assuring me that this will all be over by Tuesday. I haven't found any such reassurance yet. This morning I found myself moderately uplifted by a piece in *The Times* explaining that acetone peroxide, the explosive that London bombers favour, has a shelf-life of less than a week. It's cheap, though, and available in any half-decent hardware store, so it's not all good news.

Anyway, in this context it seems something of a miracle that I've finished any books at all. Jess Walter, a wonderful writer of whose existence I was previously unaware, sent me *Citizen Vince* in the hope that I might start a third list at the top of this page, a list entitled 'Books Foisted Upon Me', so I was immediately intrigued by his novel; as a freelance reviewer I get sent a ton of books, but nobody to date has expressed an ambition to appear in a *Believer* list. If I hadn't actually gone and read the thing I might have been tempted.

The clincher for me was an enthusiastic blurb by the great Richard Russo, and he didn't let me down, because *Citizen Vince* is fast, tough, thoughtful and funny. (Right at the beginning of the book there's a terrific scene involving an unwilling hooker and her unsatisfied customer, a scene culminating in an interesting philo-sophical debate about whether there's such a thing as half a blow job.) It's about a guy who's moved from New York City to Spokane, Washington, under the Witness Protection Program; he's going about his business of making doughnuts and committing petty fraud when it becomes apparent that a man who may or may not be connected to Vince's past wants to kill him. And this guy, the bad guy, he's really, *really* bad. He threatens to do something so vile to a small child that you can't read on until you've started breathing again.

Citizen Vince would have worked fine as 'just' a thriller, but Walter has ambitions on top of that, because it's also about voting, believe it or not; Vince has been registered by the authorities, and for the first time in his life he has to decide who he wants as President. The book's set in 1980, so the choice is between Carter and Reagan, and Vince is paralysed by it; this is hardly surprising, seeing as Walter suggests that the choice is between the America you ended up with, and another America, one that vanished when poor, decent, hopeless Jimmy was beaten. In a couple of bravura passages, Walter leaves his gangsters and petty crooks to fend for themselves while he enters the minds of the candidates themselves. I loved this novel. It came through my letter box just when I was beginning to think that I'd have to write 'NONE!' under the heading 'Books Read'; it seemed to know that what I needed was pace, warmth, humour, and an artfully disguised attempt to write about a world bigger than the one its characters live in.

Miriam Toews's lovely *A Complicated Kindness* is funny, too, but it's not overly bothered about pace, not least because it's partly about the torpor that comes from feeling defeated. Last month, I believe I threatened to get religion; I may even have said that I'd gone to live in a monastery, but before anyone at a reading asks me how I'm enjoying the monastic life, I should explain that this was another of those jokes where I say that something is so when it is in fact not so. (Maybe it's a cultural thing, these jokes falling flat? But then again, I don't make anyone laugh here either.) Anyway, *A Complicated Kindness* has further delayed my plans to turn my back on this vale of tears: Nomi Nickel, Miriam Toews's narrator, is a Mennonite, or at least she comes from a family of Mennonites, and she doesn't make it sound like too much fun.

Mennonites – and everyone's a Mennonite where Nomi lives – are against the things that make life bearable: sex, drugs, rock and roll, make-up, TV, smoking, and so on; Nomi Nickel, on the other hand, is for all of those things, wherein lies both the tension and the torpor. Nomi's sister Tash and her mother have already been driven out of town by the Mennonite powers-that-be, but Nomi has stayed behind to look after her father Ray, a man who spends a lot of time sitting on his lawn chair and staring into space; Nomi, meanwhile, bounces round the town off the diamond-hard disapproval she meets everywhere, getting into all the trouble she can, which isn't so much, in a town that doesn't even have a bus station – it was removed because the more rebellious spirits kept wanting to go places. One of the joys of the book, in fact, is the desperate ingenuity of its characters, looking for ways to express themselves in a culture that allows no self-expression. 'That was around the time our Aunt Gonad asked Tash to burn her *Jesus Christ Superstar* soundtrack. Tash could do a hilariously sexy version of "I Don't Know How to Love Him" where she basically worked herself into a complete fake orgasm during that big crescendo.' You may think that you don't want to read about the problems of being brought up Mennonite, but the great thing about books is that you'll read anything that a good writer wants you to read. And the voice that Miriam Toews finds for her narrator is so true and so charming that you don't even mind spending a couple hundred pages in a town as joyless as Nomi's East Village.

I bought *A Complicated Kindness* in the Powell's bookstall at the Portland, Oregon, airport, after several fervent recommendations from the Powell's staff who looked after me at my signing. Did you know that you have the best bookshops in the world? I hope so. Over here in England, the home of literature ha-ha, we have only chain bookstores, staffed by people who for the most part come across as though they'd rather be selling anything else anywhere else; meanwhile you have access to booksellers who would regard their failure to sell you novels about Mennonites as a cause of deep personal shame. Please spend every last penny you have on books from independent bookstores, because otherwise you'll end up as sour and as semi-literate as the English.

I bought *The Diary of a Country Priest* in a fit of post-*Gilead* enthusiasm, although I have to say that at the moment, my chances of reading it, at least in this life, are slim. I was tempted, however, by the following review on the Amazon site:

> *This book has had an enormous impact on my life. Having had to read it as part of my French A-level course (in French!) it left me psychologically scarred. Grinding through each passage was like torture, making me weep with frustration and leaving me with a long-burning and deep-felt resentment against my French teacher and the A-level exam board. This resulted in a low grade for my French lit paper, which offset a decent language paper, resulting in a 'C' which wasn't good enough for my chosen university. So I had to switch from French to business studies, so changing the course of my life. To say I detest this book is an understatement.*

You see the profound effect that literature can have on a life? Who says it's all a waste of time? If only I could produce one book that left someone with that kind of ferocious grievance. If you have read one of my books, you probably feel cheated out of however much money it might have cost you, and you'll certainly begrudge the time you wasted on it. But even at my most bullish and self-aggrandizing, I can't quite make myself believe that I've actually wrecked someone's life. Any documentary evidence to the contrary will be gratefully received. ✷

CITIZEN VINCE

by JESS WALTER

✱ ✱ ✱

Eighty-seven bars in greater Spokane, serving three hundred thousand people. One taxicab company: eight cabs. So on a Tuesday morning just past two a.m., last call, the economics are clear: more drunks than the market can bear. They leach out onto the sidewalks and stagger and yawn to their cars – those who own them and remember where they're parked. The rest walk from downtown to the neighborhoods, scattering in all directions across bridges, through underpasses, beneath trestles, up hills to dark residential streets, solitary figures beneath thought bubbles of warm breath and cigarette smoke. Rehearsed lies.

Vince Camden concentrates on his own thoughts as he walks sober and rested among the drunk and tired. Stout downtown brick and brownstone give way to low-rent low-rise strips – karate dojos, waterbed liquidators, erotic bookstores, pawnshops, and Asian massage – then a neighborhood of empty warehouses, rail lines, vacant fields, and a solitary two-story Victorian house, an after-hours cards and rib joint called Sam's Pit. This is where Vince hangs out most nights before his shift begins at the donut shop.

Vince was only in town a few months when Sam died. Thirty-seven. The new owner is named Eddie, but everyone calls him Sam – it being easier to change one's name to Sam than to change the faded Pepsi sign on the old house from SAM'S to EDDIE'S. Just as old Sam did, new Sam opens the Pit when the rest of the city closes, after Last Call. The place works like a drain for the city; every morning when the bars close, the drunks and hookers and lawyers and johns and addicts and thieves and cops and cardplayers

— as old Sam used to say, 'Evergodambody' — swirls around the streets and ends up here. It's why the cops don't sweat the gambling and undercounter booze. It's just nice to know that at three a.m., everyone will be gathered in one place, like the suspects in a seamy British drawing room.

The Pit lurks behind high, unkempt shrubs, the only thing on a block of vacant lots, like a last tooth. Behind, a rutted dirt field functions as a parking lot for Sam's and a factory showroom for the half-dozen professional women who gather here each night for last tricks. Inside, pimps play cards and wait for their cut.

Gravel cracks beneath Vince's shoes as he angles for Sam's Pit. Six cars are parked randomly in his weed-covered field, girls doing business in a couple. A car door opens fifty feet from Vince, and a woman's voice skitters across the weedy lot: 'Let go!'

Vince stares straight ahead. *Not your business.*

'Vince! Tell this guy to let go of me!'

Beth's voice. At the door, Vince turns and walks back across the lot toward a tan Plymouth Duster. Inside, Beth Sherman is wrestling with a guy in a white turtleneck sweater and a navy sport coat. As he walks up to the car, Vince can see the guy's pants are open and that he's trying to keep Beth from getting out of the car. She swings at him with the frayed, dirty cast on her right forearm. Barely misses.

Vince leans down and opens the car door. 'Hey, Beth. What's going on?'

The guy lets go and she pulls away, climbs out of the car and past Vince. He is amazed again how pretty she can be, triangular face and round eyes, bangs cut straight across them. She can't weigh a hundred pounds. Odd for a woman in her line of work to actually look younger than she is, but Beth could pass for a teenager — at least from a distance. Up close — well, the lifestyle is tough to hide. Beth points at the guy in the car with her cast. 'He grabbed my ass.'

The guy is incredulous. 'You're a hooker!'

'I'm in real estate!'

'You were blowing me!'

Beth yells around Vince at the man: 'Do you grab your plumber's ass when *he's* working?'

Vince steps between Beth and the john, and smiles disarmingly at the guy. 'Look, she doesn't like to be touched.'

'What kind of hooker doesn't like to be touched?'

Vince can't argue the premise. But he wishes the guy had just kept his mouth shut. He knows how this will go now, and in fact Beth steps around him, fishes around in her pocket, and throws a twenty-dollar bill in his face.

The guy holds up the twenty. 'I gave you forty!'

'You got half,' she says. 'You get half your money back.'

'Half? There's no such thing!' He looks up at Vince. 'Is there such thing as half?'

Vince looks from Beth to the guy and opens his mouth without the slightest expectation that anything will come. He looks back at Beth and their eyes catch long enough for both of them to note.

About Beth Sherman: she is thirty-three, just leaving 'cute', with brown hair and eyes that dart from attention. Her dislike of contact notwithstanding, Beth is well respected among the working women at Sam's, mostly for one big accomplishment – she quit heroin without methadone, cold fucking turkey, exactly nineteen months and two weeks ago, on the very day she found out she was pregnant. Her boy, Kenyon, is a little more than a year now and he seems fine, but everyone knows how she watches him breathlessly, constantly comparing him to the other kids in the park and at his day care, looking for any sign that he is slow or stunted, that her worst fears are realized, that the junk has ruined him, too. And while she is clearly on her way out of this life – she fired her pimp, *in writing* – Beth continues to turn tricks, maybe because there are so few ways for a high school dropout to support herself and her son. Anyway, she's not the only hooker at Sam's who introduces herself as something else. It's a place full of actresses and massage therapists, models, students, and social workers, but when Beth says she's in real estate, people actually seem to believe it.

When he first arrived, Vince purchased Beth's services (he tried a few of the girls) and found himself intrigued by her cool distance, the way she bristled under his hands. Then one night six months ago, she and Vince drank two bottles of wine and spent a night together *without* the exchange of money. And it was different – alarming and close. No bristle. But since then everything has been out of sorts – Beth not wanting to charge him, Vince wary of becoming involved with a woman with a kid. And so they haven't slept together in three months. The worst part is that it feels like cheating to be with the other women, and so Vince is in the midst of his longest stretch of celibacy that doesn't involve a jail cell. The whole thing has proven to him the old axiom among the professional class: *Free sex ruins everything.*

In the parking lot, Beth stalks away from the angry, unsated john – her tight jeans beneath a coat that stops midriff. Vince watches her go, then takes one of the bags of dope from his pocket, bends down, and holds it up to the window. The Bible says that even the peacemaker deserves a profit. Or it says something anyway.

After a second, the guy shrugs and holds up the twenty. 'Yeah, okay,' he says. As they exchange dope for money, the guy shakes his head. 'Never heard of a hooker who didn't want to be touched.'

Vince nods, although in his estimation the world is made of only such people, pot-smoking cops, thieves who tithe 10 per cent, society women who wear garters, tramps who sleep with stuffed bears, criminal donut makers, real estate hookers. He remembers a firefighter in the old neighborhood named Alvin Dunphy who was claustrophobic. Died when a burning apartment building collapsed on him. Thirty-eight.

OCTOBER 2005

BOOKS BOUGHT:
None

BOOKS READ:
* *Blood Done Sign My Name:
  A True Story* – Timothy B.
  Tyson
* *Candide* – Voltaire
* *Oh the Glory of It All* – Sean
  Wilsey

I want to take back some things I said last month. Or rather, I don't so much want to take them back as to modify my tone, which is a pretty poor show, considering that writing, especially writing a column, is all about tone: what I'm essentially saying is, don't read last month's column, because it was all wrong. I was way too defensive, I see now, about my relative lack of literary consumption (two books, for the benefit of those of you who are too busy busy busy to retain the minutiae of my reading life from one month to the next). Shamefully – oh, God, it's all coming back to me now – I tried to blame it on all sorts of things, including the London bombs, but the truth is that two books in a month isn't so bad. There are lots of people who don't get through two books a month. And anyway, what would happen if I had read no books? Obviously, I'd lose this job (although that's assuming one of the Spree noticed). But apart from that? What would happen if I read no books ever? Let's imagine someone who reads no books ever but polishes off every word of the *New Yorker*, the *Economist* and their broadsheet newspaper of choice: well, this imaginary person would do more reading than me, because that's got to be a couple of hundred thousand words a week, and would also be a lot smarter than me, if you use that rather limited definition of smart which involves knowing stuff about stuff. The *New Yorker* has humour in it and also provides an introduction to contemporary fiction and poetry. So the only major food group not covered is starch: in other words, the classics. And what would happen if we never read the classics? There comes a point in life, it seems to me, where you have to decide whether you're a Person of Letters or merely someone who loves books, and I'm beginning to see that the book lovers have more fun. Persons of Letters have to read things like *Candide* or they're a few letters short of the whole alphabet; book lovers, meanwhile, can read whatever they fancy.

I picked up *Candide* because my publishers sent me a cute new edition, and though that in itself wouldn't have persuaded me, I flicked through it and discovered it was only ninety pages long. Ninety pages! Who knew, apart from all of you, and everybody else? A ninety-page classic is the Holy Grail of this column, and when the Holy Grail is pushed through your letter box, you don't put it on a shelf to gather dust. (Or maybe that's exactly what you'd do with the Holy Grail. Is it ornamental? Has anyone ever seen it?) Anyway, I have now read *Candide*. That's another one chalked off. And boy, does Voltaire really have it in for Leibnizian philosophy! Whoo-hoo! Now, there's a justification for reading *Candide* right there. Many of you will have been living, like Leibniz, in the deluded belief that all is for the best, in the best of all possible worlds (because you believe that God would have created nothing but the best), but I have read Voltaire, and I can now see that this is a preposterous notion that brings only despair. And it's not only Leibniz who comes in for a kicking, either. Oh, no. Corneille, the Jesuits, Racine, the Abbé Gauchat, Rousseau . . . Just about everyone you've ever wanted to see lampooned in a short novel gets what's coming to them. You lot are probably all familiar with the Abbé Gauchat, the Theatines, the Jansenists and the literary criticism of Élie-Catherine Fréron, but I'm afraid I found myself flicking frantically between the text and the footnotes at the end; I was unhappily reminded of the time I had to spend at school reading Alexander Pope's equally mordant attacks on poetasters and so forth. Literary types will tell you that underneath all the contemporary references, you will recognize yourselves and your world, but it's not true, of course. If it's this world you're after, the one we actually live in, you're better off with Irvine Welsh or Thomas Harris.

The trouble with *Candide* is that it's one of those books that we've all read, whether we've read it or not (cf. *Animal Farm, 1984, Gulliver's Travels, Lord of the Flies*). The meat was picked off it and thrown to the crowd in the eighteenth century, and . . . I'll abandon this metaphor here, because I suspect that it must inevitably conclude with digestive systems and the consumption of ancient excrement. The point is that we are familiar with silly old Dr Pangloss, just as we know that some animals are more equal than others. Satires and allegories tend to have been decoded long before we ever get to them, which renders them somewhat redundant, it seems to me. *Panglossian* is the sort of word you might find from time to time in the *Economist* and the *New Yorker*, and in any case, if ever anyone lived in an age that had no need for a savage debunking of optimism, it is us. We believe that everything everywhere is awful, all the time. In fact, Voltaire was one of the people who first pointed it out, and he was so successful that we find ourselves in desperate need of a Pangloss in our lives. Bitter footnote: just after I'd finished my cute hardback, I found an old paperback copy on my shelves (unread, obviously): a hundred and thirty pages. Oh, the pain! I'd never have read − or paid, as you have to think of it in this case − three figures. I was tricked, swindled and cheated by my own publishers, who clearly scrunched everything up a bit to dupe the innocent and the ill read.

Book length, like time, is an abstract concept. Sean Wilsey's *Oh the Glory of It All* is a good four times the length of *Candide*, and I enjoyed it probably four times as much, even though all book logic suggests that the reverse might have been the case. I'm sure young Sean would be the first to admit that there's some sag around the middle, but like many of us, it's lovable even at its saggiest point. And also, you never once have to laugh at the pomposities of the French Academies of the eighteenth century, a prerequisite, I now understand, for any book. (In fact, publishers should use that as a blurb. 'You never once have to laugh at the pomposities of the French Academies of the eighteenth century!' I'd buy any book that had that on the cover.)

Oh the Glory of It All is a memoir, as those of you who live in the Bay Area may already know; Wilsey was brought up in San Francisco by squillionaire socialites, although after his parents' divorce, the silver spoon wasn't as much use as he might have hoped: his mother devoted her time to saving the world, and dragged Sean off around the world to meet the Pope and various scary old-school Kremlin types; meanwhile his dad married a scary old-school stepmother who treated Wilsey like dirt. (Hey, Dede! You may be a bigshot in a little bit of San Francisco, but nobody has ever heard of you here in London! Or anywhere else! I'm sorry, but she got me so steamed up that I had to get back at her somehow.) He got chucked out of every school he attended, and ran away from a creepy establishment which didn't allow you to utter the names of rock bands out loud.

American lives seem, from this distance at least, very different from European lives. Look at this: Sean Wilsey's mother was the daughter of an itinerant preacher. She ran away to Dallas to be a model, an escape funded initially by the nickels from her uncle's jukeboxes and peanut machines. She was dragged off to California by her angry family, and while waitressing there she met a US Air Force major who married her on a live national radio programme called *The Bride and Groom*. She split from the major, dated Frank Sinatra for a while, married a couple of other guys – one marriage lasted six months; the other, to the trial lawyer who defended Jack Ruby, lasted three weeks. She got a TV job and she had a fan club. And then she married Sean's dad. We don't do any of that here. We don't have itinerant preachers, or peanut machines, or Sinatra. We are born in, for example, Basingstoke, and then we either stay there, or we move to London. That's probably why we don't write many memoirs.

Timothy B. Tyson's *Blood Done Sign My Name* is a memoir, too, although it's not the peculiarities of his life that Tyson is writing about, but the point at which his experiences intersect with recent American history. Tyson was brought up in Oxford, North Carolina, where his father was the pastor of the Methodist church; in 1970, Robert Teel, the father of one of Tyson's friends, and a couple of other white thugs murdered a young black man, and after the contemptible trial, wherein everyone was found not guilty of everything, there was a race riot, and great chunks of Oxford got torched. Young Tim Tyson grew up to be a professor of Afro-American studies, and *Blood Done Sign My Name* is a perfect reflection of who he is now and where he came from: it's both memoir and social history, and it's riveting. Tyson has a deceptively folksy prose style that leads you to suspect that his book will in part be about the triumph of Civil Rights hope over bitter Southern experience, but it ends with a coda, a visit to a club in Greensboro, North Carolina, in 1992 to see Percy Sledge:

Tyson's black friend is denied admission. Yes, 1992. Yes, Percy Sledge, the soul singer.

Blood Done Sign My Name is uncompromisingly tough minded, righteous and instructive (there is a terrific section unravelling the taboo that surrounded black men sleeping with white women), and it's not about people singing 'We Shall Overcome' and holding hands until black and white live together in perfect harmony. On the contrary, Tyson is very good on how the history of the Civil Rights movement is being rewritten daily until it begins to look like the triumph of liberal good sense over prejudice; nothing would have happened, he argues, without things being set on fire. 'If you want to read only one book to understand the uniquely American struggle for racial equality and the swirls of emotion around it, this is it,' says one of the reviews on the back of the book. Well, I have read only one book about the uniquely American struggle for racial equality, and this was it. But I will read another one one day soon: it would seem strange, and perhaps a little perverse, to allow a white man to provide my entire Civil Rights education. I mean no offence to the author of this memorable book, but he'd be the first to admit that Afro-Americans might have something of interest to say on the subject.

I moved house this month and have bought no books at all for the first time since I became a Believer. I have spent hour after hour finding homes for unread novels, biographies, memoirs and collections of essays, poetry and letters, and suddenly I can see as never before that we're fine for books at the moment, thanks very much. I came across quite a few of the things that have appeared in the Books Bought column at the top of these pages, and marvelled at my own lack of self-knowledge. When exactly was I going to read Michael B. Oren's no doubt excellent book about the Six-Day War? Or Dylan Thomas's letters? The ways in which a man can kid himself are many and various. Anyway, the football season has restarted, which always reduces book time. Arsenal bought only one player over the summer and sold their captain, so we've got a perilously thin squad, and Chelsea have spent squillions again, and . . . The truth is, I'm too worried to begin Hilary Spurling's apparently magnificent biography of Matisse (bought about five years ago, new, in hardback, because I couldn't wait). I won't even be able to think about picking it up until Wenger brings in a new central midfield player. And at the time of writing, there's no sign of that. ★

NOVEMBER 2005

BOOKS BOUGHT:
* *A Little History of the World* – Ernst Gombrich
* *What Good Are the Arts?* – John Carey
* *What I Loved* – Siri Hustvedt
* *Death and the Penguin* – Andrey Kurkov

BOOKS READ:
* *The Trick of It* – Michael Frayn
* *Housekeeping* – Marilynne Robinson
* *Over Tumbled Graves* – Jess Walter
* Unnameable comedy thriller – Anonymous

O n my copy of Michael Frayn's *The Trick of It*, there is a quote from Anthony Burgess that describes the novel as 'one of the few books I have read in the last year that has provoked laughter'. Initially, it's a blurb that works in just the way the publishers intended. Great, you think. Burgess must have read a lot of books; and both the quote itself and your knowledge of the great man suggest that he wouldn't have chuckled at many of them. So if *The Trick of It* wriggled its way through that forbidding exterior to the Burgess sense of humour, it must be absolutely hilarious, right? But then you start to wonder just how trustworthy Burgess would have been on the subject of comedy. What, for example, would have been his favourite bit of *Jackass: The Movie*? (Burgess died in 1993, so sadly we will never know.) What was his most cherished *Three Stooges* sketch? His favourite *Seinfeld* character? His top David Brent moment? And after careful contemplation, your confidence in his comic judgement starts to feel a little misplaced: there is a good chance, you suspect, that Anthony Burgess would have steadfastly refused even to smile at many of the things that have ever made you chortle uncontrollably.

Sometimes it feels as though we are being asked to imagine cultural judgements as a whole bunch of concentric circles. On the outside, we have the wrong ones, made by the people who read *The Da Vinci Code* and listen to Celine Dion; right at the centre we have the correct ones, made by the snootier critics, very often people who have vowed never to laugh again until Aristophanes produces a follow-up to *The Frogs*. (I haven't read James Wood's collection of essays *The Irresponsible Self: Laughter and the Novel*, but I'm counting on Woody to provide a useful counterbalance to that sort of high moral seriousness. So I'm presuming that all the comic greats – P. G. Wodehouse, the Molesworth books, George and Weedon Grossmith, and so on – are present and correct between its covers.) The world is a lot more complicated than this diagram allows, of course, but sometimes it's easy to forget that the Frog people don't know everything. If I had to choose between a Celine Dion fan and Anthony Burgess for comedy recommendations, I would go with the person standing on the table singing 'The Power of Love' every time. I'll bet Burgess read *Candide* – I had a bad experience with *Candide* only recently – with tears of mirth trickling down his face.

As you may have guessed by now, *The Trick of It* didn't make me laugh, so I'm feeling insecure. It's brilliant – witty, smart, readable and engaging; but you know that bit in *Jackass: The Movie* when the guy takes a crap in the bathroom shop? Well, gags of that quality are conspicuously absent. I suspect that it wasn't Michael Frayn's intention to provide them, either; I raise the comparison only because when you see the word 'funny' all over a paperback (Burgess was not alone in having his ribs tickled), it raises expectations to a possibly unrealistic level. *The Trick of It* is about the relationship between a young college professor and his area of expertise, a middle-aged woman novelist he refers to as JL. This relationship becomes complicated, although perhaps in some ways simplified, when he sleeps with her and then marries her: he thus becomes a part of his own research material, a chapter in her still unwritten biography. We have objected to novels about writers and writing in this column before, have we not? We are concerned that the preciousness to which these novels can be prone will alienate the last few readers left out there. But we have no complaints in this case, you and Michael Frayn will be delighted to hear. *The Trick of It* has a healthy resonance rather than a sickly insularity – anyone who has ever been a fan will recognize something in here – and if you've read Frayn's work then you will know how effortlessly clever he is, and thus you can imagine the fun he has with the hall of mirrors he has rigged up here.

I've been reading *Housekeeping* off and on since I finished Marilynne Robinson's second novel, *Gilead*, a while back, but I kept losing it and getting distracted, and in the end I put it down for a while because I was being disrespectful to a novel that people clearly love. I thought I knew what *Housekeeping* would be because I've seen Bill Forsyth's lovely film adaptation a couple of times; I thought it would be warm and quirky, like the movie, except with better prose. Indeed, during the floods in Louisiana I nearly stopped reading the book again, for the hundredth time, because there is a description of a flood right at the beginning of the book, and I was worried that warmth and quirkiness would jar, fight horribly with the scenes we were seeing on the news. So I wasn't prepared for what I actually got, which was this extraordinary, yearning mystical work about the dead and how they haunt the living; if books can work as music, then *Housekeeping* served as a soundtrack to the footage from New Orleans. The dead haunting the living, the core of the book . . . That was missing from the movie, as far as I remember. I'm not sure Bill Forsyth knew what to do about all the souls at the bottom of the lake, so he concentrated on his eccentric central characters, and how a small community finds this eccentricity hard to accommodate. It's a fine, slightly conventional theme, but now I've read the book, I can see that this is rather like making attractive ashtrays out of Kryptonite.

One of the souls at the bottom of the lake belongs to the mother of Ruth, the novel's teenage narrator, and of her sister Lucille; Helen drove into the lake, calmly and deliberately, when her daughters were young. Her father, the girls' grandfather, is down there somewhere too, along with the passengers on a train that came off the bridge that crosses the water. Ruth and Lucille never knew their father, so eventually their aunt Sylvie comes to live with them. She's not much of a mother figure, Sylvie. She sits in the dark surrounded by empty tin cans and old newspapers, and yearns to go back to travelling around on the railroads, but she stays anyway. Have you ever seen that great Stanley Spencer picture, *The Cookham Resurrection*? It depicts the dead coming alive again, sleepy and bewildered, in the small, pretty and (otherwise) unremarkable Thameside village where Spencer lived. I'm sure that Robinson must have had the painting in some part of her extraordinary mind when she wrote *Housekeeping*. There is that same strange fusion of the humdrum and the visionary, and though Fingerbone, the bleak little town where the novel is set, clearly isn't as cute as Cookham, it still seems an unlikely location for waking dreams about a reunion of the living and all the people we have ever lost. ('Families should stay together,' says Sylvie at the end of the book. 'Otherwise things get out of control. My father, you know. I can't even remember what he was like, I mean when he was alive. But ever since, it's Papa here and Papa there, and dreams.')

It's quite clear to me now, having read her two novels, that

Marilynne Robinson is one of America's greatest living writers, and certainly there's no one else like her. I think I am using that phrase literally: I have never come across a mind like this one, in literature or anywhere else, for that matter. Sometimes her singular serious-ness, and her insistent concentration on the sad beauty of our mortality, make you laugh, in an Anthony Burgess kind of way. Pools and ponds and lakes 'taste a bit of blood and hair', observes Ruth, with customary Robinsonian good cheer. 'One cannot cup one's hand and drink from the rim of any lake without remem-bering that mothers have drowned in it, lifting their children toward the air, though they must have known as they did that soon enough the deluge would take all the children, too, even if their arms could have held them up.' She may be a great writer, but you wouldn't want her on your camping holiday, would you? (I know, I know, that's a cheap joke, and I'm making the schoolboy error of confusing narrator and author; Marilynne Robinson almost certainly spends her camping holidays singing Beach Boys songs and trying to give everyone wedgies.)

We have, from time to time in these pages, expressed our im-patience with a certain kind of literary fiction. (By 'these pages', I mean the two I'm given. And by 'we', I mean 'I'. The Spree would never express their impatience with literary fiction. In fact, 'the duller the better' is engraved on the gates, in enormous letters, at Spree Castle.) To us, it can sometimes seem overwrought, pedestrian, po-faced, monotonous, out of touch; we would argue that literary fiction must take some of the blame for the novel's sad disappearance from the centre of our culture. But sometimes, a book just can't help being literary; it can't do anything about its own complication, because its ideas defy simple expression. It took me for ever to read *Housekeeping*, but it's not possible to read this short book quickly, because it comes fitted with its own speed bumps: the neo-Old Testament prose, exactly the right language for Robinson's heart-breaking, prophetic images. And I'm glad I wasn't able to race through it, too, because the time I spent with it means that it lives with me still.

I have always prized the accessible over the obscure, but after reading *Housekeeping* I can see that in some ways the easy, accessible novel is working at a disadvantage (not that *Housekeeping* is inaccessible, but it is deep, and dark and rich): it's possible to whiz through it without allowing it even to touch the sides, and a bit of side-touching has to happen if a book is going to be properly transformative. If you are so gripped by a book that you want to read it in the mythical single sitting, what chance has it got of making it all the way through the long march to your soul? It'll get flushed out by something else before it's even halfway there. The trouble is that most literary novels don't do anything but touch the sides. They stick to them like sludge, and in the end you have to get the garden hose out. (I have no idea what that might mean. But I had to escape from the metaphor somehow.)

Neither of the other books I read this month were sludgy, at least. I read and loved Jess Walter's *Citizen Vince* recently, so I wanted to check out one of his earlier books. Unlike *Citizen Vince*, *Over Tumbled Graves* belongs firmly within the crime genre, although it's not formulaic – it actually plays cleverly with the serial-killer formula. I enjoyed it a lot, but on the evidence of the recent book, Walter is a writer who is heading for territory that gives him more freedom than genre fiction allows. Under the *Believer* guidelines, the second novel must remain nameless because I hated it so much. I was recommended it by a friend with normally impeccable taste, and he's not alone – my paperback copy contains blurbs from a couple of clever literary figures who really should know better. Is the phrase 'Deliciously politically incorrect' used with the same gay abandon in the US? You come across it all the time here, and usually it means, quite simply, that a book or a movie or a TV programme is racist and/or sexist and/or homophobic; there is a certain kind of cultural commentator who mysteriously associates these prejudices with a Golden Age during which we were allowed to do lots of things that we are not allowed to do now. (The truth is that there's no one stopping them from doing anything. What they really object to is being recognized as the antisocial pigs they really are.)

Anyway, this book is 'deliciously politically incorrect'. The narrator, who fancies himself as a cross between James Bond and Bertie Wooster, thinks it's funny to transpose the *r*s and *l*s in dialogue spoken by Chinese people, and has what he clearly regards as sound advice for women in the process of being raped: 'lie quite still, try to enjoy it. The choice is a simple one: a brief and possibly not unpleasant invasion of one's physical privacy – or a painful bashing causing the loss of one's good looks and perhaps one's life.' There may well have been men like this in the 1970s, when this book was written, but they were not clever men. It would have been torture to listen to them for two minutes at a bus stop, and you certainly don't want to hang around with them while they narrate a whole book. To compound the reader's misery, this narrator favours a jocular, florid circumlocution intended to invoke the spirit of Wodehouse, who is unwisely mentioned twice in the first fifty pages. I ended up hurling him across the room. At the time of writing, I haven't been able to confront the friend who recommended the book, but there will, I'm afraid, be bloodshed.

I really want to read every book I bought this month. That's true of every month, of course, and usually nothing happens, but this month I really *really* want to read the books I bought. I have just been to a wonderful literary festival in Iceland, where I spent time with Siri Hustvedt and Andrey Kurkov and lots of other interesting, companionable writers; and it's true that there is a slight possibility, judging from my track record, that either of these novels might fall off the bedside pile at some stage in the future, but surely they can see that the commitment is there? And the two works of non-fiction, by John Carey and Ernst Gombrich, have the most perfect titles imaginable: I desperately need to know what the uses of the arts are, and the great John Carey, who wrote the great *The Intellectuals and the Masses*, is undoubtedly the man to tell me, and thus make me feel better about the ways in which I waste my time. He may even tell me that I'm not wasting my time, as long as he manages to get solitaire and football under the arts umbrella. The title of Gombrich's book, meanwhile, cleverly isolates the precise area in which I am most ignorant. How did he know? ✶

FEBRUARY 2006

I f, as a recent survey in the UK suggested, most people buy
books because they like to be *seen* reading rather than because
they actually enjoy it, then I would suggest that you can't beat a
collection of letters by an author – and if that author is a poet, then
so much the better. The implication is clear: you know the poet's
work inside out (indeed, what you're saying is that if you read his
or her entire oeuvre one more time, then the lines would ring
round and round in your head like a Kelly Clarkson tune), and you
now need something else, something that might help to shed some
light on some of the more obscure couplets.

So there I am, reading Larkin's letters every chance I get, and impressing the hell out of anyone who spots me doing so. (Never mind that I never go anywhere, and that therefore the only person likely to spot me doing so is my partner, who at the time I'm most likely to be reading Larkin's letters is very much a sleeping partner.) And what I'm actually reading is stuff like this: 'Katherine Mansfield is a cunt.' 'I think this [poem] is really bloody cunting fucking good.' 'I have just made up a rhyme: after a particularly good game of rugger / A man called me a bugger / Merely because in a loose scrum / I had my cock up his bum.' 'Your letter found me last night when I came in off the piss: in point of fact I had spewed out of a train window and farted in the presence of ladies and generally misbehaved myself.' And so on. In other words, you get to have your cake and eat it: you look like *un homme ou femme sérieux/sérieuse*, but you feel like a twelve-year-old who's somehow being allowed to read *Playboy* in an English lesson. And what you come to realize is that the lifestyle of a naughty twelve-year-old is enervating to the max, if you're a grown-up; indeed, there are quite a few thirteen-year-olds who would find great chunks of Larkin's correspondence embarrassingly puerile.

The irony is that I was drawn to Larkin's letters through that beautiful poem 'Church Going', which makes a case for the value of churches long after organized religion has lost its appeal and its point: 'And that much never can be obsolete / Since someone will forever be surprising / A hunger in himself to be more serious.' This last line was quoted in an article I was reading in the *Economist*, of all places, and it struck a post-*Gilead* chord with me, so I reread a few of the poems and then decided that I'd like access to the prose version of the mind that created them. And yes, you can see where Larkin's hunger to become more serious came from; if I had a mouth like that, I'd have wanted to pay frequent visits to God's house, too. Larkin writes brilliantly and enthusiastically about his jazz records, and every now and again there's a peach of a letter about writing:

Poetry (at any rate in my case) is like trying to remember a tune you've forgotten. All corrections are attempts to get nearer to the forgotten tune. A poem is written because the poet gets a sudden vision – lasting one second or less – and he attempts to express the whole of which the vision is a part.

And that's the sort of thing you want, surely, when you wade through a writer's letters. What you end up with, however, is a lot of stuff about farting and wanking. Every now and again you are reminded forcibly that the ability to write fiction or poetry is not necessarily indicative of a particularly refined intelligence, no matter what we'd like to believe; it's a freakish talent, like the ability to bend a ball into the top corner of the goal from a thirty-yard free kick, but no one's interested in reading Thierry Henry's collected letters – no literary critic, anyway. And Thierry would never call Katherine Mansfield a cunt, not least because he's a big fan of the early stories. Anyway, I have given up on Larkin for the moment. The rest of you: stick to the poems.

As nobody noticed, probably, I was barred from the *Believer* again last month, this time for quoting from one of Philip Larkin's letters, more or less accurately – what's a second-person pronoun between friends? – at an editorial meeting. The Polysyllabic Spree, the seventy-eight repellently evangelical young men and women who run the magazine, 'couldn't hear the quotation marks', apparently, and anyway, as they pointed out (somewhat unnecessarily, I felt), I'm no Larkin. So I have a lot of ground to cover here – I have had several Major Reading Experiences over the last couple of months, and I've got to cram them all into a couple of measly pages, all because of those teenage white-robed prudes. Oh, it's not your problem. I'll just get on with it. I know I won't need to tell you anything about Zadie Smith's warm, moving, smart and thoroughly enjoyable *On Beauty*; Hanan Al-Shaykh was one of the authors I met on a recent trip to Reykjavik, and her lovely novel *Only in London* was a perfect reflection of the woman: surprising, fun, thoughtful.

A disgruntled Barnesandnoble.com punter slams Robert Penn Warren's *All the King's Men*: 'Oh well,' says our critic in his one-star review. 'At least it was better than the Odyssey.' This means, presumably, that the Odyssey is a no-star book; you have to admire someone prepared to flout conventional literary wisdom so publicly. I personally don't agree, and for me the Odyssey still has the edge, but Warren's novel seems to have held up pretty well. It's overwritten, here and there – Warren can't see a sunny day without comparing it to a freckly girl wearing a polka-dot dress and new shoes, sitting on a fence clutching a strawberry lollipop and whistling – and at one point, *a propos* of almost nothing, there's a thirty-page story set during the Civil War which seems to belong to another book altogether. You could be forgiven for thinking that *All the King's Men* could have done with a little more editing, rather than a little less; but the edition I read is a new 'restored' edition of the novel, containing a whole bunch of stuff – a hundred pages, apparently – that was omitted from the version originally published. A hundred pages! Oh, dear God. Those of us still prepared to pick up sixty-year-old Pulitzer Prize-winners should be rewarded, not horribly and unfairly punished.

You may well already have read *All the King's Men*; you will, therefore, be familiar with Willie Stark, Warren's central character, a demagogic Southern politician whose rise and demise deliberately recalls that of Huey Long. Me, I've just read a book about someone called Willie Talos – the name Warren originally wanted until he was talked out of it by his editor. I think the editor was right; as Joyce Carol Oates said in her *NYRB* piece about the restored edition, '"Talos" is a showy, pretentious, rather silly name in the "Stephen Dedalus" tradition, while "Willie Stark" is effective without being an outright nudge in the ribs.' But even

that, I don't think, is the point; the point is that Willie Stark is now
the character's name, whatever the author intended all those years
ago, and whichever name is better is a moot point. I feel as though
I've just read a book about David Copperbottom or Holden
Calderwood or Jay Gatsbergen. You can't mess around with that
stuff, surely? These people exist independently of the books, now
– I have, I now realize, seen countless references to Willie Stark in
reviews and magazine articles, but as the book isn't widely known
or read here in the UK, I had no idea that was who I was reading
about until after I'd finished.

Talos was, apparently, the guardian of Crete, who threw boul-
ders at people attempting to land on the island; he was also a
mechanical man attendant on the Knight of Justice in Spenser's
Faerie Queene. These are both very good reasons why Talos is a
very bad name for a Southern American politician, I would have
thought, and I can imagine that a good editor would have made
the same arguments. Noel Polk, who put this new edition
together, is of the opinion that Warren was badly served by the
editing process; in a reply to Joyce Carol Oates's piece, he claims
that 'many of us are interested in more than a good read', and
that he knows, and Oates doesn't, 'how often well-intentioned
commercial editors have altered novels for the worse'. If I were
Robert Penn Warren's editor, I'd point to a Pulitzer Prize and
sixty years in print as all the vindication I needed; we will never
know whether Polk's version would ever have endured anywhere
near as well. There is even the possibility, of course, that if
Warren had had his way in 1947, there would have been no
interest in any kind of edition in the twenty-first century. I can
see that scholars might want to compare and contrast, but I
notice on Amazon that the long 'un I read now has a movie tie-
in cover. *Caveat emptor.*

I reread John Lukacs's little book on what turned out to be the
biggest decision of the twentieth century – namely, Churchill's

decision not to seek terms with Hitler in May 1940 – because I found it on my bookshelf and realized that the only thing I could remember was Churchill deciding not to seek terms with Hitler in 1940. And I kind of knew that bit before I read it. So this time, I'm going to make a few notes that help make it all stick – it's great, having this column, because I keep the magazines, but I'd probably lose a notebook. Excuse me a moment. Norway defeat brings down Chamberlain; C becomes PM 10/5/1940. Early unpopularity of C in his own party – 'blood, sweat, toil, and tears' speech didn't go down well – 'gangsters' + 'rogue elephant'. Churchill v HALIFAX. Churchill and Lloyd George – wanted him in the Cabinet because LG admired Hitler, who might appoint him if and when . . . Dunkirk: feared max 50,000 evacuated – in the end over 338,000.

Thanks. That'll really help.

Lukacs's book is completely gripping, clear and informative, and corroborates a theory I've been developing recently: the less there is to say about something, the more opaque the writing tends to be. In other words, you hardly ever come across an unreadable book on World War II, but pick up a book on, I don't know, the films of Russ Meyer, and you'll be rereading the same impossible sentence about poststructuralist auteurism three hundred times. People have to overcompensate, you see. And *Five Days in London* also helped give a context for Philip Larkin's early letters, too. Here's Larkin, in 1942: 'If there is any new life in the world today, it is in Germany.' 'Germany will win this war like a dose of salts' (1940). 'And I agree we don't deserve to win' (1942). Lukacs points out that there was a grudging admiration for Hitler's Germany in Britain: we were clapped-out, the old order, whereas Germany was thrusting, energetic, modern. And he also notes that it was the intellectuals – and I suppose Larkin must be categorized thus, despite the farting – who were most prone to defeatism. Ha! That's the Spree, right there. They're very brave when it comes to suspending innocent columnists. But you wait until someone (and my money is on the French) lands on the West Coast. You won't see them for dust.

And the coveted 'Stuff I've Been Reading: Stuff That Stayed Read' award for the non-fiction book of 2005 goes to . . . John Carey, for *What Good Are the Arts?* It's rare, I think, for a writer, maybe for anyone, to feel that he's just read a book that absolutely expresses who he or she is, and what he or she believes, while at the same time recognizing that he or she could not have written any of it. But Carey's book — which in its first two chapters answers the questions 'What is a work of art?' and 'Is high art superior?' — is my new bible, replacing my previous bible, Carey's *The Intellectuals and the Masses.* I couldn't have written it because I — and I'm not alone, by any means — do not have Carey's breadth of reading, nor his calm, wry logic, which enables him to demolish the arguments of just about everyone who has ever talked tosh about objective aesthetic principles. And this group, it turns out, includes anyone who has ever talked about objective aesthetic principles, from Kant onwards. *What Good Are the Arts?* is a very wise book, and a very funny book, but beyond even these virtues, it's a very humane, inclusive and empathetic book: as we all know, it's impossible to talk about 'high' art without insulting the poor, or the young, or those without a university degree, or those who have no taste for, or interest in, Western culture. Carey's approach to the whole sorry mess is the only one that makes any sense. Indeed, while reading it, you become increasingly amazed at the muddle that apparently intelligent people have got themselves into when they attempt to define the importance of — and the superiority of — 'high' culture.

Just after I'd finished it, and I was looking at the world through Carey's eyes, the winner of the 2005 Booker Prize claimed that at least his was a 'proper' book — as if *Green Eggs and Ham* or *Bridget Jones's Diary* weren't proper books. And then, a few days later, the

Guardian's art correspondent launched an astonishing attack on the popular British artist Jack Vettriano: 'Vettriano is not even an artist.' (No, he's just someone who paints pictures and sells them. What do you call those people again?) 'He just happens to be popular, with "ordinary people" . . . I'm not arguing with you, I'm telling you . . . Some things about art are true, and some are false – all of which was easier to explain before we decided popularity was the litmus test of aesthetic achievement . . .'

Oh, man. That's got it all. This is not the time or the place to unravel the snobbery and the unexamined assumptions contained in those few lines; it's easier just to say that nothing about art is true, and nothing is false. And if that's scary, then I'm sorry, but you have to get over it and move on.

I read G. K. Chesterton's *The Man Who Was Thursday* because (*a*) I'd never read a word by Chesterton and (*b*) because I'd decided that from now on I'd only read stuff that John Carey recommends (in his useful little book *Pure Pleasure*). And it was pretty good, although I think that younger readers might get a little frustrated with the plotting. I don't want to give too much away. But say you were an *x*, and you believed that a group of seven people were all not *x*s but *y*s. And then you discovered that the first of these seven was actually an *x*, too. And then you found out the same thing about the second, and then the third. Wouldn't you start to get the idea? Yes, well. Anyway, I can't say anything else about it now other than that it's a novel that fundamentally believes in the decency and the wisdom of us all, and you don't find too many of those. John Carey has now made me buy a book by Kipling, and I didn't think anyone would ever manage that. ✷

MARCH 2006

So this last month was, as I believe you people say, a bust. I had high hopes for it, too; it was Christmastime in England, and I was intending to do a little holiday comfort reading – *David Copperfield* and a couple of John Buchan novels, say, while sipping an egg nog and . . .

Oh, what's the point? No one, I suppose, will remember that I began my March '05 column in this way. And if no one remembers me beginning my March '05 column in this way, then there is even less chance of them remembering that I began my March '04 column in this way, too. The tragedy is that I have come to think of those opening words as a tradition, and I was beginning to hope that you have come to value them as such. I even had a little fantasy that one of your popular entertainers – Stephen Sondheim, say, or Puff Diddle – might have set them to music, and at the beginning of March you all hold hands and sing a song called 'It Was Christmastime in England', to mark the imminent arrival of spring. I am beginning to suspect, however, that this column is making only medium-sized inroads into the American consciousness. (I have had very little feedback from readers in Alabama, for example, and not much more from our Hawaiian subscribers.) I shall keep the tradition going, but more in hope than expectation. It's the New Year here in England, and I'm sorry to say that, because of the apparent indifference of both Puff Diddle and Alabama (the whole state, rather than the band), I am entering 2006 on a somewhat self-doubting and ruminative note.

This last reading month really was a washout, though, for all the usual holiday reasons, so it was as well that, with incredible and atypical foresight, I held a couple of books back from the previous month, just to pad the column out a bit. I met Andrey Kurkov at the Reykjavik Literary Festival and loved the reading he gave from *Death and the Penguin*. (He also sat at the piano and sang a few jolly Ukrainian songs afterwards, thus infuriating one of the writers who had appeared on the same stage earlier in the evening: as I understood it, the Infuriated Writer seemed to think that Kurkov had wilfully and sacrilegiously punctured the solemnity of the occasion. You can see his point, I suppose. You can't mess around with readings by singing after them. The paying public might begin to expect fun at literary events, and then where would writers be? Up shit creek without a paddle, that's where.) I afterwards discovered that *Death and the Penguin* is one of those books that people love unreservedly. The eyes of the assistant in the bookshop lit up when I bought it, and all sorts of people have shown a frankly sickening devotion to the novel whenever I've mentioned it since.

I think I'd sort of presumed that the eponymous penguin was

metaphorical, like both the squid and the whale in *The Squid and the Whale*; my antipathy to the animal kingdom is such that even animal metaphors tend to have a deterrent effect. (What kind of person thinks in animal metaphors? In this day and age?) Imagine my horror, then, when I learned during Kurkov's reading in Reykjavik that the penguin in *Death and the Penguin* is not like the squid or the whale, but, like, an actual penguin. The penguin really is a character, who − pull yourself together, man, *which* − has moods and feelings, and has an integral part in the story, and so on. And, as if the author actually wanted me to hate his novel, it's a cute penguin, too. 'It will be a hard-hearted reader who is not touched by Viktor's relationship with his unusual pet,' says one of the quotes on the back. (Why not just include a blurb saying 'DON'T BUY THIS BOOK'?) And, of course, *Death and the Penguin* turns out to be fresh, funny, clever, incredibly soulful and compelling, and the penguin turns out to be a triumphant creation. I might read only books about animals from now on.

Misha is effectively Viktor's flatmate; Viktor adopted it (I'm not giving in on the pronoun thing) when the failing local zoo was dishing out animals to whomever could afford to feed them, and as Viktor's girlfriend had recently moved out, he was feeling lonely. (Oh, stop it. It's not that sort of book.) Misha, however, turns out to be as depressed as Viktor, and it just sort of wanders about, and occasionally disappears off to its bedroom, like a home-sick teenager on a foreign exchange programme. Viktor, mean-while, has recently started work as an obituarist: he's told to write and stockpile the obituaries of leading local figures, but the obits turn out to be needed earlier than anticipated, and Viktor eventu-ally realizes that his work is somehow bringing about the untimely demise of his subjects.

It's a neat plot, but *Death and the Penguin* isn't a plotty book: Kurkov gives himself plenty of room to breathe (it's actually more of a long, rueful sigh) and that's pretty cool in and of itself. This is a literary novel – Kurkov loves his weltschmerz as much as the next guy – but he doesn't see why weltschmerz shouldn't come bundled up with a narrative that kicks a little bit of ass. Sometimes it seems as though everything in the arts (and I include sports in the arts) is about time and space – giving yourself room to move, finding the time to play . . . My copy of *Death and the Penguin* is two hundred and twenty-eight pages long, and yet it never seems overstuffed, or underpowered, and it manages to be about an awful lot, and it never ever forgets or overlooks gesture or detail. And I already said it was funny, didn't I? What more do you want? At that length, you couldn't even reasonably want less.

Jennie Erdal's *Ghosting* is a book about writing, so, you know, if you don't want to read it because you're a plumber or a chiropodist, then I quite understand. If I were you, I would resent the repeated implication, by publishers and books pages, that my profession is more interesting than yours. Unlike most books about writing, though, this one contains a narrative that is both genuinely gripping and eccentric. Jennie Erdal was employed by a flamboyant London publisher, the sort of man who is often described as 'larger than life'. (In other words, run for the hills! And don't look back!) She began as a translator, and then worked on a huge book of interviews this guy conducted with women; finally, she wrote two novels for him. They were his novels – his name, and his name alone, was on the title page – but according to Erdal, the author took only a passing interest in their conception and execution.

His first novel, he decides, will be both thrilling and very romantic: '"It *has* to be a love story. People associate me with love . . ."' When his amanuensis asks whether he has any notion of the characters who might populate this thrilling love story, he is precise and unequivocal: they must be '"a man and a woman. Do you think I could write about *poofters*?"'

So away Jennie Erdal goes, and writes a novel, and the

flamboyant publisher publishes it, and it gets respectful reviews – partly because the flamboyant publisher is a respected figure, and partly, one suspects, because Erdal can clearly write. And, rather than breathe a huge sigh of relief, he decides to 'write' another, although this one turns out to have a higher, tighter concept than the first: he wants it to be about two women, cousins born on the same day, who are so close that when one achieves orgasm, so does the other. Pretty good, you have to admit, and as Erdal seems, inexplicably, to have ignored the idea, it's still going begging.

Ghosting is a strange and rather wonderful book, and it makes you think about all sorts of things connected with writing and the notion of authorship. The truth is, however, that it's old news. Almost nobody writes their own books these days; indeed, to do so is seen as a mark of failure in literary circles. Of course, the young have no choice, and there are, apparently, a few renegades who insist on churning out word after word: the word on the literary street is that Michael Chabon wrote every word of *The Amazing Adventures of Kavalier and Clay*, for example, presumably out of some misguided and outdated notion of honesty. But the rest of us don't really bother. I have always used an old lady called Violet, who lives in a cottage in Cornwall, in the far west of England, and who is an absolute treasure. She's getting better, too.

For some reason, I found myself up a ladder in Strand Books in NYC a couple of months ago, looking to see whether they had any copies of old William Cooper novels. I know that Philip Larkin mentions him in his letters, but there may have been another nudge from somewhere, too. Whatever the motivation, I was led as if by magic to a beautiful 1961 Scribner hardback which cost me six dollars, and which contained Cooper's first and third novels, *Scenes from Provincial Life* and *Scenes from Married Life*, published in the US as *Scenes from Life*.

I'd read them both before, twenty or more years ago, and I remembered them as being particularly important to me, although

I wouldn't have been able to articulate why. Now I can see it: Joe Lunn, the hero of these books (and Cooper's thinly disguised *alter ego*), is, in the first book at least, a schoolteacher who has ambitions to make his living from writing, and that's exactly the situation I found myself in when my sister gave me the books as a Christmas present in what must have been '82 or '83, seeing as those were the only years I was in full-time gainful employment in a school. I don't think I managed to see the connection at the time. Really. I thought I'd been enjoying them for other reasons (they are incredibly enjoyable books). I thought I should own up to that, just to help you gauge the soundness of all the other literary judgements I make on these pages.

The reason that *Scenes from Metropolitan Life*, the second novel in the sequence, isn't included in the edition I bought is that it wasn't published until 1982, even though it was written in the 1950s; Cooper's work was so autobiographical that he was threatened with legal action by the real-life version of the young woman who is Joe's girlfriend in the first book and his mistress in the second. (Is that right? The thing is, she gets married in between the two, although he doesn't. Can you have a mistress if you're not married? Can you be a mistress if your lover isn't married? Is there a useful handbook you can look these things up in?) Publication of *Scenes from Metropolitan Life* was only possible after her death, and in the meantime Cooper's career had lost all the momentum it built up after the success of the first novel. All his books are out of print now.

Scenes from Provincial Life is a lovely novel, sweet-natured, and surprisingly frank about sexual relationships, considering the book is set in 1939: Joe has a weekend cottage which he shares with a friend, and where a lot of the book is set. Joe sleeps with Myrtle, the litigious girlfriend, there; Joe's friend Tom uses it for trysts with his seventeen-year-old boyfriend Steve. See what I mean? Who knew anyone had sex in 1939, in a provincial town? Well, we all did, I suppose, but in Larkin's words, 'sexual intercourse began / in 1963' – or at least, twentieth-century mainstream British artistic representations of it did – so it's weird to read what is effectively a Kingsley Amis–style comedy of sexual manners which also talks about Chamberlain at Munich.

If *Scenes from Metropolitan Life* is a little less successful, it's partly because all the characters are a little older, and a little sadder, and they take their jobs more seriously, and those jobs are a little more dull: Joe is a civil servant in the second book. He's still trying to make up his mind whether to marry Myrtle, but Myrtle's married already, to someone stationed in Palestine, and Cooper's insouciance doesn't really seem to take the sadness of any of that on board. (My pristine secondhand copy came from my Amazon Marketplace seller with Kingsley Amis's 1982 *Sunday Times* review tucked neatly into the dust jacket, by the way. Kingsley loved the first one but gave the second a reluctant thumbs-down.) I've just started the third, and Joe's nearly forty, still single, and still looking, and you're beginning to suspect that there might actually be something wrong with him that he's not owning up to. It's hard, trying to be funny about getting older. *Scenes from Provincial Life* can afford to be cute and fresh because the characters have so little at stake; but then we grow older, more tired, more cynical, more worried; and then we die. And where's the joke in that? Oh. Ha. I've just seen it. It's pretty good.

Happy March, dear *Believer* readers. I hope you have a fantastic ten months. ✶

A *selection from*

GHOSTING

by JENNIE ERDAL

✳ ✳ ✳

I t is 1994 and we are off to France once again. This time we are
going there to write a novel. The publication of several non-
fiction books has brought Tiger a sense of fulfilment, but there has
been no lasting contentment. As the ancients knew and understood, pleasure is transient; it comes, it is savoured, and it goes.
Descartes thought that the secret of happiness was to be satisfied
with what you know you can have, and not to hanker after something you can't have. But Tiger differs from both the ancients and
Descartes in his belief that almost anything is attainable provided
you pay for it, and that by setting the sights high the chances of
pleasure being permanent are correspondingly high.

And so, from one moment to the next, anything can happen. A
moment ago a sixth volume of interviews was published, attended
by a good deal of media interest, favourable reviews, and another
round of newspaper profiles. In the *Daily Telegraph* Allan Massie
described Tiger as 'masterly and sympathetic, the most self-effacing
of interviewers and yet able to speak as an equal'. Robert Kee
called him 'a magician interviewer of the highest order'. William
Trevor wrote: 'Making real people real at second hand isn't as easy
as it seems . . . it's the subtlety of interrogation that ensures these
portraits emerge.' Tiger purred with pleasure. Everything was well
in the world. The next moment we are writing a novel and the
landscape has changed. *Sic transit Gloria mundi.*

Tiger is convinced that the way ahead 'for us' lies in a different
sort of publication. Interviews, newspaper articles, book reviews
are all very well, but *the real test* is the novel. He lowers his voice

at this point, enunciating each word slowly, a sure sign of scarcely
being able to contain his excitement, elongating the word *real* to a
disturbing length. He is captivated by the idea. This is not a whim.
I know the difference between a whim and a serious proposition.
This is a serious proposition. He will not be dissuaded. The tiger
is not for turning. I feel the familiar panic pitching its tent somewhere in my lower abdomen.

'We need to evolve,' he says.

I do not demur.

How to write a novel? How to write someone else's novel?
These two questions seem absolutely central. I wonder how I have
arrived at this point without actually meaning to.

'What sort of novel are we thinking about?' I ask.

We are in the British Airways Executive Lounge at London
Gatwick airport en route to France. The writing will be done in
France. According to Tiger, France is the best place in the world
to create a work of literature. Evidently we will have everything
we need: the best food, the finest wine, a high-tech music system,
a studio to work in, the fresh Dordogne air.

'We are thinking about a beautiful novel, very beautiful,' he says,
and he looks somewhere into the middle distance, smiling rapturously, already transported by the sheer imagined beauty of it. 'And
it will have a beautiful cover. We will make sure of that.' He taps
out the last six words on the table.

'But what genre are we talking about? Are we thinking of a
romantic novel? A thriller? (These conversations are always
conducted in the first person plural. The idiosyncratic use of
pronouns is part of the charade and has become second nature.)

'It will be thrilling, oh yes. And also romantic. *Very* romantic.
Oh, yes.'

'So, a love story then?'

'But of course! It *has* to be a love story. People associate me
with love. I am *famous* for love. Isn't it?'

In certain circumstances, the plural pronoun would switch abruptly to the singular, from *we* to *I*, from *us* to *me*. There is always a compelling reason for the shift. In this instance, the snag is that people do not associate *me* with love. Unlike Tiger, I am not famous for love.

There is a long pause. The matter might have ended there, but for my need to establish the broad nature of the project. I have to ask some more. Tiger is almost certainly concentrating on the finished product, beautifully bound and wrapped in a seductive dust-jacket. My only concern is how the finished product will be arrived at.

'What sort of love story do we have in mind?' I ask, as if we are discussing wallpaper or home furnishings and he has to pick one from a limited range. 'Is the love requited or unrequited?'

'Definitely requited. Oh yes, very requited.'

'And who are the characters?'

Even by our standards this is becoming an odd exchange.

'Sweetie,' he says, the tone long-suffering, humouring an imbecile. He takes hold of my hand in a kindness-to-dumb-animals sort of way. 'It *has* to be the love between a man and a woman. Do you think I could write about *poofters*? No, it has to be a man and a woman – a beautiful woman and very sexy. There will be lots of sex, but very distinguished. We will do the sex beautifully. Isn't it?'

'Long? Short?' I'm feeling desperate now.

He strokes his chin, weighing up the possibilities.

'Not too long, not too short.'

'And do we have a story line? Do we have any idea of what it is *about*?'

'Of course, beloved! I have thought of *everything*.' He squeals the last word in a spasm of exuberance. 'Let me tell you the idea. It is very simple. There is a man . . . he is like me somewhat . . . he is married . . . he falls in love with a woman . . . there is a *huge* passion . . . and then . . . well, we will see what happens after that, isn't it?'

There is another pause while I weigh things up. Then:

'Does he tell his wife? About the huge passion, I mean.'

'Darling, are you *mad*?' Tiger points a finger to his temple and screws it from side to side. 'Why would he tell her? Why would he hurt her?'

APRIL 2006

BOOKS BOUGHT:
* *Eustace and Hilda* – L. P. Hartley
* *Moondust* – Andrew Smith
* *Darkness Falls from the Air* – Nigel Balchin
* *1599: A Year in the Life of William Shakespeare* – James Shapiro

BOOKS READ:
* *The Dirt* – Mötley Crüe
* *The Shrimp and the Anemone* – L. P. Hartley
* *The Poet* – Michael Connelly
* *Then We Came to the End* – Joshua Ferris

'**C**haracter is fate.' *Discuss with reference to Eustace Cherrington in* The Shrimp and the Anemone *and Nikki Sixx in* The Dirt.

(It occurred to me that with the exam season coming up, younger readers might actually prefer this format for the column. I don't know how many of you are studying L. P. Hartley's *The Shrimp and the Anemone* in conjunction with *The Dirt* – probably not many. But even if it's only a couple of hundred, I'll feel as though I've provided some kind of public service. Please feel free to lift as much of the following as you need.)

In many ways, Eustace Cherrington – the younger half of the

brother-sister combo in Hartley's *Eustace and Hilda* trilogy – and Nikki Sixx, the Crüe's bass player, are very different people. Eustace is a young boy, and Nikki Sixx is a grown man; Eustace is English, middle-class and fictional, and Nikki Sixx is working-class, American and (according to the internet at least) a real person. *The Shrimp and the Anemone* is a very beautiful novel, full of delicate people and filigree observation, whereas *The Dirt* is possibly the ugliest book ever written. And yet Eustace and Nikki Sixx both, each in their own ways, somehow manage to disprove Heraclitus's maxim – or at any rate, they demand its modification. Both Hartley's novel and the Crüe bio remind us it's not *character* but *constitution* that determines our destinies. Eustace is, let's face it, a weed and a wuss. He's got a weak heart, so he can't go out much, and when he eventually steels himself to take part in a paper chase with the delectable but destructive Nancy, he collapses with exhaustion and takes to his sickbed for months. Nikki Sixx, however, is made of sterner stuff. When he ODs on heroin in LA and nearly dies – a journalist phones one of his bandmates for an obituary – what does he do? He gets home, pulls a lump of heroin out of the medicine cabinet, and ODs again. Thus we can see that Nikki Sixx and Eustace Cherrington live the lives that their bodies allow them to live. Nothing really matters, apart from this. Why do some of us read a lot of books and watch a lot of TV instead of play in Mötley Crüe? Because we haven't got the stomachs for it. It's as simple as that.

It was a mistake, reading *The Dirt* straight after *The Shrimp and the Anemone*. (Is it just a coincidence, by the way, that whole shrimp/anemone/squid/whale combo? Because even though Hartley's sea creatures are little ones, unlike writer-director Noah Baumbach's monsters, they serve pretty much the same metaphorical function: the novel opens with a gruesome and symbolic battle to the death. Anyway, where's the meat? Can anyone think of a way to get a little artistic surf'n'turf action going?) *The Dirt* shat and puked and pissed all over the memory of poor Eustace's defenceless introspection – indeed, so grotesque are the characters and narrative events described in the Mötley Crüe book that it's very difficult to see any ideal circumstance in which to read it. I certainly recommend not reading anything for a month before, because the strong flavours of Nikki, Tommy Lee and the other two will overwhelm pretty much any other literary delicacy you may have consumed; and you probably won't want to read any fiction for a month after-wards because it will be hard to see the point. There are moments in *The Dirt* that render any attempts to explain the intricate workings of the human heart redundant, because there are no intricate workings of the human heart, clearly. There are only naked groupies, and endless combinations of class-A drugs, and booze, and covers of 'Smokin' in the Boys' Room'. And what have you got to say about all that, Anita Brookner? No. I thought not. There is one moment in *The Dirt* so disturbingly repellent that it haunts me still, but I'm unsure whether to quote it or not, for obvious reasons. What I think I'll do is reproduce the offending line in tiny writing, and if you want to read it, you'll have to go and fetch a magnifying glass – that way, you have participated in your own corruption. I advise you not to bother. This, then, from the early days:

We'd scrounge up enough money to buy an egg burrito from Noggles. Then we'd line the sand off and stick our dicks into the warm meat to cover up the smell of pussy, so the our girlfriends didn't know we were fucking anything stupid or drunk enough to get into Tommy's van.

I'm afraid I have various questions about this. In America, are showers not cheaper than egg burritos? Does Noggles itself (we don't even have the establishment here in England, let alone the Noggles-associated behaviour) not have a washroom? And didn't the girlfriends ever wonder . . . actually, forget it. We've gone far enough. It could be, of course, that this episode is a fabrication, but without wishing to add to the contemporary furore about the falsification of real lives, I'd argue that this is of a whole new order: anyone depraved enough to imagine this is certainly depraved enough to do it.

So why read it at all? Well, I read it because my friend Erin gave it to me for Christmas, and she had taken quite a lot of trouble to track down a nice hardback copy. Why Erin thought this was an appropriate gift with which to commemorate the birth of our Lord I'm not sure; why she thought that it was an appropriate gift for me is even less clear and somewhat more troubling. Certain passages, it is true, were uncannily reminiscent of certain nights on my last book tour, especially the Midwest readings. I had hoped that what went on there was a secret between me and the women whose names began with the letters A through E (so many broken-hearted Felicitys!) at the signings in question, but clearly not.

And weirdly, *The Dirt* isn't a bad book. For a start, it's definitive, if you're looking for the definitive book on vile, abusive, misogynistic behaviour: if there are any worse stories than this in rock and roll, they aren't worth telling, because the human mind would not be capable of comprehending them without the aid of expert gynaecological and pharmaceutical assistance. It's very nicely put together, too. *The Dirt* is an oral biography in the tradition of *Please Kill Me,* and Neil Strauss, the Studs Terkel of hair metal, has a good ear for the band's self-delusions, idiocies and fuck-ups. Strauss, one suspects, has class. (Wilkie Collins provides the book's epigraph, for example, and I'm guessing that this wasn't Tommy Lee's idea.) 'I decided to have the name of the album, *Till Death Do Us Part,* carved into my arm,' recalls the hapless John Corabi, who replaced singer Vince Neil for one unsuccessful album. 'Soon afterward they changed the name of the album to just *Mötley Crüe.*' Unexpectedly, *The Dirt* contains real pain, too. None of these characters have childhoods that one might envy, and their adult lives seem every bit as bleak and as joyless – especially if you are cursed with a constitution that prevents anything more than an occasional night in the Bank of Friendship.

The real victim here, however, is *The Shrimp and the Anemone*, which never stood a chance. It was fantastic, too. I picked it up after my friend Wesley Stace, whose first novel *Misfortune* has been picking up a distressing amount of attention, recommended it. (Not personally, of course – he's beyond that now. He gave it a mention in a *Guardian* questionnaire.) I'm going to read the whole *Eustace and Hilda* trilogy, and I'll write about it more when I've finished. Suffice to say that after last month's entirely felicitous William Cooper experience, I'm happy with my run of lost mid-century minor classics. And just as, a while back, I vowed only to read things recommended by Professor John Carey, I am now determined only to read things blurbed by John Betjeman. He is quoted on the back of *Eustace and Hilda*, just as he is on *Scenes from Provincial Life*, and on Nigel Balchin's *Darkness Falls from the Air*, purchased this month after a tip-off. He was missing from the jacket of the Crüe book, which should have served as a warning. He clearly didn't like it much.

I was not able to heed my own advice and take time out after rubbing my nose in *The Dirt*: this column, as Nikki Sixx would say, is insatiable, a nymphomaniac, and I had to press on. I couldn't return to Hartley, for obvious reasons, so I went with Michael Connolly's clever serial killer – I needed the moral disgust that thriller writers cannot avoid when dealing with dismembered children, etc. There was one twist too many for me at the end, but other than that, *The Poet* did a difficult post-Crüe job well. I did end up thinking about how evolving technology makes things tough for contemporary crime-writers, though. *The Poet* was first published in 1996 and contains an unfortunate explanation of the concept of digital photography that even my mum would now find redundant; the novel ends with an enigma that DNA testing would render bathetically unenigmatic within seconds. Filmmakers hate setting movies in the recent past, that awkward time when things are neither 'period' nor contemporary. The recent past just looks wrong. Characters have cell phones the size of bricks and listen to music on Discmen. The same principle applies here: at these moments, *The Poet* feels anachronistic. Surely people who know their way around a laptop can do a spot of DNA testing? But no. I now see why my thriller-writing brother-in-law has run off to ancient Rome and barricaded himself in. He's not daft.

Still trying to dispel the memory of the egg burrito, I picked up Andrew Smith's *Moondust*, a book about what happened to the astronauts who walked on the moon after they fell to earth, on the grounds that you wouldn't be able to see Nikki Sixx from space. (And even if you could, you wouldn't be able to see what he was doing.) I put it down again in order to read a proof copy of a terrific first novel, Joshua Ferris's *Then We Came to the End*. Young Ferris and I share a publisher, and *Then We Came to the End* came with a ringing endorsement from a colleague. She wasn't after a blurb – she just talked with infectious and intriguing enthusiasm about the book, and this enthusiasm is entirely understandable. This book is going to attract a lot of admiration when it comes out later this year. I'm glad I read it before everybody else, because I would otherwise have been deterred by the hype (and here 'hype' is an envious and dismissive substitute for 'praise', which is how the word is usually used).

The author will, I suspect, become sick of descriptions of his novel, all of which will use the word 'meets', or possibly the phrase 'rewritten by'. As *Then We Came to the End* has not been published yet, however, he is unlikely to be sick of them yet, so I can splurge. It's *The Office* meets Kafka. It's *Seinfeld* rewritten by Donald Barthelme. It's *Office Space* reimagined by Nicholson . . . Oh, that'll do. The book is written in the first-person plural (as in 'we', for those who never got the hang of declining nouns), and I was reminded of Barthelme because of his two brilliant stories 'Our Work and Why We Do It' and 'Some of Us Had Been Threatening Our Friend Colby', neither of which is narrated in the first-person plural, but which, as you may have noticed, refer to 'us' or 'we' in the titles. So you could be forgiven for thinking that the resemblance is somewhat superficial. Barthelme, however, did have the very great gift of being able to make the mundane seem mysterious, and Ferris can do that when he wants to: his novel is set in an advertising office, and the rhythms and substance of a working day are slowly revealed to have the rhythms and substance of life itself. The novel, almost incidentally, feels utterly authentic in its depiction of office life – a rare achievement in fiction, seeing as most writers have never done a proper day's work in their lives – but the authenticity is not the point of it, because underneath the politicking and the sackings and the petty jealousies you can hear something else: the sound of our lives (that collective pronoun again) ticking away. And before I put you off, I should add that the novel is awfully funny, in both senses of the phrase. It's about cancer, totem poles, Emerson and grief, among many other things, and you should preorder it now. It's our sort of book.

Oh, but what do any of these things matter? Is it really possible that Mötley Crüe have destroyed all the literature in the world, everything that came before them, and everything written since? I rather fear it is. Please don't go looking for that magnifying glass. Save yourself while there's still time. ✲

A *selection from*

THEN WE CAME TO THE END

by JOSHUA FERRIS

✳ ✳ ✳

You Don't Know What's in My Heart

We were fractious and overpaid. Our mornings lacked promise. At least those of us who smoked had something to look forward to at ten fifteen. Most of us liked most everyone, a few of us hated specific individuals, one or two people loved everyone and everything. Those who loved everyone were unanimously reviled. We loved free bagels in the morning. They happened all too infrequently. Our benefits were astonishing in comprehensiveness and quality of care. Sometimes we questioned whether they were worth it. We thought moving to India might be better, or going back to nursing school. Doing something with the handicapped or working with our hands. No one ever acted on these impulses, despite their daily, sometimes hourly, contractions. Instead we met in conference rooms to discuss the issues of the day.

Ordinarily jobs came in and we completed them in a timely and professional manner. Sometimes fuck ups did occur. Printing errors, transposed numbers. Our business was advertising and details were important. If the third number after the second hyphen in a client's toll-free number was a six instead of an eight, and if it went to print like that, and showed up in *Time* magazine, no one reading the ad could call now and order today. No matter that they could go to the web site, we still had to eat the price of the ad. Is this boring you yet? It bored us every day. Our boredom was ongoing, a collective boredom, and it would never die because we would never die.

Lynn Mason was dying of cancer. She was a partner in the agency. Dying? It was uncertain. She was in her early forties. Breast cancer. No one could identify exactly how everyone had come to know this fact. Was it a fact? Some people called it rumor. But in fact there was no such thing as rumor. There was fact, and then there was what did not come up in conversation. Breast cancer was controllable if caught in the early stages but Lynn may have waited too long. We recalled looking at Frank Brizzolera and thinking he had six months, tops. Old Brizz, we called him. He smoked like a fiend. He stood outside the building in the most inclement weather, absorbing Old Golds in nothing but a sweater vest. Then and only then, he looked indomitable. When he returned inside, nicotine stink preceded him as he walked down the hall, where it lingered long after he entered his office. He began to cough, and from our own offices we heard the working-up of solidified lung sediment. Some people put him on their Celebrity Death Watch every year because of the coughing, even though he wasn't an official celebrity. He knew it, too, he knew he was on death watch, and that certain wagering individuals would profit from his death. He knew it because he was one of us, and we knew everything.

We didn't know who was stealing things from other people's workstations. Always small items – postcards, framed photographs. We had our suspicions but no proof. We believed it was probably being done not for the loot so much as the excitement – the shoplifter's addictive kick, or maybe it was a pathological cry for attention. Hank Neary, one of the agency's only black writers, asked, 'Come on – who could want my travel toothbrush?'

We didn't know who was responsible for putting the sushi roll behind Joe Pope's bookshelf. The first couple of days Joe had no clue about the sushi. Then he started taking furtive sniffs at his pits, and holding the wall of his palm to his mouth to get blowback from his breath. By the end of the week, he was certain it wasn't him. We were smelling it, too. Persistent, high in the nostrils, it became worse than a dying animal. Joe's gorge rose every time he entered his office. The following week the smell was so atrocious the building people got involved, hunting the office for what turned out to be a sunshine roll – tuna, whitefish, salmon, and sprouts. Mike Boroshansky, the chief of security, kept bringing his tie up to his nose, as if he were a real cop at the scene of a murder.

We thanked each other. It was customary after every exchange. Our thanks were never disingenuous or ironic. We said thanks for getting this done so quickly, thanks for putting in so much effort. We had a meeting and when a meeting was over, we said thank you to the meeting-makers for having made the meeting. Very rarely did we say anything negative or derogatory about meetings. We all knew there was a good deal of pointlessness to nearly all the meetings and in fact one meeting out of every three or four was nearly perfectly without gain or purpose but many meetings revealed the one thing that was necessary and so we attended them and afterward we thanked each other.

Karen Woo always had something new to tell us and we hated her guts for it. She would start talking and our eyes would glaze over. Might it be true, as we sometimes feared on the commute home, that we were callous, unfeeling individuals, incapable of sympathy, and full of spite toward people for no reason other than their proximity and familiarity? We had these sudden revelations that we were far from our better selves. Should we quit? Would that solve it? Or were those qualities innate, dooming us to nastiness and paucity of spirit? We hoped not.

Marcia Dwyer became famous for sending an e-mail to Genevieve Latko-Devine. Marcia often wrote to Genevieve after meetings. 'It is really irritating to work with irritating people,' she wrote once. There she ended it and waited for Genevieve's response. Usually when she heard back from Genevieve, instead of writing her again, which would take too long – Marcia was an art director, not a writer – she would head down to Genevieve's office, close the door, and the two women would talk. The only thing bearable about the irritating event involving the irritating person was the thought of telling it all to Genevieve, who would understand better than anyone else. Marcia could have called her mother, her mother would have listened. She could have called one of her four brothers, any one of those South side crowbars would have been more than happy to beat up the irritating person. But they would not have understood. They would have sympathized, but that was not the same thing. Marcia needed understanding, and Genevieve would only need to nod for Marcia to know that she was getting through. Did we not all understand the essential need for someone to understand? But the e-mail Marcia got back was not from Genevieve. It was from Jim Jackers. 'Are you talking about me?' he wrote. Amber Ludwig wrote, 'I'm not Genevieve.' Benny Shassburger wrote, 'I think you goofed.' Tom Mota wrote, 'Ha!' Marcia was mortified. She got sixty-five e-mails in two minutes. One from HR cautioned her about the dangers of sending private e-mails. Jim wrote a second time. 'Can you please tell me – is it me, Marcia? Am I the irritating person you're talking about?'

Marcia wanted to eat Jim's heart because some mornings he shuffled up to the elevators and greeted us by saying, 'What up, my niggas?' He meant it ironically in an effort to be funny but he was just not the man to pull it off. It made us cringe, especially Marcia, especially if Hank was present.

In those days it was rare that someone pushed someone else down the hall really fast in a swivel chair. Most of the time there were long, long pauses during which we could hear ourselves breathe as we bent over our individual desks, working on some task at hand, lost to ourselves – a long pause before Benny, bored, came and stood in the doorway. 'What are you doing?' he'd ask.

It could have been any of us. 'Working,' was the usual reply.

Then Benny would tap his topaz class ring on the doorway and drift away.

How we hated our coffee mugs! Our mouse pads, our desk clocks, our daily calendars, all the contents of our desk drawers. Even the photos of our loved ones taped to our computer monitors for uplift and support turned to cloying reminders of time served. But when we got a new office, a bigger office, and we brought everything with us into the new office, how we loved everything all over again, and thought hard about where to place things, and looked with satisfaction at the end of the day at how well our old things looked in this new, improved, important space. There was no doubt in our minds just then that we had made all the right decisions, whereas most days we were men and women of two minds. Everywhere you looked, in the hallways and bathrooms, the coffee bar and cafeteria, the lobbies and the print stations, there we were with our two minds.

There seemed to be only the one electronic pencil sharpener in the whole damn place.

MAY 2006

I have a bookshelf over my bed, which is where I put the Books Bought and others that I have a serious intention of reading one day. And inevitably, over time, some of these are pronounced dead, and taken gently and respectfully either to the living room shelves downstairs, if they are hardbacks, or the paperback bookcase immediately outside the bedroom door, where they are allowed to rest in peace. (Do we have a word for something that looked like a good idea once? I hope so.) I'm sure you all knew this, but in fact books never die – it's just that I am clearly not very good at finding a pulse. I have learned this from my two younger children, who have taken to pulling books off the shelves within their reach and dropping them on the floor. Obviously I try not to notice, because noticing might well entail bending down to pick them up. But when I have finally and reluctantly concluded that no one else is going to do it, the book or books in my hand frequently look great – great and unread – and they are thus returned to the bookshelf over the bed. It's a beautiful, if circular, system, something like the process of convectional rainfall: interest evaporates, and the books are reduced to so much hot air, so they rise, you know, sideways, or even downstairs, but then blah blah and they fall to the ground . . . something like, anyway, although perhaps not exactly like.

This is precisely how Michael Ondaatje's *Running in the Family* was recently rediscovered. It turns out that I own a beautiful little Bloomsbury Classics hardback, as attractive to a small child, clearly, as it was to me. Indeed it's so attractive that it wasn't even placed back on the bookshelf over the bed: I began reading it fresh off the floor, as if it weren't rainfall after all, but a ripe, juicy . . . enough with the inoperable imagery. *Running in the Family* is a fever dream of a book, delirious, saturated with colour; it's a travel book, and a family history, and a memoir, and it's funny and unforgettable. Ondaatje grew up in Sri Lanka, then called Ceylon, and it would not be unkind to describe his father as nuts – now and again, dangerously so. He pretended to have gone to Cambridge University (he sailed to England, stayed in Cambridge for the requisite three years, read a lot, and hung out with students without ever bothering to enrol); he was banned from the Ceylon Railways after hijacking a train, knocking out his travelling companion, who happened to be the future Prime Minister of the country, and bringing the entire railway system to a standstill; he was a part-time alcoholic, prone to epic drinking bouts, who buried scores of bottles of gin in the back garden for emergencies.

Ondaatje helps us to float over all this emotional landscape so that it feels as if we were viewing it from a hot-air balloon on a perfect day; someone with a different temperament (or someone much younger, someone who still felt raw) could have written – and been forgiven for writing – something darker and more troubling. 'I showed what you had written to someone and they laughed and said what a wonderful childhood we must have had, and I said it was a nightmare,' says an unnamed sibling at the end of the book, which tells you pretty much all you need to know about the theory and practice of memoir: it ain't the meat, it's the motion. The passage describing the death of Lalla, Ondaatje's grandmother, who was swept away in a flood, is one of the most memorable accounts of someone's last moments that I can remember. I'm grateful to my children for all sorts of things, of course, things that will inevitably come to me immediately after I have finished this column and sent it off; but I'm extremely grateful that one of them dropped this wonderful book on the floor. Actually, that may well be it, in terms of what my sons have given me, which puts a different complexion on the experience. I loved *Running in the Family*, and I mean the author no disrespect. But it's not much to show for twelve years of fatherhood, really, is it?

I've been losing a lot of books recently, so I am glad that nature has been bountiful, whether that bounty takes the form of fruit or rain. I have no idea where I've put *Eustace and Hilda*, the L. P. Hartley trilogy I was reading and loving, and Andrew Smith's book about the Apollo astronauts, *Moondust*, which I started and stopped a while back, was missing for most of this month, and as a consequence I haven't quite finished it. (It turned up in a drawer.) Lots of people are reading it here at the moment – it's a Richard and Judy book, Richard and Judy being our equivalent of Oprah – which is both weird and great, because in many ways *Moondust* is an eccentric book, with a set of references (Bowie, Neil Young, Updike, Rufus Wainwright, Eric Hobsbawm) that perfectly reflect the author's interests without necessarily reflecting the tastes of a mass reading public.

Smith knows that his obsession with the moon landings is about something else, and he is particularly good at teasing out the personal and global meanings of the Apollo missions – hell, there are even a few cosmic meanings in there – without ever sounding mad or pretentious. The author argues that when Apollo died in 1972, the dreams of the '60s died with it (and David Bowie is quoted as saying that the '70s were the start of the twenty-first century, which means that the twentieth century, perhaps uniquely, contained only seven decades), and there's a nostalgia for what the future used to represent and no longer can, and there's all sorts of stuff about ageing and ambition. Despite the astronauts' protestations to the contrary, it's clearly been a struggle, flying to the moon and back in your thirties and forties, and then having to live out the rest of your life earthbound.

There's something in *Moondust* that I'd never thought about before, and it's haunted me ever since I read it. I had always felt rather sorry for Michael Collins, Richard Gordon and the other four guys who flew all the way to the moon but then had to stay in the Command Module. I'd always had them down as close-but-no-cigar Pete Best types, doomed to be remembered for all time as unlucky. And yet their Apollo mission was surely every bit as extraordinary as those of the guys who got to put up flags and drive around in little golf buggies: forty-seven minutes of each lunar orbit that the Command Module took was spent on the far side of the moon, 'out of sight and unreachable and utterly, utterly alone'. The six Pete Bests were, as one NASA employee put it, the loneliest men 'since Adam'. Charles Lindbergh actually wrote to Collins, saying that walking on the moon was all very well, 'but it seems to me that you had an experience of in some ways greater profundity'. I find that it takes most of my courage simply to contemplate their pitch-black solitude. The closest I have ever come, I think, was last Christmas Day, when I walked round the corner to buy cigarettes and my whole neighbourhood was utterly deserted. I'm not suggesting for a moment that my existential terror rivalled theirs, but it was a pretty creepy couple of minutes, and I was certainly glad to see the guy in the shop.

There are now nine people in the world who have walked on the moon, and unless something dramatic happens (and I'm talking about a governmental rethink rather than a cure for death), it won't be too long before there are none. That might not mean anything to a lot of you, because you are, I am led to understand, young people, and the moonwalks didn't happen in your lifetime. (How can you be old enough to read the *Believer* and not old enough to have seen Neil Armstrong live? What's happening to the world?) But it means a lot to me, and Andrew Smith, and when the Apollo missions, the future as we understood it, become history, then something will be lost from our psyches. But what do you care? Oh, go back to your hip-hop and your computer games and your promiscuity. (Or your virginity. I forget which one your generation is into at the moment.)

Kurt Vonnegut's *A Man Without a Country* was an oddly fitting companion to Smith's book, perhaps because the quirky humanist hope that one used to discern in Vonnegut's novels – several of which were written just as men were trying to get to the moon, and which frequently took an extraterrestrial view of our planet – is all but extinguished here. It's a charming, funny, wise little book, of course, because Vonnegut is incapable of writing anything that doesn't possess these qualities, but it's sad, too. Perhaps the questionable advantage of old age – Vonnegut is in his eighties now – is that you can see that hope is chimerical, and *A Man Without a Country* is devastatingly gloomy about the mess we have made of the world. I know he's right, but there is something in me, something callow and unrealistic (and something connected with the little boys who pull books off the shelves and drop them on the floor), that stops me from *feeling* that he's right. It has a very good smoking joke in it, though, this book. 'Here's the news,' says Vonnegut. 'I am going to sue the Brown & Williamson Tobacco Company, manufacturers of Pall Mall cigarettes, for a billion bucks! Starting when I was only twelve years old, I have never chain-smoked anything but unfiltered Pall Malls. And for many years now, right on the package, Brown & Williamson have promised to kill me. But I am now eighty-two. Thanks a lot, you dirty rats.'

It's been kind of a gloomy month, all in all, because Marjane Satrapi's two brilliant, heartbreaking graphic novels, *Persepolis: The Story of a Childhood* and *Persepolis 2: The Story of a Return*, aren't likely to lift the spirits, either. The story of Satrapi's childhood is also the story of the Iranian revolution, so she witnessed one violent and repressive regime replacing another; I got the same feeling I had while reading Jung Chang's *Wild Swans*, that the events described are so fantastical, so surreal and horrific, that they no longer seem to belong to the real world but to some metaphorical Orwellian dystopia. We know very little of the real world, though, those of us who live in the US and Europe, just our small and relatively benign corner of it, and though we can see that the Guardians of the Revolution are human, just like us, it's pretty hard to find a way in to their humanity. Satrapi follows the trail of blood that leads from the overthrow of the Shah, through the fatuous and tragic war with Iraq, and on to the imprisonment, torture and eventual murder of the leftists who helped bring about his downfall. And as the free-thinking daughter of left-leaning parents, Satrapi is able to use the small frames of her own life to create the bigger picture without contrivance or omission. (If the first book is slightly more successful than the second, it's because Satrapi spent some of the 1980s in Austria, so her personal and national histories take divergent paths.)

Satrapi draws in stark black-and-white blocks which bring to mind some of Eric Gill's woodcuts, and these blocks quickly begin to make perfect sense; in fact, it would be pretty hard not to draw post-revolutionary Iran without them – what with the beards and the robes and the veils, there was and still is a lot of black around. You know how bad things were for young Marjane and her mates? A poster of Kim Wilde comes to represent freedom, and who wants to live in a place where that's been allowed to happen? I know myself well enough to understand that I would never have read a prose memoir describing this life and these events – I wouldn't have wanted to live with this amount of fear and pain over days and weeks. I'm glad I understand more than I did, though, and these books, it seems to me, provide an object lesson in all that's good about graphic novels.

I picked up Bernard Levin's *The Pendulum Years*, about Britain in the '60s, because there's a little story in it that I'd always thought would make a good film, and I wanted to remind myself of the details. But then I remembered that the book contained one of my favourite pieces of comic writing, Levin's account of the Lady Chatterley trial, so I reread that, and a few of the other chapters. The piece on the Lady Chatterley trial made me laugh all over again, but it struck me this time that, even though Levin does a great job, it's not so much his writing that's funny as the trial itself; it's hard to go wrong with this material. For the benefit of young people: at the beginning of the 1960s, Penguin Books published Lawrence's *Lady Chatterley's Lover*, the first time it had been available to the general public since 1928, and the publishers were promptly prosecuted. Penguin won the ensuing court case, but not before some very English (and, it has to be said, extremely dim) lawyers argued, with unintentional comic élan, that the book had no literary merit, and therefore Penguin couldn't justify its obscene content. The law's notion of literary merit was both revealing and instructive – Mr Griffith-Jones, for the prosecution, doubted, for example, that any book which contains a misquotation from the 24th Psalm could be said to be much good. 'Do you not think that in a work of high literary merit . . . he might take the trouble to look it up?'

Mr Griffith-Jones was also perturbed by Lawrence's repeated use of the words *womb* and *bowels*, taking the view that your absolutely top authors, your greats, if you will, would get the thesaurus out. 'Then a little bit further down page 141, towards the bottom, at the end of the longish paragraph the two words "womb" and "bowels" appear again . . . Is that really what you call expert, artistic writing?' This really happened, honestly.

I was going to point out the bleeding obvious (as I prefer to do whenever possible, because it takes less effort, but fills up the space anyway) – I was going to say that a decade that began like this ended with man walking on the moon. Things aren't quite that cheerily progressive, though, are they? Because we're not landing men on the moon, or anywhere else in space – indeed, we no longer even possess the proper technology. There are plenty of people out there, however, who don't want us reading about wombs and bowels. Just ask Marjane Satrapi. ✷

A selection from

PERSEPOLIS

by **MARJANE SATRAPI**

★ ★ ★

THE BICYCLE

MY FAITH WAS NOT UNSHAKABLE.

THE YEAR OF THE REVOLUTION I HAD TO TAKE ACTION. SO I PUT MY PROPHETIC DESTINY ASIDE FOR A WHILE.

TODAY MY NAME IS CHE GUEVARA.

I AM FIDEL.

AND I WANT TO BE TROTSKY.

WE DEMONSTRATED IN THE GARDEN OF OUR HOUSE.

DOWN WITH THE KING!

DOWN WITH THE KING!

THE REVOLUTION IS LIKE A BICYCLE. WHEN THE WHEELS DON'T TURN, IT FALLS.

WELL SPOKEN!

AND SO WENT THE REVOLUTION IN MY COUNTRY.

TO ENLIGHTEN ME THEY BOUGHT BOOKS.

I KNEW EVERYTHING ABOUT THE CHILDREN OF PALESTINE.

ABOUT FIDEL CASTRO.

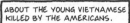

ABOUT THE YOUNG VIETNAMESE KILLED BY THE AMERICANS.

ABOUT THE REVOLUTIONARIES OF MY COUNTRY...

BUT MY FAVORITE WAS A COMIC BOOK ENTITLED "DIALECTIC MATERIALISM."

IN MY BOOK YOU COULD SEE MARX AND DESCARTES.

THE MATERIAL WORLD DOESN'T EXIST, IT'S ONLY A REFLECTION OF OUR OWN IMAGINATION.

SAYS YOU!

261

262

THE FIREMEN DIDN'T ARRIVE UNTIL FORTY MINUTES LATER.

THE BBC SAID THERE WERE 400 VICTIMS. THE SHAH SAID THAT A GROUP OF RELIGIOUS FANATICS PERPETRATED THE MASSACRE. BUT THE PEOPLE KNEW THAT IT WAS THE SHAH'S FAULT!!!

EXIT

JUNE 2006

L ast month I read Marjane Satrapi's two Persepolis books and Kurt Vonnegut's *A Man Without a Country*, and I seem to recall that I described the experience as somewhat gloomy. Ha! That was nothing! I didn't know I was born! I now see that the time I spent in Satrapi's horrific postrevolutionary Iran, and the time I gave over to Vonnegut telling us that the world is ending, were the happiest days of my life. The end of the world? Bring it on! With the honourable exception of *Freakonomics*, the most cheerful book I read this month was Jon Krakauer's *Into the Wild*, the story of how and why a young man walked into the Alaskan wilderness and starved (or perhaps poisoned) himself to death. *Into*

the Wild wins the Smiley Award because it has a body count of
one. Ken Dornstein's memoir *The Boy Who Fell Out of the Sky*
begins and ends with the Lockerbie disaster in 1988, when a Pan
Am plane blew up over a Scottish village, killing all 259 passengers, including the author's older brother David. And E. L.
Doctorow's novel *The March* describes William Sherman's journey
from Atlanta up to North Carolina, and just about everybody dies,
some of them in ways that you don't want to spend a long time
thinking about.

I was actually in North Carolina when I finished *The March* —
this is something I like to do when I'm particularly enjoying a
novel, despite the cost. (Did you know that there's no such planet
as Titan? Vonnegut just made it up. They could have put that on
the jacket, no? Oh well. You live and learn.) A couple of days later
I passed the book on to one of my travelling companions, Dave
Bielanko of the mighty band Marah, and he in return gave me the
Krakauer book. It's what you do when you're on the road. Oh,
yeah. There's a lot of, like, brotherhood and stuff. We were actually
on the road between Memphis, Tennessee, and Oxford, Mississippi,
a journey that takes approximately ninety minutes, and those
forty-five minutes were the only chunk of road I experienced. But
never mind! I was there, swapping books, and, you know, looking
out of the window. (And Oxford, Mississippi, is yet another place
in the US that I want to move to. Everyone there is a writer, or a
musician, or someone who hasn't yet bothered doing either thing
but could if he or she wanted to. And the mayor runs the bookstore, and in Faulkner's house you can read the plot outline he
wrote in pencil on the wall, and you can see the can of dog repellent he kept by his desk, and the sun shines a lot.)

It's a strange experience, reading Ken Dornstein's memoir
immediately after I'd finished *Into the Wild*, because there were
occasions when it seemed as though Dornstein and Krakauer
were writing about the same young man. Here's Chris

THE COMPLETE POLYSYLLABIC SPREE

McCandless, the doomed explorer, at college: 'During that final year in Atlanta, Chris had lived off campus in a monkish room furnished with little more than a thin mattress on the floor, milk crates and a table.' And here's David Dornstein: 'David's room was a classic writer's Spartan cell – a desk, a chair, a mattress on the floor, books stacked all around.' Both David Dornstein and McCandless spend an awful lot of time underlining meaningful passages in classic literature; these passages will later be discovered by future biographers, and both of these young men seemed to presume that there would be future biographers, because they left hundreds of pages of notes. David Dornstein, who wanted passionately to write, frequently imagines that his future biographer will have to piece together his work from these notes (chillingly, more than once he imagines himself killed in a plane crash); McCandless refers to himself in the pseudonymous third person – he was 'Alexander Supertramp'. Both of them have a taste for a slightly affected mock-heroic voice. And both of them seem doomed.

David Dornstein wasn't doomed in the same way as Chris McCandless, of course. McCandless chose to walk almost entirely unequipped into deadly terrain in order to live out some half-baked neurotic Thoreau fantasy. David Dornstein simply got on a routine passenger flight from London to New York, but what is remarkable about Ken Dornstein's memoir is that his brother's tragic and ungovernable fate seems like an organic part of the story he's telling. Someone sent me a proof copy of *The Boy Who Fell Out of the Sky* a while back, and I didn't think I was going to read it, partly because I couldn't imagine how it could be a *book*. To put it crudely and brutally, my anticipated problem was all in the title: whatever David's story was, it would be ended by a random, senseless explosion. (I'd been afraid of exactly the same thing with my brother-in-law's novel *Pompeii* – how can you create a narrative arc when you're just going to dump a load of lava on people's heads?) I don't know whether it's tasteless to say that the end of his life makes sense, but that's the unlikely trick that his brother pulls off.

Creating narrative coherence out of awful accident is, I suppose, a textbook way of dealing with this sort of grief (and grief, of course, is mostly what this book is about). It's partly Dornstein's skill as a writer that makes the raw material seem tailor-made for the form he has chosen, but the lives examined here are also freakishly appropriate for this kind of examination. It's not just the notes that his brother left, the half-finished stories and abandoned novels and instructions to literary executors, the letter to David from his father that explains and explores the story of Daedalus and Icarus. Ken ends up married to David's college girlfriend, but before they get there the two of them have to work out, slowly and painfully, whether there's any more to their relationship than a shared loss. And David wanted Ken to become the writer he feared he would never be, so the very existence of *The Boy Who Fell Out of the Sky* provides another layer of complication. It's a compelling, sad, thoughtful book, and I'm glad I picked it up.

Sixty passengers killed in the Lockerbie bombing fell on to the roof and garden of one particular house in the town. (The woman who lived there, perhaps understandably, moved away.) We can't imagine horror on that scale intruding into our domestic lives, but in Doctorow's novel *The March* it happens all the time. A still, hot morning, everything in its place, and then suddenly the sound and soon the sight of an avenging army come to fuck up everything you own and hold dear, and then the flames, and quite often something worse on top. And of course one has every right to be troubled by everything being held dear Down There, but this needn't prevent a sense of wonder at the sheer scale and energy of the devastation. (One of the things I kept thinking as I read the novel was, how on earth did you manage to create a country out of this mess?) In Doctorow's novel, Sherman's march absorbs turncoat soldiers just trying to get through, and freed slaves, and bereft Southern widows, and cold-eyed surgeons; they're all eaten up and digested without a second thought. The violence, and violence of feeling, in this novel is on occasions so intense that it becomes kind of metaphysical, in the way that the violence in *King Lear* is metaphysical; the pitiful soldier with a spike protruding from his skull who has no memory of any kind, who lives every single second in the now, takes on an awful weight of meaning. And he ends up killing himself in the only way he can.

Lincoln turns up at the end of the book, as he has to, and in Chapel Hill, North Carolina, I bought a used copy of his letters and speeches. He must have been an annoying person to live with, no? Yes, there's the Gettysburg address. But there's also this letter to a young family friend: 'I have scarcely felt greater pain in my life than on learning from Bob's letter, that you had failed to enter Harvard University . . . *I know not how to aid you . . .*' [itals mine]. Come on, Abe! Is that really true? You couldn't pick up the phone for a pal? You can take this 'honest' stuff too far, you know.

It would be easy, if unfair, to parody the post-Gladwell school of essays (and it's not unfair to say that *The Tipping Point* and *Blink* both paved the way for *Freakonomics*). You take two dissimilar things, prove – to your own satisfaction, at least – that they are not only not dissimilar but in fact more or less indistinguishable, suddenly cut away to provide some historical context, and then explain what it all means to us in our daily lives. So it goes something like this:

> On the face of it, World War II and Pamela Anderson's breasts would seem to have very little in common. And yet on closer examination, the differences seem actually much less interesting than the similarities. Just as World War II has to be seen in the context of the Great War that preceded it, it's not possible to think about Pammie's left breast without also thinking about her right. Pamela Anderson's

breasts, like World War II, have both inspired reams of comment and analysis, and occupied an arguably disproportionate amount of the popular imagination (in a survey conducted by the American Bureau of Statistical Analysis, more than 67 per cent of men aged between thirty-five and fifty admitted to thinking about both World War II and what Anderson has under her T-shirt 'more than once a year'); both World War II and the Anderson chest are becoming less *au courant* than they were. There are other, newer wars to fight; there are other, younger breasts to look at. What does all this tell us about our status as humans in the early years of the twenty-first century? To find out, we have to go back to the day in 1529 when Sir Thomas More reluctantly replaced Cardinal Wolsey as Lord Chancellor in Henry VIII's court . . .

They're always fun to read (the real essays, I mean, not my parody, which was merely fun to write, and a waste of your time). They pep you up, make you feel smart but a little giddy, occasionally make you laugh. *Freakonomics* occasionally hits you a little too hard over the head with a sense of its own ingenuity. 'Now for another unlikely question: what did crack cocaine have in common with nylon stockings?' (One of the things they shared, apparently, is that they were both addictive, although silk stockings were only 'practically' addictive, which might explain why there are comparatively few silk-stocking-related drive-by shootings.) The answer to the question of whether mankind is innately and universally corrupt 'may lie in . . . bagels'. (The dots here do not represent an ellipsis, but a kind of trumpeting noise.) Schoolteachers are like sumo wrestlers, real-estate agents are like the Ku Klux Klan, and so on. I enjoyed the book, which is really a collection of statistical conjuring tricks, but I wasn't entirely sure of what it was about.

I don't think I have ever had so many books I wanted to read. I picked up a few things in US bookstores; I was given a load of cool-looking books by interesting writers when I was in Mississippi and ordered one or two more (Larry Brown's *On Fire*, for example) when I came home. Meanwhile I still want to go back to L. P. Hartley's *Eustace and Hilda* trilogy, but Hartley seems too English at the moment. And I have a proof copy of the new Anne Tyler, and this young English writer David Peace has written a novel about 1974 as seen through the prism of Brian Clough's disastrous spell in charge at Leeds United. (Brian Clough was . . . Leeds United were . . . Oh, never mind.) So I'd better push on.

Except . . . a long time ago, I used to mention Arsenal, the football team I have supported for thirty-eight years, in these pages. Arsenal was occasionally called in to provide an excuse for why I hadn't read as much as I wanted to, but up until a month or so ago, they were rubbish, and I couldn't use them as an excuse for anything. They weren't even an excuse for a football team. Anyway, now they're — *we're* — good again. We have the semifinals of the Champions League coming up in a couple of weeks, for the first time in my life, and I can see books being moved on to the bench for the next few weeks. Ah, the old dilemma: books versus rubbish. (Or maybe, books versus stuff that can sometimes seem more fun than books.) It's good to have it back. ✶

ACKNOWLEDGEMENTS

Thanks to: Andrew Leland, Vendela Vida, Heidi Julavits and the Spree, Charlotte Moore, Tony Hoagland, Zelda Turner, Tony Lacey, Joanna Prior, Rosie Gailer and Caroline Dawnay.

Thanks also to Dave and Serge Bielanko, Nick Coleman, Sarah Vowell, DV DeVincentis, Wesley Stace, Harry Ritchie, Tony Quinn, Rachel Cooke, Eli Horowitz, Gill Hornby, Robert Harris and everyone else who has recommended a book to me.

Grateful acknowledgement is made to the following for permission to reprint previously published material. A selection from Charlotte Moore's *George and Sam: Autism in the Family* appears courtesy of Viking Penguin. Tony Hoagland's 'Impossible Dream' from *What Narcissism Means to Me*, published by Graywolf Press, appears courtesy of the author. A selection from *Twenty Thousand Streets Under the Sky* appears courtesy of the estate of Patrick Hamilton. A selection from Anton Chekhov's *A Life in Letters*, translated by Rosamund Bartlett and Anthony Phillips, appears courtesy of Penguin. A selection from Sarah Vowell's *Assassination Vacation* appears courtesy of Simon & Schuster. A selection from Jess Walter's *Citizen Vince* appears courtesy of Hodder & Stoughton. A selection from Jennie Erdal's *Ghosting* appears courtesy of Canongate. A selection from Joshua Ferris's *Then We Came to the End* appears courtesy of Little, Brown & Co. and Penguin. A selection from Marjane Satrapi's *Persepolis* appears courtesy of Jonathan Cape.

INDEX OF STUFF HE'S BEEN READING